Argyll

ARGYLL

The Making of a Spiritual Landscape

Ian Campbell Bradley

SAINT ANDREW PRESS
Edinburgh

First published in 2015 by
SAINT ANDREW PRESS
121 George Street
Edinburgh EH2 4YN

Copyright © Ian Campbell Bradley, 2015

ISBN 978-0-86153-838-6 (paperback)
ISBN 978-0-86153-940-6 (hardback)

The opinions expressed in this book are those of the author and do not necessarily reflect those of the publisher.

British Library Cataloguing in Publication Data
A catalogue record for this book is available from the British Library.

It is the publisher's policy to only use papers that are natural and recyclable and that have been manufactured from timber grown in renewable, properly managed forests. All of the manufacturing processes of the papers are expected to conform to the environmental regulations of the country of origin.

Typeset by Regent Typesetting

Printed and bound in the United Kingdom by
Ashford Colour Press, Gosport, Hampshire

This book is dedicated to the memory of my mother, Mary Campbell Tyre (1910–1998) and her seven siblings, especially Margaret (or Pearlie, as I knew her), all of whom grew up in Argyll and who inspired me with its romance and with their faith.

Contents

Acknowledgments

I am indebted to all those who have shared their knowledge of Argyll with me and especially to Ruth Black, Rachel Butter, Alistair Campbell of Airds, Robert Campbell Preston, Father William Fraser, Ann Galliard, Calum Macfarlane-Barrow, Lady Mary MacGrigor, Lorn Macintyre, David Mackenzie, John Lowrie Morrison, Dane Sherrard, Iain Thornber and Peter Yeoman. I am also grateful to Tim Congdon and to the elders and office bearers of Jura Parish Church for their hospitality. Ann Crawford has been an exemplary editor.

I am especially grateful to John Lowrie Morrison for allowing me to reproduce his painting 'An evening gloaming, Carsaig Bay, Knapdale' on the front cover of this book.

I first seriously worked out several of the themes for this book when leading a week in Iona Abbey in September 2006 for representatives of churches from across Argyll. I am very grateful to the late Murdoch MacKenzie for inviting me to think about Argyll's distinctive spirituality and to my co-leader, Martin Shaw, for his insightful comments.

My research visits to Argyll have been greatly helped by grants from the Deas Fund and The Carnegie Trust for the Universities of Scotland.

Introduction – Evangelical Simplicity and Liberal Mysticism

This book is a labour of love. Indeed, it represents the consummation of a life-long love affair. Perhaps its origins can even be traced back before my birth. I was conceived, so my parents informed me, in the Argyll Arms in Inveraray. Carsaig Bay, which is illustrated on the front cover, is where I hope to be laid to rest when I die, next to my mother, who was born in nearby Tayvallich, my father, my brother and generations of my Campbell ancestors, who were tenant farmers at Barnashalg, now a ruin in the wooded hillside above. It overlooks Jura, where my great-great-great grandfather, Alexander Kennedy, was minister from 1823 to 1849 and where I have undertaken a number of locum ministries. Another Argyll island, Iona, has been perhaps the single most important source of my spiritual refreshment and growth over the last twenty-five years.

Given these links, it is perhaps not surprising that I find Argyll to have a more markedly and distinctively spiritual landscape than anywhere else I have been. It is a landscape of presences and prophecies, of premonitions and intimations of mortality and immortality. Both its natural and its man-made features prompt spiritual stirrings of a kind and intensity that I have not experienced elsewhere. Within its bounds are located seven of my own 'top ten' sacred places in the British Isles – the graveyard at Carsaig Bay; Iona Abbey; Jura Parish Church; Kilmartin valley; St Columba's cave at Ellary; the Roman Catholic Cathedral at Oban; and St Conan's Kirk on Loch Awe. For me Argyll is above all a landscape of ruins and ghosts. Three examples of this particular combination come to mind although there are many others. At the southernmost tip of the Mull of Kintyre the stark shell of the burned-out Keil School stands on the shore near to where Columba's footprints are supposedly carved in the rock under the forbidding crag of Dunaverty where more than 300 men were brutally massacred in 1647, their bodies hurled into the sea below. Near Slockavullin in mid-Argyll the spooky silhouette of Poltalloch House provides an eerie backdrop to the prehistoric burial sites below that make Kilmartin valley more than anything else a landscape of the dead. On Iona, those stepping ashore off the ferry at the jetty are at once confronted with a landscape of ghosts and ruins – to the left Martyrs' Bay, scene of the slaughter of sixty-eight monks by Vikings in 806, to the right the ruined nunnery with its echoes of the half-forgotten faith and deeds of the Augustinian sisters and beyond it the Street of the Dead, a place of burial for the great and the good and a processional way for pilgrims venerating the shrine of Columba.

Laying aside my own feelings, a very good case can be made for regarding Argyll as one of the most distinctive and important spiritual landscapes in the British Isles. As well as having the most significant concentration of prehistoric religious sites in Europe, it can justly claim to be the cradle of Christianity not just in Scotland but for much of Britain. This book explores ways in which Argyll's spiritual landscape has moulded and expressed the faith of its inhabitants. It is about the relationship between landscape and belief and the spiritual significance of certain distinctive features in the make-up of Argyll, geographical, physical, social, cultural, tribal and familial. It charts how successive movements of belief and religious practice have left marks on the landscape still very evident today. It is by no means an exhaustive and comprehensive gazetteer of the region's sacred sites. Argyll is already well covered in this respect, not least by the very detailed set of volumes on its ancient monuments produced by the Royal Commission on the Ancient and Historical Monuments of Scotland between 1975 and 1992 and the superb on-line record of sites, www.canmore.rcahms.gov.uk. This book is more selective and impressionistic, focusing on certain places and people of particular interest and significance and also indicative of broader trends and themes.

I should make clear at the outset that I take Argyll to encompass essentially the area which took that name before local government reorganisation in the latter part of the twentieth century. It includes the northern areas of Ardnamurchan, Morvern, Sunart and Ardgour and the northern portion of Lorne, comprising South Ballachulish, Glen Etive and Rannoch, which were transferred to Highland region in 1975. It does not include the islands of Arran and Bute and that part of Dunbartonshire transferred into the new unitary council area of Argyll and Bute in 1996, although I do make an exception for the area around Luss on the western shores of Loch Lomond, which really does belong in Argyll's spiritual landscape. Essentially Argyll is the territory of the ancient kingdom of Dál Riata, embracing Lorne, mid-Argyll, the Cowal and Kintyre peninsulas and the inner or southern Hebridean islands of Mull, Iona, Lismore, the Garvellachs, Coll, Tiree, Colonsay and Oronsay, Jura, Islay and Gigha as well as the 'small isles' of Muck, Rum, Canna and Sanday which were transferred to Inverness-shire in 1891.

I grew up in Kent, which with its Jutish origins is just about as far culturally, as well as geographically, from the Gaelic heartland of Dál Riata as it is possible to be in the United Kingdom. Yet even as a boy living in the English Home Counties, Argyll was deeply imprinted on my youthful consciousness, and my unconsciousness. I was taken there at the age of 15 months to be baptised in Toward parish church with its unusual stained-glass window depicting the death of Columba. I spent family holidays with aunts and uncles in Innellan, Lochgoilhead and Lochgilphead. Although the school chapel where I came to faith and was confirmed was dedicated to St Augustine of Canterbury, it was always Columba of Iona who fascinated me, perhaps because of the painting of him sitting in his cell copying the Psalter which hung in the front hall of our house. It was a gift from my father to my mother on the eve of their wedding at St Columba's Church of Scotland in London, later the venue for my own marriage.

My mother did not just teach me about Columba. Along with her siblings she embodied and epitomised a theological and religious outlook which mixed open-minded liberalism and romantic mysticism with a high moral seriousness and evangelical simplicity in a way that I have not found in any other strain of Christian thought or practice, either during my youthful engagement with various hues of Anglicanism and English Nonconformity, or in my later encounters with many different varieties of Scottish Christianity. This particular combination seems to me to be distinctive to Argyll – certainly my mother told me that she found it lacking in both the Anglicanism of southern England and the Presbyterianism of Fife which she experienced towards the end of her life. A question which has long fascinated me – and which this book sets out to answer – is why the Christianity of Argyll is so different from that found in neighbouring regions. It is altogether gentler and less judgemental than the Christianity of the Western Isles and Northern Highlands and altogether simpler and more mystical than that found in Central and Eastern Scotland. I am not the only person to feel this difference. In his fascinating contribution to *The Argyll Book*, Donald Meek, the distinguished Gaelic scholar who himself hails from Tiree, notes that Argyll was regarded as a rather 'moderate' region by evangelicals from other parts of the Highlands. He goes on to attribute its open 'liberal and liberating atmosphere' to both its distinctive religious complexion and geographical position.[1]

My experiences of undertaking locum ministries over the Christmas period in the Outer Hebrides and on the Argyll island of Jura underline the contrast between the Christianity of these two regions. Only a handful of the large regular weekly congregation in the parish church in the Western Isles were members and took communion. This was because church membership was open only to those who abstain utterly from drinking, dancing and singing secular songs. I was visited one morning in the manse and upbraided by a senior elder for attending a pre-Christmas ceilidh in the community hall and compounding the offence by publicly singing (in a completely sober state) Andy Stewart's 'A Scottish Soldier'. There was some debate as to whether to have either a Christmas Eve or Christmas Day service in the church, and attendance at both was sparse, perhaps reflecting lingering suspicions that they are Popish if not pagan intrusions. The atmosphere on Jura could not have been more different. At the Christmas Eve Watchnight service over which I presided the parish church was packed with a congregation that was made up of people from many different denominations and backgrounds. There were candles galore, a tree decked with fairylights, a crib at the door and a baby doll lying in a manger in front of the Communion table. After the Christmas morning service many of the worshippers decamped to the island's one and only hotel for a drink.

The difference of outlook and approach between the Christianity of Argyll and that of the Western Islands and north west Highlands goes back a long time. Reminiscing about his grandfather's ministry in Morvern between 1770 and 1824, Norman MacLeod wrote: 'One characteristic of the manse life was its constant cheerfulness. One cottager could play the bagpipes, another the violin, and a dance in the evening by his children was his delight. If strangers were present, so much the better. He had not an atom of that proud fanaticism which connects virtue with suffering.' By contrast, MacLeod commented that the minister in a parish in the Western Isles once told him that 'on religious grounds' he had broken the only fiddle on the island. MacLeod went on to note: 'His notion of religion, we fear, is not rare among his brethren in the far west and north'. At around the same time as the Morvern minister was encouraging music making in his parish, a minister on Skye set fire to a pile of bagpipes and fiddles as big as a house on the shores of Loch Eishart with the remark 'Better is the little fire that warms in the day of peace than the great fire that consumes on the day of wrath'. Criticising such killjoy attitudes Norman MacLeod asked 'What next? Are the singing birds to be shot by the kirk sessions?'[2]

It would be quite wrong to characterise Argyll's Christianity as frivolous, easy-going or casual. It has always had a deeply serious side. There is a strong and unmistakeable evangelical strain which goes back to the austere asceticism of Columba, sleeping on the bare earth of his cell at Torr an Aba on Iona with a stone for his pillow, and the solitary hermits who built their beehive cells on the Garvellachs. The theological temper of Argyll has never been narrowly judgmental, however. Rather it has been notably liberal. There can be few places where heretics are venerated as much as saints – yet such is the treatment accorded to Alexander Robinson, thrown out of the Church of Scotland in 1897 for over-emphasizing the humanity of Christ, who is commemorated by a stained-glass window in Kilmun Church where he was minister. Another Argyll-born minister arraigned for heresy for preaching the doctrine of universal love rather than limited atonement, John McLeod Campbell, is similarly celebrated in a window in Rhu Church (pages 153–4). It is significant that the Church of Scotland congregations on the islands of Barra and South Uist, feeling themselves very different in theological and liturgical outlook from those in the more northerly of the Western Isles, have recently successfully petitioned to leave the Presbytery of Uist and join the Presbytery of Argyll with which they feel much more affinity.

Perhaps Argyll's distinctive spiritual atmosphere is the result of a blending of the best of the surrounding traditions – the evangelical simplicity and mysticism of the northern Highlands and Outer Hebrides without its harsher side and tendency towards judgmentalism, and the enlightened moderatism of Eastern and Lowland Scotland without its over-rational suspicion of the romantic and mystical. There are other respects in which Argyll brings different traditions together – sometimes they stand in juxtaposition like the Highland and the Lowland churches in Campbeltown and the English and Gaelic speaking division of Inveraray Parish Church. More than in any other region of Scotland, there is an intermingling of the pagan and primal with the Christian and of the Protestant with the Catholic. The former is graphically illustrated by the two figures carved high on the south wall of Muckairn Parish Church in Taynuilt, one a grinning ecclesiastic and the other a 'Sheela-na-gig' mother goddess and female fertility symbol. The latter juxtaposition finds unintentional confirmation in the series of roundels from the High Kirk of Dunoon now propped up against an outside wall where John Knox finds himself next to a very Catholic looking angel.

Argyll is a very Presbyterian place. There are several reasons for this, not least the dominance of the Campbells. Episcopalianism has never had a strong hold, other than for a time in Appin and Ardnamurchan, while the historic heartland of West Highland Catholicism is centred just across the border into the old county of Inverness-shire in Moidart and Arisaig. The majority of the parishes in the Diocese of Argyll and the Isles, which today comprises only 1.6 per cent of the total Catholic population of Scotland, are still to be found in Lochaber and in the Southern Hebrides. Argyll's Presbyterianism has had a distinctive character, markedly more mystical, more liturgical and more liberal than that found in other areas, especially of the Highlands. Several factors may account for this – the lingering influence of Columba and the other Irish missionaries and saints; the fact that unlike so many clan chieftains and lairds, the Dukes of Argyll remained loyal to the Kirk and did not forsake it for

Episcopalianism; and the region's loyalty to the Established 'Auld Kirk' with the consequence that the influence of the Free Church has been less keenly felt than further north. Climatic, geographical and linguistic factors have also played a part, from the soft mild rain that makes Argyll so green to its location as the borderland between Highland and Lowland Scotland and its position as a stronghold of Gaelic language and culture.

The Gaelic contribution to Argyll's spiritual landscape is immensely important, not least in providing its name. The word Argyll comes from the Gaelic 'Airer Goídel' (or Earra Ghaidheil) meaning the border region of the Gaels. As the thirteenth-century work *De Situ Albanie*, an early history of Scotland, put it: 'the name Arregathel means margin of the Scots or Irish'. There is much debate as to whether the Gaelic speaking kingdom of Dál Riata was the result of immigration from northern Ireland, or the homeland of a more settled population who had long spoken the same language as those living in Ireland. There is also debate as to exactly when and why the term Airer Goídel came in to use, with some suggesting that it was taken up in the ninth century to distinguish the mainland area from the islands, which had largely come under Norse control and were known as Innse Gall (Islands of the Foreigners). Either way, Argyll was a border or frontier region between the Gaels and both the Norse and the Lowland Scots. It was also where the Gaelic language was first spoken and established in what was to become Scotland. Although there are very few Gaelic speakers left, the language has left a considerable mark on its spiritual landscape. To give just two examples, Carnasserie Castle is remembered as the place where John Carswell translated the Book of Common Order, the very first book to be printed in Gaelic, and Bunessan in the Ross of Mull has given its name to the tune associated with one of the best loved Christmas hymns, 'Child in the Manger' or 'Leanabh an Aigh' written by Mary MacDonald who lived there throughout her eighty-three-year life.

The Gaelic word airer also means coast, so Airer Goídel could equally well signify the coast of the Gaels. It is a region dominated by lochs and sea – Argyll's coastline is longer than that of France – and water has been very important in fashioning its spiritual as well as its physical landscape. So also has another factor conveyed by the

Gaelic word airer – its position as a marginal border region. Percy Grainger, the Australian-born composer who holidayed in Kintyre, described Argyll as 'the penumbra of Europe', presumably having in mind its position on the edge, away from the heat and centre of the sun, a place in the shadow and yet shining like a beacon when the rest of Europe was dark.

It is thanks to Gaelic that there are so many place names that testify to Argyll's particularly spiritual landscape, not least the large number beginning with the prefix 'Kil', which comes from the Old Irish term 'Cell' meaning a church, ecclesiastical settlement or religious burial ground. There are far more 'Kil' names in Argyll than in any other part of Scotland, twenty-eight of them in South Kintyre alone. They are very often paired with the name of a saint and associated with a medieval chapel. There are many other place names in Argyll which testify to a sense of the sacredness of place. They include Glen Aray, which means the Glen of Worship, and Holy Loch, originally called Loch Shiant from the Gaelic word 'Seunta' meaning sacred. The idea of sacred places has long been particularly important in Argyll. One of the earliest Christian treatises on the subject, *De Locis Sanctis*, was written towards the end of the seventh century on the island of Iona by Adomnán, ninth abbot of the monastery founded there by Columba. Today Argyll is in the forefront of the revival of interest in sacred places through pilgrimage, with over 250,000 people coming to Iona each year and significant new initiatives taking place at Luss and in the development of pilgrim routes through Kintyre and Cowal, and from Iona to St Andrews.

The Gaelic influence on Argyll's spiritual landscape goes much deeper than language. More than any other region of Scotland, Argyll has exhibited those features which are associated with Celtic religion in its primal as well as its Christian forms. It is the land of second sight – the ability to see events at a distance either in time or space – and of the evil eye. Its geographical position as 'a land that lies westward', to quote from George Campbell Hay's poem '*Tir Thàirngaire*', looking towards the setting sun and with its islands in the western sea, has given it particular associations, in Celtic understanding, with the Otherworld, variously described in Gaelic as Tír na mBeo (the Land of the Living), Mag Mell (Delightful Plain), and Tír na nÓg (the Land of the Young). This is a land without sickness, old age or death where happiness lasts forever. It is also to the west that people have traditionally gone to die and there is much in Argyll's landscape of ghosts and ruins that speaks of death.

The spiritual landscape of Argyll combines pre-Christian and Christian features. Pagan folklore and superstition have been as important to its formation as Catholicism and Calvinism. It is a landscape populated by fairies and banshees, glastaigs, brownies and hags, water horses and kelpies as much as by saints, priests and preachers. These primal presences remain and they have not always been repudiated or rejected by Christian ministers, who have often, in fact, been among the most assiduous in collecting folklore and preserving ancient traditions. They have been adapted and appropriated into new belief systems in a constant process of re-imagining and re-incorporation. Stones from megalithic burial sites were incorporated into medieval chapels and later into Reformed kirks. Recent research has shown that early Christian churches were often built deliberately near to the shrines and sacred places of pre-Christian belief systems. It may or may not be true that Columba constructed his monastery on Iona on the site of a Druidic college but if he did, he was acting in conformity with a trend, found throughout Argyll's religious history, of looking back to past traditions and taking over, re-using and adapting their monuments and artefacts rather than either destroying them or preserving them untouched.

This process of constant borrowing and re-working comes out of a mindset very different from our modern approach towards ancient buildings and structures, which is either to knock them down to make way for completely new replacements or else to conserve and preserve them as museum pieces. What happened throughout thousands of years in Argyll was rather a constant process of reinterpreting and re-creating the sacred landscape, informed by a strong sense of provisionality. At Ardchattan on the northern shore of Loch Etive five successive parish churches were built in a little over 500 years, each new building re-using stones from the previous one – the original thirteenth-century chapel was re-built substantially in the fifteenth century, followed by the Priory Church in the seventeenth century, a new parish church in 1730 and then another, still in use today, in 1836. When the inhabitants of Taynuilt heard of Nelson's great victory at Trafalgar in 1805, they dragged a megalithic standing stone from the field where it had stood for thousands of years and re-erected it near the church as the first monument to the great naval battle anywhere in the British Isles.

Argyll exhibits in particularly dramatic form the characteristics of what, for better or worse, has come to be known as Celtic spirituality. Its spiritual landscape is imagined and imaginal. By this I do not mean that it has been constructed on the base of false and fictitious myths, although there have been plenty of those. Romantic fantasy has certainly played a part in the creation of its landscape. The county has more than its fair share of quixotic follies, such as McCaig's Tower above Oban, and of buildings which are not what their names suggest, like Glenbarr Abbey, rightly described by Frank Walker as 'an abbey only by romantic assumption'.[3] In describing it as imaginal, what I have in mind is rather the extent to which Argyll's spiritual landscape has a dimension beyond the physical and material. It is informed and enriched by imagination, a landscape not just of mountains, lochs and stones but of supernatural presences and intimations of another world.

The Irish mystical theologian, Noel Dermot O'Donoghue, who taught for many years at Edinburgh University, distinguished four regions of what he called 'imaginal reality' in the Celtic tradition: the world of fairies; the world of elemental presences; the world of the living dead and the world of angels.[4] All four have been prominent features of Argyll's spiritual landscape. There is certainly no shortage of places said to be the haunts of the sithich, or fairies. They include the Fairies Hill near Kintraw, the Fairy Islands in Loch Sween, with their ancient oak trees covered in lichens and mosses which still today have an atmosphere that is enchanted as much as enchanting, and the 'fairy well' of Tobar an t-Sithein near Baile à Chlamhain on Islay, where until relatively recently people reported seeing fairies dancing. Dun Bhuirg on Mull and Dunnuilg near Loch Craignish are among the hills said to be the dwelling places of fairies who occasionally come down to help mortals, especially women with their weaving. A story set on the shores of Loch Awe tells of fairies from Kilchrenan taking a child to nearby Nant Wood. Her father reclaimed her by drawing a furrow round the fairy hillock with his plough. Another man whose wife and children were stolen by fairies discovered that they were imprisoned inside Beinn Iadain in Morvern. He found a way into the fairy mountain through a back door and rescued them by tying three knots in the black silk handkerchief which his wife had worn on her wedding day. There are also numerous stories of people being transported great distances across Argyll by a flying host (sluagh in Gaelic) of fairies.

Argyll is especially rich in glastaigs, mortal women put under enchantment and given a fairy nature. Haunting both pastures and households, and appearing in the guise of thin little creatures with long yellow hair and dressed in green, they often guided herds of sheep or cattle or undertook housework when people were asleep, but they could also be disruptive and act like poltergeists if upset or disturbed. They have left their mark on the landscape, as in the hollow in the ground near Balnahard on Colonsay where libations of new milk were said to have been poured as offerings to the glastaig who had charge of the local sheep and cattle. Their male equivalents, brownies, were not so common and rarely harmful. Belief in banshees, the fairy women who began to wail if someone was about to die and who were seen as omens of death and messengers from the underworld, is attested in such place names as Toll na Caointich, 'the pool of the banshee', near Port Wemyss on Islay. Argyll also has its demons as well as its fairies. The devil makes regular appearances in its folklore, manifesting himself to a shepherd in Benderloch in the form of a large bundle of ferns rolling down the hillside and, in a story which is located both at Kilneuair Kirkyard and Saddell Abbey, leaving a handprint in the stone after appearing to a tailor stitching a pair of trousers while seated on a tomb.

Elemental presences abound in Argyll – hardly surprising when the region is subjected to some of the wildest, windiest and wettest weather in the British Isles. Natural and climatic forces were personified in the form of Cailleachan, fearsome ancient women sometimes known as storm hags, who were seen as having a direct influence on both landscape and weather. The Cailleach Bheir, who lived in a cave in the rocks on Ben Cruachan, was believed to control the flow of the spring near its summit by covering it over with a stone every evening. One evening she was distracted from this nightly task because her herd of goats had wandered off on to Rannoch moor and she had to round them up. As a result, the waters cascaded down the mountain to form Loch Awe. She was punished by being turned into a granite boulder, Creag na Caillich Bheir (the Old Wife's Rock), which can still be seen on the side of Loch Etive. Another cailleach, called Bhéarra, was believed to usher in winter weather by washing her great plaid in the whirlpool of Coire Bhreacain (Coryvreckan) north of Jura. This process took three days, during which the roar of the coming tempest was heard twenty miles away. When she finished, her plaid was pure white and snow covered the land.

The dead are a very obvious continuing presence in Argyll. No other region of the British Isles has a greater concentration of burial sites, elaborately carved grave slabs, mausoleums and monuments, many of them prominently displaying the stark injunction '*memento mori*' (remember death). If the Kilmartin Valley and the Street of the Dead on Iona are the most dramatic examples of ritual landscapes of the dead, there are many other equally powerful physical reminders of human mortality. Among the most sombre is the monument to the Gaelic poet Duncan Ban Macintyre, which stands on a hillside south of Dalmally. A harsh granite block surmounted by a circular henge, it broods over the dark waters of Loch Awe and the heavily wooded island graveyard of Inishail.

Monument to Duncan Ban Macintyre

Another island graveyard, Eilean Fhianain, or the Green Island, in Loch Shiel, which for long formed the boundary between Argyll and Inverness, is the oldest place of burial in Western Europe still in use today. More than 60,000 bodies are said to be interred there. Modern burials there invariably involve the digging up and displacement of the bones of those previously laid to rest. Perhaps it is their ghosts who ring the ancient bell lying on the altar of St Finnan's Chapel which is sometimes heard by those fishing on the loch when there is not a living soul on the island.

Angels, too, have left their mark on the topography of Argyll, most famously on Cnoc nan Aingeall, the Hill of the Angels which stands in the middle of the island of Iona. This is where, according to his biographer Adomnán, Columba was seen by a fellow monk conversing with angels who had flown down from heaven in white robes as he stopped to pray on his way down to the machair on the west coast of the island. Known also in Gaelic as Sìthean Mòr, or the large fairy mound, it is one of many places in Argyll with both Christian and pre-Christian associations. There has been an unusually strong devotion in Argyll to the Archangel Michael who was frequently invoked in incantations and charms and depicted on gravestones.

The intermingling of folklore and Christian faith persisted not just through the Middle Ages but well beyond the Reformation. As late as 1650, parishioners of Craignish were rebuked by the Kirk Session for 'going sungates around the Kirk' before entering for divine service. Although there were some other similar complaints from church authorities, overall there is a striking lack of censure or even concern on the part of Argyll's Presbyterian ministers about the survival of pre-Christian beliefs and practices. Indeed, several seem to have found no incompatibility in embracing manifestations of primal beliefs such as second sight and the existence of elemental presences like the Cailleachan alongside their Christian faith. John Frazer, minister of Coll and Tiree in the early eighteenth century, compiled a collection of examples of the phenomenon of second sight and wrestled with the question as to whether it was inherited or came as a direct gift from God. In 1791 Charles Stewart, minister of Strachur and Strathlachlan, suggested that two mudslides in the hills north of Loch Eck, which had destroyed dwelling places, were caused by a water spout produced by the Cailleach Bheir. Some of the most comprehensive collections of Scottish folklore and superstitions were made by Argyll ministers in the nineteenth and early twentieth centuries, notably John Gregorson Campbell of Tiree and Kenneth MacLeod of Gigha. Bordering on the syncretistic, their attitude to the material which they found and preserved for posterity was different both from the unease generally, although not universally, displayed by the more conservative and Calvinistic ministers of the Western Isles and Northern Highlands and the sceptical rationalism which tended to prevail in the Lowlands.

Argyll is a region where the next world can seem very close. Its westward orientation, suggesting proximity to the Otherworld, its location on the fringe and at the edge, the strange almost ethereal quality of its light brought about by the interplay of mist, rain, sun and cloud on its lochs and mountains, and the intermingling of so many spiritual influences combine to make it, in the (borrowed) words that George MacLeod famously applied to Iona, 'a thin place'. At the south end of Jura, Geata Àth nam Marbh – the Gate of the Ford of the Dead – supposedly provides a passage between this world and the afterlife. If Argyll often feels close to heaven, then it has also been taken to provide ways to the underworld and to hell. There is a legendary tunnel leading to hell at Clach-Tholl, a raised natural arch located south-west of Port Appin at the end of the Appin peninsula. Another legend locates the home of the ocean gods far below the Coryvreckan whirlpool. Once, in a storm, a sow which belonged to this underwater realm was tossed up in a turbulent sea. She swam ashore to Scarba and had nine piglets, from whom all the wild boar in Scotland are said to have descended.

There is more to the spiritual landscape of Argyll than the effects of mystical Celtic spirituality and the evangelical austerity of Columba and his successors. Physical and climatic factors have also played a key role, fashioning a terrain which is at once less barren and desolate than that of the more northerly highlands and islands and more rugged and muscular than the smooth contours of the Lowlands. They have also provided the two elements which have literally shaped Argyll more than any others – stone and water. It is no coincidence that it was in Argyll, in the course of his tour of the Highlands and Islands, that Dr Johnson made his famous observation to his Scottish host that 'Your country consists of two things, stone and water. There is, indeed, a little earth above the stone in some places, but a very little; and the stone is always appearing. It is like a man in rags; the naked skin is still peeping out.'⁵

Stone and rock have been hugely important in the making of Argyll's spiritual landscape. As well as containing some of the oldest known rocks on the earth, formed over 2,800 million years ago, the region contains the greatest concentrations in Europe of prehistoric cup and ring markings and standing stones. The standing stones found in particular profusion in the Kilmartin Valley are enigmatic and mysterious. What was the purpose in uprooting these great blocks from their original habitat, hauling them many miles and planting them singly or in groups upright in the ground? Do they point to the alignment of the stars or connect with some complex system of solar worship? Do they stand as silent witnesses and prayers to the gods or do they have a more prosaic purpose as boundary markers? Many archaeologists suggest that their primary role may well have been as grave markers and burial places. In that case, they form one of the earliest expressions of that distinctive Argyll landscape of ghosts and ruins, the forerunners of all those chapels, mausoleums and cemeteries with their incised crosses and carved grave slabs. Argyll's spiritual landscape has literally been chiselled out of stone – not just the standing stones and the cup and ring markings but also the hermits' caves, the high-standing crosses, the monastic cloisters and the simple but sturdy post-Reformation kirks. There is a hardness and a greyness to that stone which has made for plainness and lack of ostentation as well as for durability. But there are also other stones found in profusion along the coast of Argyll that sparkle with colour and vitality, like the smooth rounded pebbles on the shore of Port a'Churaich (the Bay of the Coracle) on Iona that modern pilgrims either pick up to take home as talismans or cast into the sea to rid themselves of a curse or burden.

The greyness and hardness of the stone in Argyll is tempered by the greenness and the softness of the ferns, lichens and moss that grow over and around every rock face and boulder. Argyll's predominant colour is not grey but rather green from the lushness of its vegetation. That lushness is a result of the Gulf Stream and in particular of the rain which falls so often in this part of Scotland. It accounts not just for the 'vile bogs' which Dr Johnson singled out as main product of 'too much water', but also for the ferns and bracken, the rhododendrons and foxgloves that heighten its mysterious, mystical atmosphere, providing the carpets and canopies for fairy glens and enchanted forests.

Water has made its mark on Argyll in many different ways. It has provided a third dominant colour alongside grey and green in the blue of its lochs and seascapes. Nowhere in Argyll is more than twelve miles from either a loch or the sea. The interplay of rain, mist, sun and cloud enhances its otherworldly, supernatural atmosphere. In his most famous hymn, 'O Love that Wilt Not Let Me Go', written as he sat in his manse at Innellan on the East Cowal coast, the blind minister George Matheson traced the rainbow through the rain, something that it is often possible to do in Argyll. To the Free Church minister, Thomas Ratcliffe Barnett, who travelled as a pilgrim through Argyll in the early decades of the twentieth century, cloud and rain created a landscape always misty and melancholy, 'which moves the soul and fills the eyes with tears', perfectly suited 'to a Celtic dreamer' whose 'sunshine is a rainbow. The romance is drenched in pain. Rain-swept mountains; mist on the tops; white foam leaping up the red-wrack rocks; rolling seas breaking over the bow of the boat'.[6]

Holy wells have long been an important feature in Argyll's spiritual landscape. The town of Tobermory on Mull takes its name from Tobar Maire, Mary's well. Tobar na Slainte, which issues from a limestone cliff on the north east shore of Lismore at the point where Moluag is said to have landed, is one of many wells associated with saints and credited with healing properties that were frequented until the later nineteenth century. In the 1850s a local minister channelled a natural spring through a lion's head outlet on rocks half way down the twisting single-track road known as Hell's Glen that corkscrews down to Lochgoilhead. He named it 'Moses' Well', giving Biblical cachet to what must have been a welcome place for weary travellers to stop and quench their thirst. Rivers, too, have played an important part in Argyll's religious history, not least the lazily snaking Add up which both Columba's coracle and royal galleys probably made their way to Dunadd.

Islands have always been especially important in Argyll's spiritual landscape. The isles of the western ocean have their special associations with death and the next life, while the spiritual power of off-shore islands like Eilean Mór in the mouth of Loch Sween, Eileach an Naoimh in the Garvellachs, Jura and Colonsay is enhanced by the ruins which testify to their early use as retreats by monks and hermits. Iona is, of course, par excellence the sacred isle. Scarcely less important are the islands in the middle of inland lochs, like Inishail and Eilean Fhianain. Several Argyll parish churches were situated on islands to which worshippers rowed or sailed until well on in the eighteenth century.

The importance and the hazards of water-borne transport, which was only really superseded in Argyll by overland travel seventy years or so ago, are well illustrated in my own family history. My mother's father owned three coaches and six horses which met the steamer from Glasgow at Ardrishaig pier and transported passengers, freight and mail to and from their destinations around North Knapdale. She herself had to catch the steamer from Ardrishaig to Dunoon every Monday morning to get to the nearest secondary school and often reminisced about dancing on the decks to the music of a piper on the Friday afternoon return journey. She also told me about the untimely death of her uncle who was drowned coming back to Eilean Righ in Loch Craignish after attending Sunday morning worship at Kilmartin Church. Despite the ever-present danger of drowning, journeying by sea and across lochs was much preferred to overland travel. John Marsden's book *The Sea Road of the Saints* shows the extent to which cross-water routes provided the medieval motorways across the West Highlands and Islands. This is why so many important monasteries and churches, and so many of the magnificent carved stones that they produced, are to be found at island and coastal sites which seem remote and inaccessible in our motorcar-dominated age.

It is appropriate that one of the great visual symbols of Argyll should be the sea-going galley also known as the lymphad or birlinn. An amalgam of the Viking long ship and the earlier Irish currach or coracle, the West Highland galley was in many ways the most tangible and lasting legacy of the period of Norse occupation of the region. Especially in the form of the Galley of Lorne, it is depicted at sacred sites across Argyll – scratched on the walls of Kilchattan Chapel on Luing; carved on numerous late medieval grave slabs; represented twenty times in the windows, gates and railings of St Conan's Kirk on Loch Awe; glowing in the massive stained-glass

Depictions of galleys:
Top left: etched on the wall of Kilchattan Chapel, Luing
Top right: carved on a gravestone, Kilmory Knap
Bottom left: in a window in Southend Church
Bottom right: on the war memorial, Inverary Church

window in Southend Parish Church commemorating the eighth Duke of Argyll; silhouetted in the sanctuary lamp of St Columba's Roman Catholic Cathedral in Oban; glittering in the burnished copper war memorial in Inveraray Parish Church; prominent in the panels on the front of the local government offices in Dunoon Castle; and sailing forth on the coats of arms of several clans, Argyll and Bute Council and the Roman Catholic Diocese of Argyll and the Isles. As well as pointing to the importance of Argyll's seafaring tradition, the symbol of the galley has spiritual significance. Seen by some historians of heraldry as having its origins in a Scandinavian crescent-moon-shaped galley which was the male embodiment of the pagan earth mother goddess, and standing through the Christian centuries for pilgrimage and journeying to the next world, it has been the object of mystical experiences and supernatural happenings.

Symbol of the ancient Norse kingdoms of the Isles, the Galley of Lorne was used by Somerled as a heraldic charge, adopted by the Macdonald Lords of the Isles and MacDougall Lords of Lorne and later inherited through marriage by the Campbells, who incorporated it in their coat of arms. In forming a link between these powerful rival clans, it symbolizes another important theme in the spiritual landscape of Argyll that has been shaped as much by the religious and political leanings of its lairds as by its geography. While other dynasties like the MacLeods of Morvern have left an important mark, it is the MacDonald and Campbell clans and their chiefs who have been the pre-eminent influences in this respect. As Lords of the Isles, the MacDonalds did much to preserve and enhance the sacred landscape of Argyll in the Middle Ages, not least through building and supporting the great monastic houses of Iona, Saddell and Ardchattan. The contribution of the Campbells, and especially of successive earls and dukes of Argyll, has been more controversial but more enduring. Accused, not altogether justly, of iconoclastically destroying many of the religious artefacts of the Middle Ages, they established the towns of Campbeltown, Inveraray, Bowmore and Port Ellen as planned model settlements embodying the ordered principles of Presbyterianism and generously endowed numerous parish churches. More broadly, through the strength of their own convictions, their extensive patronage and their continuing loyalty to the Established Church, they have been one of the dominant influence behind the creation of Argyll's distinctive liberal, mystical Presbyterianism.

More than any other Scottish clans, the Campbells and MacDonalds have been traditionally locked in bitter feuding and violent animosity. The fact that both have contributed significantly to the development of Argyll's sacred landscape serves as a reminder that not all is sweetness and light in its religious history and as a warning against over-romanticising its spiritual story. Mary McGrigor is quite right to subtitle her book about Argyll 'land of blood of beauty'. Bitterly divided as they have been, MacDonalds and Campbells seem to me to have provided complementary strands in Argyll's spiritual make-up – the former contributing to its medieval Catholic foundations and the latter to its distinctive post-Reformation combination of liberal and mystical Protestantism. In doing so, they have perhaps modelled in microcosm those apparently conflicting forces, Highland and Lowland, Celtic and Calvinist, Protestant and Catholic, which have shaped its spiritual landscape and held together, sometimes in tension and sometimes through a synthesis and fusion, what are often perceived as opposites.

The Celtic Cross symbol used as the logo for Argyll and Bute Council on the side of the Islay–Jura ferry berthed at Port Askaig

Visitors coming into Argyll today are greeted by a simple ringed Celtic cross which appears on road signs, vehicles and ferries and is the official corporate logo of Argyll and Bute Council. It is the only local authority in the United Kingdom of which I am aware with an unmistakably Christian symbol, and nothing but that symbol, as its badge of identity. This image appears again and again across the region: in its earliest incarnation going back more than a thousand years in the form of the incised cross stones found in ancient burial grounds like Cladh a' Bhile near Ellary and the great high-standing crosses on Islay and Iona; then in the later medieval crosses like those now erected in the middle of Inveraray and Campbeltown; and more recently in thousands of gravestones, like that for my own mother, father and brother in Carsaig Bay. At one level, it is a starkly simple Christian symbol, bold in its evangelical message and uncompromisingly proclaiming Christ's death as the ultimate salvific act. Yet in its Celtic form it also introduces an element of mystery with the unending scrolls and spirals of the knotwork and an added liturgical dimension with the elaborately carved depictions of Biblical scenes and characters.

There is one particular cross which for me epitomises Argyll's spiritual landscape. Maclean's Cross, dating from the fifteenth century, stands half way along the road between the ferry jetty and the Abbey that is traversed by nearly all the quarter of a million visitors who come to Iona each year. Those who pause as they pass by it probably register the classic Celtic interleaved foliated designs that cover the side that faces the road. Most probably miss the stark portrayal of the Crucified Christ on the other face. A good many almost certainly also miss the building which forms its background, the simple parish church built to the standard design of Thomas Telford in 1828. The image of the Kirk framed by the Cross, which can also be seen at Lochaline in Morvern where a fourteenth- or fifteenth-century disc-headed cross is silhouetted against a background of another simple church built in 1898, sums up the diverse and apparently discordant strands which have together fashioned Argyll's spiritual landscape: Celtic and Calvinist, Catholic and Reformed. This dramatic visual juxtaposition encapsulates what are perhaps its two dominant features – evangelical simplicity and liberal mysticism.

Maclean's Cross, Iona, with the parish church behind

1

Entering Argyll – St Conan's Kirk

There are two main road routes into Argyll. The more southerly skirts the western shore of Loch Lomond and then branches off along the A83 through Arrochar before rising up over the Rest and Be Thankful and swooping down to Cairndow and the head of Loch Fyne. Recent boundary changes mean that Argyll is now entered relatively early along the shores of the bonnie, bonnie banks, with the first major settlement reached being the village of Luss. It is associated with Kessog who, if local claims are to be believed, is the earliest known Argyll saint and spiritual figure, having apparently arrived in the area in AD510. A relatively new arrival in Argyll, where there have been significant recent initiatives in the promotion of pilgrimage, Luss will have its moment of glory towards the end of this book.

The other main overland route into Argyll, followed by the railway line as well as the road to Oban, is via Crianlarich and Tyndrum where the A85 branches off to follow the River Lochy before skirting the northern shore of Loch Awe and squeezing through the Pass of Brander under the flank of Ben Cruachan on its way to Loch Etive and the Firth of Lorne. On this more northerly approach, the first significant settlement reached after entering Argyll is Dalmally, with its unusual octagonal church. Just a few miles further along the A85, perched somewhat precariously on the edge of Loch Awe with the railway line below, stands St Conan's Church. Arguably the most quirky, atmospheric and intriguing ecclesiastical building in Scotland, it provides a perfect introduction to Argyll's distinctive spiritual landscape.

Many of those passing by in coaches or cars en route to Oban or the islands probably gain the impression that this is an ancient medieval church which has stood for centuries, maybe even since the time of Conan, a somewhat shadowy seventh-century saint who seems to have been active in this part of Lorne. In fact, St Conan's Kirk is a twentieth-century building, the creation of Walter Douglas Campbell, an eccentric and well-connected architect born in 1850, who lived with his sister and brother in a mansion house of his own design on Innis Chonain, an island in the north of Loch Awe connected to the mainland by a bridge. Apparently in response to his mother's complaints that the long drive to the parish church in Dalmally was too much for her, he built a small and relatively simple church on the north side of the loch in the 1880s. He later decided to extend and transform it into something much grander, beginning work to his own designs in 1907. When Campbell died seven years later the new church was less than half completed. Work was suspended during the First World War and thereafter his sister Helen supervised construction until her own death in 1927. The church was finally completed in 1930.

St Conan's Kirk is an extraordinary and evocative monument to Walter Campbell's eclectic romanticism. Built out of local Cruachan granite boulders, which were rolled down from the hill above, split and roughly shaped on site, it is a hotchpotch of different architectural styles. Especially on a drizzly or misty day, of which there are plenty around Loch Awe, its turreted and pinnacled exterior resembles a cross between Hogwarts School and one of the castles built by mad King Ludwig of Bavaria. The large Saxon tower is modelled on Monkwearmouth Church in Durham with its associations with the Venerable Bede. Another, smaller tower is said to be based on a Norman church in Picardy. Built on the steeply sloping banks of Loch Awe, the south wall is held up by a mass of flying buttresses and retaining walls which enhance the church's fairy-tale atmosphere and appearance. Perched on a buttress below the smaller tower, and next to an elaborate Romanesque doorway, the figure of St Conan, sculpted by Alexander Carrick, looks out over the loch. Steps from the doorway lead down to a series of terraces, the lowest of which is called St Modan's Walk.

The church is best entered through cloisters that could have come straight from one of Argyll's medieval monasteries. An elaborately carved Norman archway leads into the South Aisle, also known as St Columba's Aisle, which is flanked by side chapels dedicated to St

The apse of St Conan's Kirk

Conval and St Bride. Beyond it, continuing along the south side of the church, is another aisle, dedicated to St Fillan, from which projects a large side chapel containing a larger than life-size wooden effigy of Robert the Bruce. A spacious nave, the main remnant of the original 1880s building, gives way to a vast chancel, enclosed at its east end by a semi-circular apse, said to have been inspired by St John's Chapel in the Tower of London. It is made up of ten granite pillars carrying high stilted arches in the Romanesque style and wrapped around by a five-sided ambulatory with clear glass windows looking out on the mountains of Glenorchy and Glenstrae. A cavernous crypt below the chancel adds to the Cathedral-like atmosphere and air of dark mystery that hangs over the whole building.

The eclectic feel of St Conan's is enhanced by the provenance of many of its adornments and furnishings as much as by the variety of its architectural styles. Built into its walls are stones from the old medieval church of Inchinnan in Renfrewshire and the surrounds of a window from Iona Abbey. The oak beams in the cloister roof come from two old battleships, the *Caledonia* and the *Duke of Wellington*. Among the artefacts which decorate the various chapels are two slabs of Levantine marble, the original west window from St Mary's Church, South Leith, two screens from Eton College Chapel and a large bell from the Skerryvore Lighthouse. A striking set of four chairs in the chancel apse, their sides carved in sweeping Art Nouveau curves flaring from the mouths of dolphins, appear to be of Venetian origin and other chairs in the chancel come from Greyfriars Kirk and Old Corstorphine Church in Edinburgh. The font is a model of a Breton fishing boat.

If this hotchpotch quality primarily reflects Walter Campbell's eccentric and eclectic tastes, it also introduces a theme that has characterized the making of Argyll's spiritual landscape – the mixing up, re-use and adaptation of very different and even incongruous elements. Borrowings from the past – sometimes rather indiscriminate and maybe even inappropriate – have nearly always been preferred to repudiations of it. There are several other more specific features of the bizarre architecture of St Conan's which are also characteristic of the wider spiritual landscape of Argyll as a whole. Among them is an openness to and embrace of the primal pagan Celtic past, symbolised by the replica prehistoric stone circle erected near the approach to the church from the elegant gate-lodge and now sadly in disarray. Inside, the organ screen, carved by Campbell himself, at the west end of the nave represents a similar fusion of primal and Christian Celtic symbols. At its base are grotesque monsters representing creatures of pagan times and a belt of interlaced ribbonwork symbolising eternity. Higher up, crosses in Celtic ribbon-work represent Christianity and at the top of the screen are emblems of the four heavenly creatures, lion, calf, man and eagle, described in Revelation 4.7. The small central organ is supported by pelicans, symbolising self-sacrifice, and the wings of time bound together by the Celtic knot of the Holy Trinity.

Another prominent theme in the architecture of St Conan's, as it is throughout the spiritual landscape of Argyll, is the veneration of Celtic saints. Five saints have specific parts of the church dedicated to them – Modan, Conval, Bride, Fillan and Columba – and Conan is remembered in the church's name and the statue on the exterior south wall. The golden age of Celtic Christianity is also celebrated in the huge replica high-standing cross, carved in the characteristic Celtic style with leafy interlacing on the faces and knotwork around the two cross-head bosses, which Campbell erected in memory of his mother near the roadside above the church.

Death also looms large in this church. Visitors entering from the Cloister Garth are immediately confronted by two dark and forbidding funeral chapels – one containing the tomb of Walter Campbell and his sister Helen and the other the tomb of his nephew, Archibald Douglas Campbell, the fourth Lord Blythswood, who carried on the work of construction after their deaths. Death also features prominently alongside the theme of muscular Christianity in the striking stained-glass windows along the south side of the church. The McCorquodale window in St Fillan's Aisle depicts the Sword of the Spirit piercing evil creatures and a heroic warrior who has put on the whole armour of God bearing the shield of faith, his faith so strong that he does not even look at the fiery darts coming at him through the brambles and smoke. In the central light, under the words 'I have finished my course', angels take from his hands the helmet of salvation and the weeds and smoke at his feet turn to roses.

Muscular Christianity re-surfaces in the towering armour-clad effigy of Robert the Bruce. It was from the hillside above the kirk that he dispatched the outflanking column under the Earl of Douglas that went on to inflict a decisive defeat on John of Lorne in the Pass of Brander, neutralising a major threat to his kingship. Bruce has other Argyll connections – it is said to have been at Ugadale in Kintyre that he saw a spider making six attempts at climbing the roof a barn, inspiring his famous aphorism, 'if at first you don't succeed, try and try and try again'. He is not the only royal figure commemorated in St Conan's Kirk. A stained-glass window at the far end of the South Aisle containing the Royal Arms emblazoned with those of the Dukes of Argyll serves as a memorial to Princess Louise, daughter of Queen Victoria, who married the Marquess of Lorne, eldest son of the eighth Duke of Argyll, in 1871. A marble bust of her faces the pulpit. Princess Louise, who was a talented artist, is thought to have been responsible for designing two of the windows on the south side of the church. One, in St Columba's Aisle, shows green-scaled dragons succumbing to St Michael's sword, a motif found on several of Argyll's medieval carved tombstones. The other depicts St George with a six-headed green scaly monster at his feet. With one hand he holds his sword high, while in the other he carries a balance, sitting in which is an extraordinary winged fairy-like creature. It serves as a reminder of the enduring role played by fairies in Argyll folklore and belief well into the twentieth century. Perhaps rather more overtly Christian, although no less romantic and mystical, are the pink-cheeked angels and cherubs painted by Helen Campbell in the rose window high above the organ screen.

St Conan's Kirk is a supreme example of Argyll's imagined and imaginal spiritual landscape. At one level it is an exercise in wild romantic fantasy. Walter Campbell maintained that the tiny room accessed from St Bride's Chapel through a small Saxon doorway was the cell of St Conan himself. Yet at the same time it is also a very ordered and very Presbyterian place. Although the Church has never been part of the Church of Scotland and is maintained by a group of trustees, the services are taken predominantly by the local parish minister. This may be the only Presbyterian church in Scotland to display a relic – let into the base of the effigy of Robert the Bruce is a small

Detail of window in St Conan's Kirk

ossuary containing a bone taken from his tomb at Dunfermline Abbey – but it has a clear Reformed atmosphere in terms of its liturgical layout. At the east end of the apse is an oak communion table rather than a marble altar. Quirky as it is, it embodies the open, liturgical, mystical Presbyterianism that has been particularly characteristic of Argyll.

It is also unmistakeably a Campbell creation in its ethos and its echoes. Walter Campbell was immensely proud of his Camp-bell ancestry. His father had reverted to the old family name of

Campbell instead of that of Douglas which had been assumed by one of his ancestors when he inherited the estate of Blythswood, which had been in Campbell hands since the time of Charles I, in 1838. St Conan's is filled with emblems of the clan and reminders of their dominant position in Argyll. The double row of carved stalls in the chancel, carved from Spanish chestnut, show the full coats of arms of local chiefs with the two main branches of the Clan Campbell, Argyll and Breadalbane, in pride of place. The Galley of Lorne is carved on the memorial tablet to Walter and Helen Campbell on the exterior west wall and makes numerous appearances inside – I have counted twenty but there may well be more – notably in the stained-glass window commemorating the uniting of the Royal family and the Dukedom of Argyll, on the wrought iron gates and railings in St Fillan's Aisle guarding the entrance to the crypt, and over the gates to the Campbells' tombs in St Conval's Chapel. We are never allowed to forget that this church was conceived and built by a Campbell.

St Conan's atmosphere of slightly whimsical devotion is summed up by the three gargoyles on the outside roof of the south wall which show a dog chasing two hares. Presumably they are among all those creatures called on to glorify God's name in the quotations from the Benedicite that are inscribed on a series of panels on the walls of St Modan's Walk below. From the Walk itself, and the terrace above it, there are spectacular view down Loch Awe that, like the Celtic Saints and the Campbells, has been a dominant feature of Argyll's spiritual landscape and history. Big, brooding and somewhat forbidding, though never in a sinister way, the loch encompasses mythical, pre-Christian and Christian themes within its deep dark waters, islands and densely wooded banks. We have already recounted the legend of how it was formed when a spring high up on Ben Cruachan overflowed because of the momentary negligence or distraction of the Cailleach Bheir (pages 11–12). On its banks are pre-Christian sites like Fianna-charn (Fingalians' Mound) and early Christian sites like Kilneuair, also known as Cill an Iubhair, the Chapel of the Yews, which is possibly where Columba established a monastery. There are also strange places which seem to straddle the worlds of paganism and Christianity, like Kilmaha, roughly half way up the west side of the loch, where there is a chapel and burial ground containing a very unusual rock carving of a ringed cross flanked by two long-robed figures whose heads resemble birds rather than humans.

Visible from the terrace running along the south side of St Conan's Kirk are the islands in the northern part of Loch Awe, which have their own special significance in Argyll's spiritual landscape. Nearest to the shore is Innis Chonain, the home of Walter Campbell with its associations with St Conan himself. Further away is Inishail, known variously as the Holy Isle and the Island of Rest, and surely one of the region's most evocative spiritual places. Said to have been the site of an early nunnery, it became a significant mecca for medieval pilgrims who walked up Glen Aray and fell to their knees at the first sight of the island. Local folklore tells of a particular kneeling rock on the slopes above the eastern bank of the loch, but its precise location has proved impossible to determine.

St Conan's Kirk is at one level *sui generis*, the unique testament to one individual's faith and romantic imagination. Yet it also echoes other great projects across Argyll where people have placed stone upon stone for the glory of God. Among the most extraordinary is Kilneuair Church at the other end of Loch Awe, which dates back at least 600 years before Walter Campbell began to realise his vision. If local legend is to be believed, it was an even more quixotic enterprise, built in the manner of Solomon's Temple in Jerusalem without a hammer or chisel being laid on a single stone on site so that there was no desecration of its sanctity through the noise of construction. This was achieved by all the stones being cut and dressed twelve miles away at Killevin on the shores of Loch Fyne. A human chain was formed over the hill between Killevin and Kilneuair and each stone passed from one man to another. It is doubtless a fanciful story – as was the lingering belief among local people that the walls of the church were haunted by the Spirits of the dead and souls released from Purgatory – but it testifies to the long-standing attachment in Argyll to sacred places and buildings. That attachment was perhaps first shown in the creation of the great megalithic monuments in the Kilmartin Valley, which form the earliest known spiritual landscape in Argyll.

2

Kilmartin Valley and the Spirituality of Stone

Situated almost at the geographical centre of Argyll, Kilmartin Valley provides one of the oldest and most extraordinary spiritual landscapes, not just in the British Isles but in the whole of Europe. Nowhere else has such a concentration of prehistoric ritual monuments. Initially constructed nearly 6,000 years ago, they continue to exude an awesome sense of primal power and mystery.

Part of Kilmartin Valley's unique atmosphere is provided by geographical and topographical features. It was formed at the end of the last Ice Age 10,000 years ago. Melting ice and rising sea levels produced the Mòine Mhór, or 'Great Moss', one of the last remaining raised peat bogs in Britain, stretching from the gravel terrace on which the village of Kilmartin is sited down to Loch Crinan where it turns into a salt marsh. The River Add flows sluggishly through the valley in giant serpent-like loops. Although the Mòine Mhór was drained 200 years ago for farming, its designation as a National Nature Reserve since 1987 has allowed water levels to rise and its distinctive springy sphagnum moss to flourish. An important contributor to the battle against global warming, it absorbs huge amounts of carbon dioxide which is stored in the peat. This is in no sense a desolate landscape – it does not have the barren bleakness of the much more boggy land that covers so much of the Northern Highlands and the Outer Hebrides – but teems with wildlife and especially with wild flowers. It does, however, have an undeniably primaeval other-worldly quality. In part, this comes from the mist that so often rises and gathers over it. It is not difficult to imagine dinosaurs lumbering out of the gloom. Watery sites like mosses, bogs, rivers and lakes have always been places of veneration and seen as the dwelling places of spirits and divinities. In the case of the Mòine Mhór, it is more than just dampness which creates a mysterious atmosphere. The moss can feel safe and reassuring – especially at its southern boundary where the beautifully painted locks and houses along the towpaths of the Crinan Canal create an ordered toytown landscape – but it can also feel eerie and haunted – perhaps nowhere more so than on its wooded western slopes where the ruins of Poltalloch House, built in Jacobean style between 1849 and 1853 and partially demolished in 1957, protrude spookily through dense trees and shrubs.

What makes Kilmartin Valley such a spiritual landscape is its extraordinary concentration of prehistoric monuments. Around 800 have been recorded, ranging from standing stones, burial cists and henges to incised rock faces. Curiously, amidst all these archaeological remains, there is virtually no evidence of any human settlement in terms of domestic dwellings, food remains or activities like metal-working. This has led archaeologists to suggest that the valley may have been deliberately laid out as a ritual landscape and that no one actually lived there. It is, indeed, well described in the video shown at the Kilmartin House Museum, opened in 1997 in the old manse, as 'the valley of ghosts'.

This ritual landscape was laid out, adapted and reconfigured over a period of around 3,000 years between 4000 and 1000BC. Evidence of human habitation in Argyll in fact goes back long before this – flint tools and waste found in a cave in Kilmelford in the 1950s suggest humans were living there as early as 11,000BC in the Upper Palaeolithic period before the ice had finally retreated from mainland Scotland, and there is evidence of human settlement around 9800BC during the Mesolithic period on Colonsay and Oronsay, in caves near Oban and in mid-Argyll. It is not until the later Neolithic period, around 4000BC, that there is clear archaeological evidence of human activity in the Kilmartin Valley. This was a period of transition in human evolution from nomadic hunter gatherer to the more settled activities of growing crops and tending animals. With this transition came a much greater sense of investment in place. People began clearing forests, planting crops and building homes. In the case of the Kilmartin Valley, this investment showed itself not in such domestic activities but rather in a new sense of the sacredness of place, expressed through the building of ritual funerary monuments. As the archaeologist Graham Ritchie has pointed out, Argyll's earliest agricultural communities have left their mark on the landscape, not through fields or farms, but with the burial places of their dead.[1]

Possibly the earliest of the monuments built in the Kilmartin Valley were two parallel lines of timber posts erected along a 400-metre stretch of gravel terrace at Upper Largie, just half a mile north of Kilmartin village, which are thought to date from around 3800BC. They have been variously interpreted as marking a ceremonial route or delineating a boundary between the worlds of the living and the dead. Either way, they signal the beginning of a process by which the valley was laid out as a ritual landscape specifically associated with death. We will, of course, never know the precise nature of the rituals which took place within this designated sacred space, but later constructions make clear that the valley's primary function was as a place of burial and strongly suggest that part at least of its purpose was both to delineate and to connect the worlds of the living and the dead.

Other early monuments were certainly built to house the dead, like the twenty or more chambered cairns, which date from around 3700BC. These massive cairns, built out of boulders, were places of communal burial where grave goods like pottery and tools were placed alongside the bodies. Around 3000BC a new phenomenon emerged in the valley in the form of two circles at Temple Wood, originally built with wood and later with stone. These do not seem originally to have been built as burial places, although they were subsequently adapted for that purpose, but rather perhaps, like the later standing stones erected in the valley, to have had a role in ritual and worship through marking the positions of sun, moon and stars.

Next in time chronologically, dating probably from between 2900 and 2500BC (although some archaeologists have suggested from as early as 3500BC), came the rock art that provides one of the most fascinating and distinctive aspects of the spiritual landscape of this part of Argyll. Several exposed rock faces around the Kilmartin Valley and on its surrounding slopes are covered with indentations 'pecked' into the surface with a pointed tool made of quartz, most commonly the so-called 'cup and ring' markings which consist of a bowl-like hollow or cup surrounded by concentric circles or spirals and often with a gutter or groove protruding like a tail. There are also spirals on their own, ringed stars and parallel grooves. The most dramatic and prolific concentration of this rock art, the largest of its kind in Europe, is to be found at the south east edge of the valley on two stone outcrops at Achnabreac, which can be accessed via a signposted minor road off the A816 two miles north of Lochgilphead. There are also good examples at Ormaig near Loch Craignish; behind the hotel at Cairnbaan; and, most easy to access, on a rock just behind the primary school playground in Kilmichael Glassary.

Cup and ring markings, Achnabreac

Numerous theories have been put forward to explain the significance of these strange indentations. They have been seen as markers of the positions of stars and the courses of the sun and moon, as receptacles to collect sacrificial blood and as symbols of male potency and female fertility. Marianna Lines has suggested that they may have been associated with a worship practice akin to that of the Tibetan prayer wheel whereby a stone ball is set into a cupped stone and rotated sun-wise (*deiseil*) to speed prayers on their way.[2] It has even been postulated that they were simply doodlings with no great significance, the Neolithic equivalent of graffiti. This seems somewhat unlikely given the considerable physical effort that went into their creation. It is also intriguing as to why certain rock faces were privileged and singled out to be covered with indentations while others were left untouched. Ultimately, like other aspects of Argyll's prehistoric past, they remain a mystery.

Another significant change took place in the ritual landscape of the Kilmartin Valley around 2500BC, during what is known as the Chalcolithic period, with a move from communal to individual graves. Rising individual wealth and status meant that people were no longer all buried together and that certain prominent individuals were singled out for special treatment. Significantly, this period marked the transition from Stone Age to Bronze Age. The arrival of metal weapons and implements probably facilitated the emergence of a military and commercial élite whose status was demonstrated through the construction of conspicuous individual funerary monuments. This may explain the building, between 2500 and 1500BC, of what is known as the linear cemetery, a line of seven cairns through the middle of the valley floor. The most northerly, Glebe Cairn, can clearly be seen from Kilmartin House Museum and the most southerly, Ri Cruin, has a name which suggests that it was the burial place of a king, although this is probably anachronistic. Each of these cairns consists of a cist, or box-like tomb, dug into the ground and sealed with a stone capping slab, with water-smoothed stones heaped over the top. As with the timber posts erected 1,500 or so years earlier, but this time on a larger scale, the intention in constructing these cairns spaced out down the valley floor was surely to create an ordered ritual landscape centred on the themes of death and burial.

The valley continued to be used as a place of burial through the Middle and Later Bronze Age. The stone circles at Temple Wood were adapted for this purpose during this period. Between 2300 and 2000BC two cist graves covered by small cairns were constructed outside the north east circle and later a massive cist grave was built in the centre of the south west circle. Somewhere around 1450–1200BC new burial monuments, known as 'kerb cairns' were built to contain the ashes of cremated bodies. Also in this period a massive timber circle was constructed on the Upper Largie gravel terrace and groups of standing stones were erected at Ballymeanoch and Nether Largie.

The Kilmartin Valley provides no archaeological evidence of the worship of gods and goddesses, as one might expect at such a primal

Burial cists in Temple Wood

and important ritual site. Rather, the overwhelming sense that the modern visitor gains from wandering among its many prehistoric monuments is of reverence for ancestors, the significance attached to the rite of burial and the more general and ubiquitous presence of the dead. This is, indeed, a valley of ghosts and a landscape peopled by the dead who continue to haunt it as invisible beings. Even those monuments, such as the standing stones and circles, which would appear originally to have had more of an astrological purpose, built to mark or predict movements of sun and moon and perhaps even to provide an early calendar to help with planting crops, seem later to have been pressed into service as burial sites. Cists were added to the circles at Temple Wood and traces of cremated human bone, carbon-dated to between 1400 and 1050BC, have been found around the base of one of the Ballymeanoch standing stones. Indeed, it has been suggested that the standing stones in the valley were themselves primarily funereal rather than astrological in purpose – eighteenth century antiquarians took them to be early grave markers, commemorating those who had fallen in conflict, and more recent experts have postulated that they may have marked the boundaries of processional routes associated with either the disposal or commemoration of the departed. We are never, it seems, far from death in this, the earliest of Argyll's spiritual landscapes.

Ballymeanoch Standing Stones

The development of the Kilmartin Valley over the three millennia from 4000BC exemplifies two themes that we will encounter again and again as we explore Argyll's spiritual landscape. It was ordered rather than random and at the same time, despite its timeless primal atmosphere today, it was constantly changing. Monuments were re-adapted and re-fashioned, with cists being inserted into chambered cairns and stone circles to change their use, just as stones were taken from early sites to be re-used and incorporated into later structures. This approach is alien to us now when the emphasis is on preserving and conserving ancient monuments. It does not, however, betoken a casual attitude to the past. Indeed, in many ways it illustrates a more reverential approach than ours. We label ancient sacred monuments and seek to classify and describe them. Our ancestors until not so long ago – the great change came in the nineteenth century – respected their spiritual power and ritual meaning and sought to harness and re-interpret it to fit their own beliefs. The sacred landscape was revisited and re-used while remaining sacred. Carved rocks were used as communion tables by seventeenth century Covenanters. Following in this tradition, one contemporary charismatic Christian congregation has picked up the spiritual resonances of the Kilmartin Valley landscape and not simply treated it as a museum piece. Just opposite Kilmartin Parish Church and the Kilmartin House Museum is the Living Stones Christian Centre, its sign carved on a replica standing stone. Opened in 2002, it is the base of a Christian group, originally known as The Renewal Fellowship, formed in 1973 in the early days of the charismatic revival movement. It represents an interesting modern attempt to plug into the spiritual landscape of this area and re-orient its prevailing atmosphere from death to life.

Among archaeological finds in other parts of Argyll, two give a further insight into beliefs in the pre-Christian era. A life-size female figure carved from a single piece of alder with quartz eyes, discovered under moss at north Ballachulish in 1880 and now in the National Museum of Scotland in Edinburgh, has been dated to between 840 and 397BC. Perhaps a fertility figure, or an Iron Age goddess, the intertwined branches and twigs which covered it suggest a wicker-work container and have even prompted speculation that this could have been an early 'wicker woman', symbolic of that strange and terrifying pagan cult explored in the 1973 cult film 'The Wicker Man' set on the fictional Hebridean island of Summerisle. A primitive stone head discovered in a garden at Port Appin in 1982, which now grins enigmatically from its display case in the Kilmartin House Museum, possibly testifies to the importance of the Celtic head cult. Belief among Iron Age Celts that the essence of a person resided in his or her head led them to sculpt images of heads in stone and to bury skulls in the ground.

Although Kilmartin Valley has by far the greatest concentration of prehistoric monuments, they are to be found right across Argyll, not least on the island of Colonsay, which has a rich collection of stone circles and standing stones. They reinforce the importance of stone in Argyll's sacred landscape, represented in prehistoric times by the great standing stones and circles erected with considerable human effort, and the cup and ring markings so carefully and deliberately chiselled into bare rock faces. Thousands of years on, they still speak powerfully if silently of mysterious worship and awe in the face of the elements. Equally evocative are the stones untouched by humans, the bare rock faces which have no carvings on them and the billions of pebbles and boulders which strew the beaches of Argyll. These too preach their own sermons of stone.

3

Dunadd and Dál Riata

Sometime between 1200 and 1000BC, during the period of transition from the Bronze to the Iron Age, ritual activity seems to have ceased in Kilmartin Valley. The erection of burial mounds and standing stones gave way to the building of hill forts and duns, small defensive hill-top structures with disproportionately thick walls. Suggestions put forward to explain this dramatic change in the man-made landscape include the theory that the coming of iron weapons produced a more aggressive society focused on defending territory rather than remembering the dead, and the effects of climate change with wetter weather leading to the expansion of the peat bog. Whatever the reason, by the early centuries AD the valley had become a place where the emphasis was no longer on honouring dead ancestors but rather on protecting the living. Rachel Butter calls it 'a tense landscape now not known by reference to gods and ancestors but by reference to living political leaders and petty tyrants'.[1]

Of the thirty hill forts and duns built around Kilmartin Valley, the best-known and most significant by far is Dunadd. It stands on an outcrop of metamorphosed igneous rock which rises dramatically out of the boggy valley floor. Easily accessible via a signposted track off the A816 three miles north of Lochgilphead, it is well worth climbing the steep path that leads through natural fissures in the rock and man-made walls and mounds to the rock face at the very top with its mysterious carvings and spectacular view. Unlike the valley from which it springs, Dunadd was a landscape of the living rather than the dead, populated by warriors, tribal chiefs and kings. While chiefly evoking the tense atmosphere of conflict and power politics, it also has a sacred aspect. It stands at the heart of the story of the creation of the Gaelic kingdom of Dál Riata, the conflict between

Gaels and Picts, and the coming of the new faith of Christianity into Scotland.

Dunadd is located almost at the geographical centre of Argyll – make it the point of a compass and you can trace a circle which goes out as far as Colonsay to the west, Loch Lomond to the east, Morvern to the north and the Mull of Kintyre to the south. From its summit you can see the Paps of Jura, the hills of Arran, and Ben Cruachan at the far end of Loch Awe. It is appropriate that nearby Lochgilphead is now the administrative centre of Argyll and Bute. The surrounding parishes, Kilmartin, Glassary and Craignish, were long thought of as being the real Argyll, and described as such as distinct from the other named areas of Kintyre, Cowal, Knapdale, Lorne and the islands. As recently as 1902 John Gregorson Campbell observed that 'the district forming the parishes of Kilmartin and Kilmichael, at the west end of the Crinan Canal, is known in the neighbourhood as Argyle (Earra-Ghaedheal) ... The people, for instance, of Loch Aweside say of a person going down past Ford that he is going down to Argyle. In course of time the name has been extended to the county'.[2]

Dunadd is not an obvious strategic site like Dumbarton Rock, Dundurn or Dunollie, all of which were situated in direct relation to major land and water routes. Rather, its selection for fortification seems to have owed much to its proximity to the prehistoric sacred monuments of the Kilmartin Valley. It seems deliberately to have been sited in a pre-existing spiritual landscape. The fortifications as they stand now are thought to be the result of at least five distinct stages of building and re-building defensive earthworks, walls and enclosures. Dunadd was probably first fortified in the Iron Age, perhaps, like the many other hill forts in the area, being set up and garrisoned in response to the coming of a more lawless and violent society prone to local skirmishing and cattle rustling. The earliest radiocarbon dating for deposits found on the summit is for the period between 400 and 200BC. There seems to have been further fortification between 100BC and AD100 when a substantial stone structure was built on the summit, but the major period of construction was between the fourth and tenth centuries AD. Indeed, it can probably be dated more specifically to between the sixth and eighth centuries when Dunadd's power and prestige were at their height. It is from this period that high status gold and silver jewellery and decorated beads and glasswork have been found during excavations. The discovery of these and other artefacts suggests that Dunadd became a major metalworking, manufacturing and trading centre, with, for example, a higher concentration of wheel-turned French pottery than has been found in any other site in Britain or Ireland. It also became a place of considerable strategic importance as is clear from two contemporary references in the late seventh and early eighth century. Both come from the Annals of Ulster, almost certainly compiled by the monks of Iona. An entry for 682 (correctly 683) mentions a 'siege of Dún Att' and another for 735 (correctly 736) describes Oengus, king of the Picts, laying waste the territory of Dál Riata and seizing Dún Att.

The most striking evidence for Dunadd's possible political and spiritual importance is the collection of carvings found on the bare rock face at the highest point of the hill, accessed by a stairway cut into the stone from the grassy summit terrace. They consist of a bowl or basin, two footprints, a human head and a wild boar along with an indecipherable line of Ogham script. Both the footprints face north and are in alignment with the summit of Ben Cruachan, the highest mountain in Argyll. The less distinct of the two is close

Footprint on the summit of Dunadd

41

to the boar carving and consists of a lightly pecked outline of a right foot with a pronounced taper to the heel. The better preserved and slightly larger footprint, further north and closer to the Ogham inscription, is big enough to fit a foot clothed in a shoe or boot. It is difficult to determine how old these carvings are – it has been argued that the feinter footprint and rock-cut basin may date from the Iron Age with the boar, the deeper footprint and the Ogham inscription being added later in the seventh or eighth century and the human head a much more recent addition. Their significance seems to be enhanced by the fact that the surface on which they are carved forms part of the skyline when viewed from the lower part of the fort.

Archaeologists and historians are agreed that these carvings mark Dunadd out as a special place. Some have argued that they played a vital role in royal inauguration rituals in which new kings put their feet into the carved footprints to symbolise their connection with the land. This is certainly what happened several centuries later at Finlaggan on Islay (pages 116–17). There is no hard evidence that Dunadd was used for royal inaugurations but the nature of its summit carvings, together with the archaeological and literary evidence of its considerable wealth and strategic importance, have generally been taken to support the thesis that it may very well have been the capital and royal palace of the Gaelic kingdom of Dál Riata, which grew to encompass most of modern Argyll. The noted Victorian antiquary and historian of Celtic Scotland, William Skene, was one of the first to put forward this idea. In a lecture at nearby Poltalloch in 1850 he argued that Dunadd was the *caput regionis* mentioned by Adomnán as the place where Columba met sailors from Gaul. Although subsequent scholars have been less emphatic in making this claim, Alan Lane and Ewan Campbell conclude their substantial monograph based on extensive excavations in the early 1980s by saying that Dunadd may well have been the chief seat or principal royal centre of Dál Riata.[3]

As with so many other places in Argyll, legend and imagination have played as big a part as historical facts in constructing the story of Dunadd's spiritual and ritual significance. The 'Stone of Destiny', that iconic symbol of kingship used for the coronation of Scottish, and later British, monarchs, has even been dragged into the story. According to some legends, originally the pillow on which Jacob slept when he had his dream of the ladder leading up to heaven, it was brought to Ireland, via Egypt and Spain, and sited at Tara, the holy hill on which Ireland's high kings were crowned. A piece of the stone was broken off and taken to Dál Riata, possibly even by Columba who, according to some stories, used it as his pillow or altar on Iona. It is said to have been housed for a time on Dunadd, where it was used for the crowning of Dál Riatan kings, before being taken to Dunstaffnage Castle near Oban and thence to Scone in Perthshire where Scottish kings sat on it for their enthronement. There are good grounds for thinking that from at least the late seventh century abbots of Iona presided over Christian services to consecrate kings of Dál Riata, using as a precedent the possibly apocryphal ordination of King Aédán by Columba on Iona in 574 described by Adomnán. Ewan Campbell's book *Saints and Sea-Kings* includes a modern artist's impression of a royal inauguration on Dunadd, with the new king placing his foot in the rock-cut footprint while the abbot of Iona and other monks and warriors look on.[4] While there is no direct evidence that it was the location for such ceremonies, Dunadd undoubtedly took on the aura of a special and sacred place during the Middle Ages, not least because of its supposed association with royal inaugurations. In 1506 the Earl of Argyll, acting as the king's lieutenant with almost vice-regal powers, chose it as the place to issue proclamations by James IV about the future governance of the isles.

There is considerable debate as to whether the Dál Riata, the Gaelic speaking inhabitants of Argyll who gave their name to the kingdom which flourished there from the sixth to the ninth centuries, came over as immigrants from Ireland or were indigenous to the West Highlands. The idea that an Irish dynasty moved to western Scotland in the early sixth century, triggering a much broader movement of migration, is largely dependent on an account in a tenth-century manuscript, *Miniuguíd Senchusa fher nAlban* (History of the Men of Scotland), which is thought to be based on mid-seventh-century genealogies. It tells of Fergus Mór mac Eirc, a Gael living in County Antrim, invading what was to become Argyll around AD 500. His three sons, Angus, Loairn, or Lorne, and Fergus macEirc, are said to have established their capital at Dunadd and to have carved out between them the territory which they had conquered. The kindred of Angus went on to occupy Islay and Jura and those of Lorne to settle the northern part of Argyll, which now bears that name. Fergus macEirc had two sons, Comghall, who established himself on and gave his name to the Cowal peninsula, and Gabrán, who took Knapdale and Kintyre and was acknowledged as the first king of Dál Riata as a whole, which he ruled from his fort at Dunadd. Other important strategic strongholds were established at Dunaverty in Kintyre, Tarbert on Loch Fyne and Dunolly overlooking what is now Oban. One of Lorne's grandsons, Baodan, later took Morvern.

The purpose of this story is very clearly to provide an origin legend for what was to become Argyll, suggesting that the whole area was settled by members of one family and their descendants, known in Gaelic as cenéla. It gives priority to three groupings of kindred – the Cenél Gabrán in Kintyre, the Cenél Loairn in North Argyll and the Cenél Angus in Islay. By the early seventh century, led by the descendants of these three groups, the Dál Riata had become the dominant force in an area stretching from Ardnamurchan in the north to Arran in the south, the region which would later be given the name airer Goídel, the coastland of the Gael. There is an intriguing footnote to the story about Fergus in one of the carvings on the summit of Dunadd. Between the less distinct footprint and the boar, now almost impossible to discern, is a lightly incised outline of a human figure smoking a pipe and wearing a crown with the inscription 'King Fergus' written above. This is generally thought to be a piece of early twentieth century graffito although it is possible that there was an earlier carving underneath it.

Although it is still common to read that the Gaelic kingdom of Dál Riata came about as a result of Irish immigration into what is now Argyll, an increasing number of historians are profoundly sceptical of this interpretation of its origins. They point to the fact that all the place names in Argyll are Gaelic apart from some later Norse names. There are no Pictish names, which seems strange if Irish Gaels ousted the Picts, nor are there any Brittonic names suggesting an affinity with the inhabitants of the Strathclyde region to the south. On the basis of this evidence, Ewan Campbell maintains that throughout the Iron Age the inhabitants of what was to become Argyll spoke Gaelic and were much closer linguistically and culturally to their neighbours across the Irish Sea than they were to their land neighbours to the north, east and south.⁵ The mountainous region which divided Argyll from the Pictish territories of central, eastern and northern Scotland perhaps provided a greater linguistic and cultural barrier than the short sea crossing separating it from Ireland.

It is in fact quite possible that while the inhabitants of Argyll were Gaelic speaking long before AD500, there may have been some migration from Ireland around then on the part of a ruling elite. It certainly seems to be the case that the history of Argyll in the sixth and seventh centuries centred around territorial and familial disputes between the three cenéla said to have descended from Fergus Mór mac Eirc. As well as being at the centre of Dál Riata as a whole, Dunadd may also have been located on the border between the territories of Cenél Gabran and Cenél Loairn and may have oscillated between their spheres of influence. It also seems to have played a key role in bigger battles being waged by the Gaels of Dál Riata against the Strathclyde Britons, the Anglians of Northumbria and the Picts to the north and east. Some historians suggest that that the siege mentioned in the first reference in the Annals of Ulster may have involved the Cenél Loairn trying to throw off incursions by either the British or Northumbrians. The second reference specifically mentions the seizure of the fort by the Pictish king Oengus in 736. This seems to have been a crucial episode in a wider conflict in the mid eighth century that resulted in the Pictish conquest of Dál Riata. Pictish kings may well have been inaugurated on the top of Dunadd in the wake of this conquest – indeed some archaeologists date the carvings from this period, pointing to the strongly Pictish appearance of the boar in particular. Pictish domination of Dál Riata continued for perhaps as much as a hundred years before the emergence in the mid ninth century of a Gaelic dynasty under Cinnead macAilpín (Kenneth McAlpine) who ruled a combined Scottish and Pictish kingdom which, from around 900, was known as Alba and subsequently as Scotland. While retaining its legendary aura and mystery, Dunadd lost its strategic and political importance with this development, as the centre of gravity of the new kingdom moved eastwards to Forteviot, Scone and Dunkeld.

While Dunadd's century or so of occupation by the Picts from around 740 to 850 should not be forgotten, and may even have produced some of its iconic summit carvings, it is right that the hill fort is remembered first and foremost as a stronghold and symbol of Scots Gaeldom. Whether they had recently come over from Ireland or had long been resident on the west coast of Scotland, Argyll's Gaelic speaking inhabitants in the early Middle Ages were clearly culturally and linguistically close to their kinsmen across the water in Ireland, known to the Romans as the Scotti. Many proudly traced their ancestry back to Fionn macCumhaill (Fingal) and his followers, the Fianna or Féinn, a word which can be translated as warriors, giants or heroes. Dunadd has its own place in the stories that were told of these legendary Celtic fighting men. In some of them, one of the footprints on its summit is said to have been made where Ossian, the legendary son of Fingal who in later life became a blind bard, landed after leaping across the valley from Rhudil hill, over half a mile away. According to one version, Ossian was hunting along Lochfyneside when he was suddenly charged by a stag. To escape, he ran up the hill above Kilmichael and from there leapt to the top of Rhudil, where he left his right footprint, before making the leap to Dunadd where he left his left footprint.

The rock-cut footprint was also long known locally as 'The Fairy's Footmark' testifying to the notion that Dunadd was the dwelling place of fairies. It is not the only supposed fairy footprint in the vicinity. At the northern end of Loch Loran, four miles or so to the east of Dunadd, are five flat stones bearing what may be natural markings improved by light pecking. Two of them, which lie close together with what look like heels pointing across the loch, are called the 'Fairy Footprints'. The left foot has what could well be artificially added toes. Behind them are two oval stones with hollows which suggest large hoof-prints.

Through these and other associations, Dunadd has become part of the primal and mythical spiritual landscape of Argyll. Its fortifications and carvings speak of different values and priorities from those expressed by the prehistoric monuments that litter the valley below – of warriors and fighting men and the inauguration of kings rather than the worship of sun and stars and the veneration of the dead. Yet if the incised footprints on its summit suggest a radical departure from the cup and ring markings and standing stones in the valley below, they share that characteristic feature of Argyll's landscape, the spirituality of stone. Is it too fanciful to see the Ogham inscription as the voice of the rock proclaiming the rightful king after he has made his solemn covenant with the land by placing his foot in the carved footprint during the inauguration?

Dunadd does not just reflect Argyll's early primal and pagan religion. It also embraced and nurtured the new religion of Christianity that came over from Ireland in the sixth and seventh centuries. Among the artefacts found in archaeological digs on the site are a slate disc dating from between 600 and 800 inscribed with the words '*I nomine*', short for 'In the name of God', and a cross-incised quern, or grinding stone, of a distinctive style found on Iona and suggesting links with the monastery there. Further possible evidence for monks being resident on Dunadd is provided by the discovery of orpiment, a pigment used in the production of illuminated manuscripts. Viewed from a broader perspective, Dunadd is at the centre of a Christian landscape – there are twenty-six sites in its vicinity with evidence of early Christian activity, including nineteen with 'kil' names, denoting a church or ecclesiastical establishment, among them the immediately adjoining parishes of Kilmartin and Kilmichael Glassary. Within close proximity there are also eighty-three Christian carved stones dating from between the sixth and ninth centuries. Could it be that these symbols of the new faith were deliberately sited next to the many monuments to older primal religion in the Kilmartin valley and to the sacred hilltop fort in their midst?

There is one further feature of Dunadd worthy of mention. A well at the foot of a deep gully directly below the summit on the west side of the hill (the opposite side from the access route and difficult to reach) is known as St Columba's Well. How far back this dedication goes is uncertain but whatever its provenance and antiquity, it links Dunadd to the first towering spiritual giant of Argyll whose footprints still bestride the region, and who may indeed have visited the hill fort itself when it was the *caput regionis* of Dál Riata.

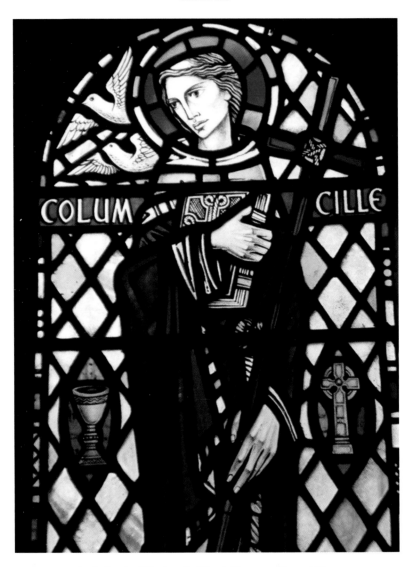

St Columba Window in North Transept, Iona Abbey

4

Columba's Footprints

No one has made a greater impact on the spiritual landscape of Argyll than Columba, the Irish monk who lived from 521 to 597. His imprint is found across the region – literally, if legend is to be believed, in the footprints that he left at the very south end of Kintyre and on a hillside in Morvern as well as in the caves, wells and chapels named after him. His Gaelic name, Choluim Chille (also variously rendered Colm, Calum or Columb Cille), prefaced by the prefix Cill or Kil, indicating an ecclesiastical site, occurs in at least eight well-attested early Argyll place names: at Tarbert on Jura; at Keil near Duror on Loch Linnhe; at Ardchattan near Benderloch at the mouth of Loch Etive; at Keil near Lochaline in Morvern; at Keil near Southend in Kintyre; in the north east of Mull; and in the parishes of Kildalton and Kilarrow on Islay. More recently, he has been commemorated in numerous stained-glass windows and church dedications across different Christian denominations. It is small wonder that Marian Pallister dedicates her book, *Lost Argyll*, to 'St Columba, whose path I keep crossing'.

Today Columba is associated primarily with Iona, the island where he established the monastery that played a central role in the Christianisation of Scotland and northern England and which is now visited by over 250,000 tourists and pilgrims every year. A bay and a hotel on the island are named after him and his story is told through displays in the north transept of the Abbey where a pair of stone feet are all that remain of a probable medieval monument to him. He is also depicted in two stained-glass windows in the Abbey, one in the north transept commemorating Kenneth MacLeod and the other high up in the east wall of the chancel. Yet virtually nothing remains on Iona from Columba's lifetime. What visitors see today is the restored Benedictine Abbey established around 1200, more than 600 years after his death. All that survive from his own monastery, which consisted of a number of simple huts made out of wood and wattle and daub, are the outlines in places of the boundary vallum or ditch and the possible site of his own austere cell on Tòrr an Aba, the mound in front of the Abbey. The high-standing crosses and dramatic Street of the Dead post-date Columba's life by at least 150 years, as does the restored shrine chapel to the left of the entrance to the Abbey where his corpse lay before being removed from the island to prevent its seizure by Viking raiders. These striking features of Iona's spiritual landscape testify to the power of a dead saint rather than to his faith or activities when alive. It is on the Argyll mainland and on some of its other islands that we can find stronger traces of the living Columba.

Historians are now generally agreed that Columba did not make directly for Iona when he left Ireland in 563. The romantic story that he left his beloved homeland as a penitential pilgrim determined never to look on it again and sailed from island to island until reaching Iona, the first from which there was no view back, only surfaced in the late eighteenth century. It is much more likely that he headed first for the mainland of Argyll. There is less agreement about what prompted the 42-year-old monk to make the journey that was to have such a decisive impact on the Christian history of Scotland and the British Isles. Was he exiled from Ireland for some crime, as several sources suggest? Did he simply desire, as his biographer Adomnán suggests, to be a pilgrim for Christ, following the call of white martyrdom which led many Irish monks to forsake the pleasures and distractions of home and take up a life of exile and renunciation? Was this a case of Celtic wanderlust or a midlife crisis? Or was he summoned by the king of Dál Riata to set up a church for his people?

This last possibility is given considerable credence by a reference in the Annals of Ulster, probably composed on Iona, to Conall mac Comgaill, king of Dál Riata from 558 to 574, granting the island of Iona to Columba in 574. It is significant that the first incident Adomnán records after describing Columba leaving Ireland is a meeting between the saint and this king. This would almost certainly have taken place at one of Dál Riata's royal palaces or forts. Dunadd has been suggested as the likeliest location although it could also have been at Dunaverty at the south end of Kintyre. Either way, it looks as though Columba was on the Argyll mainland before he went to Iona. Alfred Smyth goes so far as to suggest that he did not move to Iona until 574, at the beginning of the reign of Conall's successor, Aédán mac Gabráin, eleven years after his arrival in Argyll from Ireland.[1]

The shortest and least hazardous sea crossing between Ireland and Scotland is from the north east coast of Antrim to the southern tip of the Mull of Kintyre, a distance of just twelve miles. The notion that this was the route taken by Columba in 563 has had a powerful appeal to artists. A dramatic painting by William McTaggart entitled 'The coming of Columba', now hanging in the National Gallery of Scotland in Edinburgh, shows two white-sailed boats bearing the saint and his companions sailing into Gualdrons Bay near Machrihanish. Born near Campbeltown, McTaggart was perhaps not wholly unbiased in his choice of location – he began the painting in 1897 on one of his annual holidays in South Kintyre and depicted Columba arriving in the bay where he had played as a boy – but most historians agree that it is likely Kintyre was the saint's first port of call on leaving Ireland.

A ruined chapel and a well, both bearing Columba's name, are to be found close to the shore at Keil Point on the southern tip of Kintyre near the village of Southend. Nearby are two footprints carved on a rocky outcrop. Known as St. Columba's footprints, they supposedly mark the place where he first set foot in Scotland, having sailed into either Dunaverty or Caskay Bay. The more southerly footprint is laid parallel to the shore with the other, now largely eroded, at a ninety-degree angle to it and the date 564 carved between them. In fact, while the first footprint probably dates back to the first millennium BC, the other, more northerly, one was apparently carved by a local stonemason in 1885. He may also have added the date although there are suggestions that it was carved in the sixteenth century. Beside the footprints are what look like the outline or foundations of a small rectangular building. Could this conceivably have been a cell or chapel built by Columba when he landed here? This is unlikely – anything dating from his time would not have been built with stone. The footprints, along with the adjoining chapel and well, were

Columba's footprints, Southend

probably attributed and dedicated to Columba several hundred years after his death, either in the twelfth century or later in the Middle Ages, when the parish of Kilcomkill was established, perhaps by the MacDonald Lords of the Isles.

Yet even if Columba did not create either of these footprints himself, it is quite possible that he stood in the older one looking up towards the fortress of Dunaverty, a stronghold of the Dál Riatan kings perched on top of the rocky cliffs which loom over Keil Point. In his recent biography of the saint, Tim Clarkson speculates that the older footprint may have been used at royal inugurations with the nearby well providing water for sacred anointings, first by pagan priests and later by their Christian successors. He suggests that it may have been here that Aédán's anointing as king took place, an event which Adomnán described Columba presiding over on Iona. He also posits Dunaverty as Aédán's capital in Kintyre and the *caput regionis* where, according to Adomnán, Columba met sailors from Gaul.[2]

Others historians believe that the 'caput regionis' was Dunadd, another centre of royal power with two carved footprints on its summit, and that this was where Columba met King Conall soon after arriving from Ireland. Given his close links with Dál Riatan royalty, it seems highly probable that Columba would have visited Dunadd. An early settlement known as Kilmahumaig, less than three miles from Dunadd and at one time annexed to Kilmartin parish, seems to have been dedicated to Columba and provides further possible evidence of his association with this area. So too does the proximity of one of the most romantic and evocative places in Argyll's spiritual landscape which bears his name, St Columba's cave on the shore of

Loch Caolisport near Ellary in Knapdale. There are in fact two caves on this site. In his book *Celtic Scotland*, William Skene suggested that Columba might have used one as a chapel and the other as a dwelling place when visiting King Conall at Dunadd which is just nine miles away. Mary Donaldson believed that Conall might, in fact, have had his fortress on top of An Torr at the head of Loch Caolisport and less than two miles from the caves.[3]

Entrance to Columba's Cave, Ellary

There have even been suggestions that the bay in front of the caves rather than the Mull of Kintyre may have been where Columba first landed in Argyll. Excavations suggest that the caves were occupied as early as 5500BC. A considerable quantity of pottery from the early iron age points to more intensive use and occupation between c.500BC and AD400. The caves seem next to have been used in the seventh and eighth centuries by Christians, possibly hermits or itinerant preachers with Columban affiliations. They were probably responsible for carving the crosses which can still be seen on the rock face at the back of the main cave and turning it into a chapel by erecting an altar on a rock shelf. Several authors have attributed the carvings to Columba himself but archaeologists are disinclined to date them so early. Human remains suggest that the caves and the area around them were used for burials and the proximity of the

Altar in Columba's Cave

burial ground at Cladh a'Bhile with its important collection of early Christian gravestones may be significant (page 84). From the ninth century Norsemen apparently stored their boats in the caves and probably slept in them – a rare Viking balance has been found in the larger one. In the twelfth century Christians seem to have returned to them and in the following century a chapel was built by the entrance to the main cave, the ruins of which are still visible. Much later the caves were used by fishermen to store their nets. Like so many places in Argyll's spiritual landscape, St Columba's cave has had many different uses and incarnations. It is now once again a shrine and a place of pilgrimage, with occasional services being held there by Roman Catholics, Episcopalians and Presbyterians.

It is not just in Kintyre and Knapdale that Columba has left possible marks on the landscape. His footprint is also said to be visible on the summit of Glas Bheinn, the hill in the south east corner of Morvern, although I have to confess that neither I nor the local historians whom I have consulted have been able to find it. The story goes that he climbed the hill having crossed Loch Linnhe from Lismore with Moluag, perhaps in a demonstration of fraternal reconciliation after their rather unseemly scramble to be the first to reach that island (page 78). Columba placed his foot on the rocky summit and pointed down to a green knoll on the other side of Loch Aline as the perfect location for a new church. This is the foundation legend for the church at Keil (now Lochaline parish church) originally known as Cill Cholumchille, or Kilcolmkeil. There is a further story that as he made his way across the shallow waters of the loch to reach his chosen site, Columba stood on a flounder which told him to watch where he put his crooked legs, provoking the saint's response: 'If I have crooked legs, may you always have a crooked mouth'. This is supposedly the reason for the rather ugly facial features of this particular species of fish.

Adomnán has several stories about Columba's travels through the 'rough and rocky' district of Ardnamurchan. One describes the saint miraculously creating a spring of water and font in which to baptise a child brought to him. This is supposedly the origin of what is still called Columba's Well, a natural basin into which water drips in a cave known as Uamha Thuill near Kilmory on the north Ardnamurchan coast. It was renowned for its healing properties and resorted to by people suffering from mental illness until the mid nineteenth century. Another story tells of him standing in the sea praying and causing a storm which drowns an evil man. This is said to have taken place in 'Sharp Bay', which has been tentatively identified as Sanna Bay at the west end of the Ardnamurchan peninsula. Adomnán also suggests that Columba twice got as far as the boundary between Ardnamurchan and Moidart, the northernmost point of Argyll, in his search for good oak timber for building his monastery on Iona. On one of these visits he was delighted to find that the river where he and his companions halted was teeming with salmon. According to local folklore, he used the word 'sale' to describe the fish, thus originating the name 'Shiel' by which the river has been known ever since.

Columba's church-planting activities involved the foundation of several monasteries across Argyll. Like their Iona mother house, most of them were located on islands. The only mainland monastic foundation mentioned by Adomnán is that of Cella Diuni on the shores of Loch Awe. There is no consensus among historians as to where this was. Tom Clancy favours a site near Kilchrenan at the north end of the loch, while both Marion Campbell and Marian Pallister prefer Kilneuair, 'the Church of the Yews', which sits on a flat-topped knoll on the south east bank of Loch Awe close to an old drove road to Loch Fyne. It was known at least as far back as 1389 as 'SanctColmysKirke in Glasrie'. There have also been suggestions that Cella Diuni may have been sited at Kilmaha, roughly half way up the west side of Loch Awe, where there is a chapel and burial ground.[4]

Adomnán mentions two monasteries closely connected with Columba on Tiree –one at Artchain and the other at Mag Luinge, which was probably situated at Soroby on the south-east of the island. The latter seems to have been set up as a penitents' colony, to which Columba sent those who came to him seeking pastoral counselling and absolution for the crimes that they had committed. An incident recounted by Adomnán could be taken to suggest that Columba did not like Tiree very much. Once, while praying alone on Iona, he saw in front of him a 'line of foul black devils armed with iron spikes and drawn up ready for battle'. Realizing that they wanted to attack his monastery, he engaged them in battle all day and eventually, with the help of the angels who came to his aid, he succeeded in banishing them to Tiree where he predicted that they would invade the monasteries and bring deadly plague to the monks. In the event, thanks to prayer and fasting, only one man died in the community at Mag Luinge, although the other monasteries on Tiree were ravaged by the deadly plague as he had predicted. Columba's name is associated with several other places on Tiree. A hill near the pier is called both Cìoch Chaluim Chille (Columba's hill) and Dùn an t-Sìthein (Fort of the Fairyhill). A passer-by is said to have heard beautiful fairy music and found a door which led him inside the hill where he found fairies singing and dancing. A small flat rock to the right of the pier and in front of the parish church is known as Mallachdaig or 'The Little Accursed One'. Columba is said to have tied his coracle to seaweed on this rock on a visit to the island only to find on his return that the boat had drifted away. He cursed it and said nothing would ever grow on it again. A rocky outcrop further along the beach is named Sgeir Naomhaig or Holy Skerry because he allegedly blessed it after it proved a more reliable anchorage point.

According to local tradition Columba used to pray under a yew tree on the island of Bernera off Lismore, where he subsequently built a chapel. There are also references to him founding a monastery on an unidentified island named Elen. The location of another unidentified island called Hinba, with which Columba apparently had a close and consistent connection, has prompted much speculation. Adomnán described him founding a monastery there, to which he later sent his uncle Ernan as abbot, and making frequent visits, both to escape from the hustle and bustle of Iona by going on solitary retreat and also to meet other important Christian leaders. It was on Hinba that he celebrated the Eucharist with four prominent monastic founders, Brendan, Cormac, Cainnech and Comgall, who had come from Ireland to visit him. Hinba was also where Columba experienced, over a space of three days and nights, an intense concentration of angelic visions which revealed many secrets and made plain passages from Scripture.

Hinba clearly played an important part in Columba's life. On the basis of his reading of Adomnán, Alfred Smyth proposed that it was Columba's first base on Scotland and that he did not move from there to Iona until the beginning of Aédán's reign in 574. John Marsden also puts the foundation of Hinba before that of Iona. Gunna, which lies between Coll and Tiree; Eileach an Naoimh in the Garvellach islands in the Firth of Lorn, where an isolated early grave is said to be that of Columba's mother, Eithne; Eilean Shona in Loch Moidart; Canna, where there is a medieval church dedicated to Columba at A'Chill, the main settlement on the island; and Seil have all been proposed as the location of Hinba. Most historians, however, tend to favour either Colonsay/Oronsay or Jura. Both Alan Macquarrie, who devotes an interesting chapter to the question in his book *The Saints of Scotland*, and Richard Sharpe, editor of the best edition of Adomnán's life, opt for Oronsay/Colonsay.

I myself am strongly inclined to agree with William Watson and other Celtic scholars that Hinba is, in fact, Jura. There are several pieces of evidence supporting this theory. Adomnán states that Ernan, Columba's uncle, was abbot there. The main graveyard on Jura, on the site of what is thought to have been the earliest ecclesiastical settlement on the island, which lies above the main settlement at Craighouse and near the old crofting township of Keils, is called Kilearnadil. Local tradition has it that Ernan wished to be buried on the island and that his body was transported back from Iona where he died on a visit, landed on a rock known as Leac Earnan at the south end of Jura and carried to Kilearnadil. Both the well and the ecclesiastical settlement at Tarbert, half way up Jura, seem to have been dedicated to Columba from an early period. Lowlandmen's Bay, situated between Craighouse and Tarbert on the island's east coast, perfectly fits Adomnán's description of the Muirbolc Már, or 'great bag-like bay', on Hinba. Watson further argues that Hinba was named after the Old Irish word *inbe* meaning an incision and that this must have been suggested by some distinctive topographical feature. Jura is virtually bisected by Loch Tarbert which presents a more dramatic example of such an incision than is found on any other island off Argyll.

Columba exemplified in his faith and his lifestyle the evangelical simplicity that I have suggested has been a characteristic of Argyll's spiritual landscape. The earliest written account of him, *Amra Choluimb Chille*, an elegy written within a few years of his death by a blind Irish poet, Dallán Forgaill, described him as 'a sound, austere sage for Christ'. His rigorous, muscular Christianity is well captured in the portrayal of his nightly routine on Iona in the Old Irish life, written some centuries after his death. It describes him sleeping for just a few hours on the bare earth floor of his cell, his head resting on a stone pillow, and then rising and going down to the machair by the seashore where he would chant all 150 psalms before sunrise each morning.

Columba had a strong mystical bent and was open to supernatural experiences. There are many stories of him communing with angels, the most dramatic being the one reported by Adomnán in which a fellow monk saw 'holy angels, dressed in white robes, flying down with amazing speed and gathering around the holy man' as he stood on a little knoll on Iona praying with his arms spread towards heaven. The presumed site of this encounter, a little hill just off the road down to the machair on the west side of the island, has long been called Cnoc nan Aingeal, or the Hill of the Angels. Adomnán writes more than once of Columba being bathed in heavenly light. During the three days and nights when he experienced visitations and spiritual insights on Hinba, the hut in which he resided was filled with light which could be seen 'escaping through the chinks of the doors and through the keyholes' while inside Columba could be heard 'singing spiritual songs of a kind never heard before'. In his case, mysticism was not accompanied by the theological liberalism which later often went with it in Argyll's distinctive brand of Christianity. Whatever else he was, Columba was no liberal. The emphasis in the Latin poem, *Altus Prosator*, the most likely to be genuine of the many works attributed to him, is on the sovereignty of God, the reality of human sin, the depth of the fall of humanity, the power of divine judgement, the terrible apocalyptic nature of Christ's second coming and the reality of Hell. In theological terms, he anticipated the conservative evangelicalism found in the Western Isles rather than the gentler and more open outlook which tended to be displayed in Argyll.

It is in his interaction with the physical landscape of Argyll, rather than in his theology, that Columba stands among the founding fathers of its distinctive spirituality. He was very conscious of the power of the elements and especially of the sea, which was an ever-present force around the islands and coastal regions where he planted most of his monasteries and undertook many of his evangelistic journeys. It was not uncommon for monks to drown while sailing to and from Iona. In one of the prayers attributed to him he describes himself as 'a little man, trembling and most wretched, rowing through the infinite storm of this age'. A poem written soon after his death graphically describes him crossing 'the long-haired sea … foam-flecked, seal-filled, savage, bounding, seething, white-tipped, pleasing, doleful.'

Gaelic to the core of his being, with supposed descent from Niall of the Nine Hostages, roots in the Irish warrior aristocracy and training as a poet, Columba has often been portrayed as uniting the Celtic traditions of the *Fianna,* heroic warriors, and the *Filidhean*, poets with a priestly calling. Some modern writers have followed Charles Plummer and other earlier Celtic scholars in portraying Columba essentially as a Christianized Druid, gifted with second sight (see page 204). In this reading, the angels with whom he communed take over the role of the fairies of pre-Christian Celtic mythology. In 1693 John Fraser, Dean of the Isles, suggested that Columba had deliberately built his monastery on Iona on the site of an existing Druid school or college and even taken over this pre-Christian institution. The notion that there were already Druids on Iona, suggested by the early name of the area near Martyrs' Bay, Cladh nan Drunnich, or the Druids' Burial Place, appealed strongly to eighteenth-century syncretists and romantics who pointed out that the ancient Greek historian Plutarch had written of an island of holy men close to the coast. Recent radio-carbon dating suggests that there was an enclosure in pre-Christian times covering roughly the same area as that bounded by the later monastic vallum on Iona. The extent to which

Statue of Columba with a bishop's mitre over doorway of St Columba's Church, Poltalloch

Columba and his contemporaries consciously took over some of the roles and institutions of pre-Christian druids and bards and worked with and adapted some of their belief systems rather than repudiating them is hotly debated by scholars. It is part of a much wider debate as to whether so-called Celtic Christianity represented continuity with or radical rejection of pre-Christian Celtic religion.

It is as a towering Christian figure that Columba is most obviously and vividly remembered throughout Argyll. As a saint, he has a unique ecumenical reach, being hailed equally enthusiastically by Presbyterians, including Free Presbyterians, ever keen to point out that he never became a bishop; Episcopalians who see him as a proto-Anglican and even occasionally endow him with an episcopal mitre, as in the statue above the entrance porch of St Columba's Church on the Poltalloch estate near Kilmartin; and Roman Catholics who place him high in the pantheon of early medieval saints. Rather surprisingly, no current Church of Scotland or Roman Catholic parish churches in Argyll are dedicated to him, a strange omission given that there are several churches in both denominations dedicated to lesser-known local saints, but many have stained-glass windows in which he is depicted. The east window of Morvern Parish Church, Lochaline, puts him in extremely exalted company, with Christ above him and St John and St Paul below, and a window in Toward Parish Church on the Cowal peninsula unusually portrays him dying, his right arm being held up by his faithful servant, Diarmait, so that he can give a blessing and his eyes gazing towards heaven from where two angels have descended to meet him.

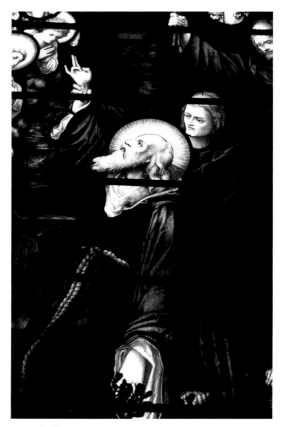

Detail of window showing death of Columba,
Toward Church

Three Episcopal churches in Argyll are dedicated to Columba:
Bridgend on Islay, Gruline on Mull, and the one already mentioned
at Poltalloch. So is the Roman Catholic Cathedral in Oban where he
makes two appearances on the oak panel behind the high altar, on
one side standing with a Celtic cross while the Pictish King Brude
kneels at his feet and on the other exchanging pastoral staffs with St
Mungo, or Kentigern of Strathclyde. The Catholic primary school in
Oban is also dedicated to him. Columba is commemorated in Oban's
Episcopal Cathedral, which is dedicated to St John, by a statue to the
right of the reredos with the face of Alexander Chinnery Haldane,
Bishop of Argyll and the Isles, who commissioned its building. He

is also a significant presence in Oban's secular landscape with the imposing red sandstone Columba Hotel standing guard over the North Pier. In the town's Tourist Information Centre, housed in what was formerly St Columba's Parish Church in Argyll Square, a stained-glass window depicts him and a companion in a small boat.

Columba is bigger than Argyll, of course. He spent more of his life in Ireland than in Scotland and he is rightly remembered there, not least at his birthplace at Lough Gartan and his monastic foundation at Derry. He is also commemorated across Scotland. In contrast to his neglect in Argyll, many Church of Scotland parish churches in other parts of the country are dedicated to him. It is, however, to Argyll, where he spent most of the last four decades of his life engaging in pastoral and missionary work and planting monasteries, that he especially belongs. In death even more than in life, he played a central role in the development of its spiritual landscape. Devotion to him throughout the Middle Ages, not least among the Lords of the Isles, led to numerous chapels, churches, wells and other natural and man-made features being dedicated to him. He was hailed as a protector by the Gaels and later by the Scots as a whole when they faced their enemies. Even the Norse enlisted him in their efforts to retain their hold over the islands off Argyll. In 1249 King Alexander II of Scotland, lying off the island of Kerrera on his way to attack King Haakon's Norse fleet in the Hebrides, was told in a vision by Columba, who appeared to him as a 'frowning figure, very bald in front', to return home. He ignored the advice and was promptly stricken with a fever. Landed on Kerrera, Alexander died on the eastern shore at a place which is still known as Ach-an-Righ, or the Field of the King. Norwegian sources credit the saint's posthumous intervention with preventing an attack on the Hebrides.

Columba will, of course, always be associated primarily with Iona where a whole ritual landscape was laid out for the many medieval pilgrims who came to venerate his relics. His allure is still the main factor drawing visitors to the island today. As we have seen, however, he also left supposed footprints across the Argyll mainland from the southern tip of the Mull of Kintyre to the northern fringes of Ardnamurchan via Ellary, Dunadd and Loch Awe. He stands as the pre-eminent representative of that good and godly company, the saints of Argyll.

5

The Saints of Argyll

More than anywhere else in the British Isles outside Ireland, Argyll is a land of saints. They have left their mark on the landscape in numerous place names with the prefix Kil and in the dedications of chapels, crosses, caves and wells. The overwhelming majority of the saints commemorated in Argyll were missionary monks from Ireland who lived in the sixth or seventh centuries. Many had an association with Columba and Iona. Their commemoration underlines the close links between Irish and Scottish Dál Riata.

Argyll has more place names beginning with Kil than any other part of Scotland – there are twenty-eight in South Kintyre and forty on Islay alone. The prefix derives from the Gaelic word 'cill' ('cell' in old Irish) denoting a church, ecclesiastical settlement or burial ground. It is thought to come originally from the Latin word 'cella' used for a cell or room in a house containing a shrine to a god. In Argyll the 'Kil' prefix is almost invariably followed by the name of a saint. This linkage has often been taken to indicate that the saint named actually visited or had a direct link with the area where he or she is commemorated. In fact, many Kil names cannot be dated with any certainty before the thirteenth century, and in some cases no further back than the sixteenth century. Stories arose to suggest the actual historical presence of a particular individual in the place where he or she was later commemorated but they are often of relatively late provenance and cannot be verified by contemporary sources.

If we cannot be certain that places named after a saint indicate that he or she was ever actually there, they do suggest local popular devotion to that particular individual. The persistence of cults of local Celtic saints was a marked and distinctive feature of the spiritual life of the West Highlands throughout the Middle Ages.

As Rachel Butter has demonstrated, some places were probably named after saints simply because that was what local people called them – 'commemoration' may be a better term than 'dedication' to describe how many of the Kil names came into being.[1] The process can perhaps be compared to the modern practice of naming streets after figures like Nelson Mandela, with the difference being that in the case of the saints' commemorations it was predominantly local rather than international figures who were honoured in what was probably mostly an expression of popular usage, not official decree, although there were cases were political factors played a part in choosing one saint rather than another to mark a territory.

Although recent scholarship has questioned the physical presence of several of these saints in Argyll, they have been a very considerable imagined presence and an important feature of the spiritual landscape as patrons, protectors and the subjects of legends and stories. In one particularly dramatic example, their activities were even believed to have directly affected the physical landscape. Distinctive features in the geology and flora of the island of Lismore were attributed to the consequences of the race between Columba and Moluag to be the first to land there.

The list that follows includes those saints thought to have been present and active in the region and the rather larger number apparently commemorated in dedications who may not always have set foot in Argyll. It does not include Biblical saints like John and Michael, who inspired dedications in Argyll as across the Christian world, nor the Virgin Mary, who is almost certainly commemorated in places named Kilmory and Kilmorie. Rather, the emphasis is predominantly on local saints, the great majority of whom hailed from Ireland. It is not an exhaustive list and, as with everything pertaining to the so called 'golden age' of Celtic Christianity in the sixth and seventh centuries, it needs to be treated with extreme caution and accompanied by a reminder that we are here in the realm of legend rather than hard historical evidence. The brief sketches of those listed below should not be treated as biographies. They are culled from hagiographical writings spread over 800 years and reflect the posthumous cults of the saints commemorated in Argyll rather than their actual historical lives. The early sixteenth-century *Aberdeen Breviary*, our best source for the lives of Scottish saints, often presents what are clearly composite figures, based on conflating material from several sources probably relating to different individuals. It can be very difficult to disentangle them.

Abbán moccu Cormaic (d. 520?)

A monk from Leinster commemorated mostly in Ireland, he is said to have retreated for solitary prayer to a cave on the island of Eilean Mór at the mouth of Loch Sween. A chapel there is dedicated to him, as was the parish church at Keills on the tip of the nearby Tayvallich peninsula. His name, localised as Macoharmaig, was used for the whole chain of islands at the mouth of Loch Sween, which are known as the McCormick Isles. According to a tradition which cannot be verified any earlier than 1797, he was buried on Eilean Mór.

Adomnán c. 627–704

A close kinsman of Columba, he was born in the north east of Ireland and probably came to the monastery on Iona around 650, becoming the ninth abbot there in 679. He is best known as Columba's biographer and author of *De Locis Sanctis*, a treatise on Christian holy places and pilgrimage sites supposedly based on information from Arculf, a Gaulish bishop who was returning from a pilgrimage to the Holy Land when his ship was blown off course and ended up in the Hebrides. Most dedications to him are in the Strathay area. Argyll commemorations are rare, among them possibly being Kileonan in Kilkerran parish in South Kintyre.

Aidan (d. 651)

Originally from Ireland, he was a monk on Iona before being sent down to the kingdom of Northumbria in 634 following the request of King Oswald to set up the monastery on Lindisfarne, or Holy Island. There were several other saints with this name, which is a diminutive of Áed, some of whom may also have been the objects of cults in Argyll.

Bathán, Baithine or Bathene c.536–600

A cousin of Columba, he was made head of the monastic house at Mag Luinge on Tiree and succeeded Columba as abbot of Iona in 597. Adomnán describes Columba prophesying that while crossing from Iona to Tiree, Bathán would encounter a large whale but that his faith in Christ would shield him from danger. The whale duly appeared and although his companions in the boat were terrified, Bathán 'without a tremor of fear blessed the sea and the waves. Immediately, the great creature plunged under the waves and was not seen again.'[2]

Berach (d. 595)

An Irish disciple of Kevin of Glendalough, he is commemorated largely in Ireland and has few, if any, Scottish associations although there is a possible commemoration at Kilberry in Knapdale. It is difficult to be certain, as there were several saints with this name.

Blane (d. 590)

He is largely associated with the Strathblane area, notably Dunblane, and also with Kingarth on Bute. There is no evidence that he was ever in Argyll but there is a possible commemoration of him at Kilblaan at Conie Glen just north of Southend, and William Watson mentions another at Glenshira in Inveraray parish.

Brendan (c. 484–c. 577)

Associated with the Irish monastic foundation at Clonfert, he is best known as 'The Navigator' because of the legendary stories of his travels across the Atlantic. Adomnán lists him as one of those present at a celebration of the Eucharist with Columba on the island of Hinba. According to his Life in the *Codex Salmanticensis*, he founded monasteries on Tiree and on an island called Ailech, which has been identified as Eileach an Naoimh in the Garvellach Islands. Creag á Bhriundain, a rocky outcrop on Tiree, is possibly named after him – local legend has it that he came there in 514 – and he is said to have established a church on the island called Bledach. The date of his foundation of the monastery on Eileach an Naoimh is usually put, without very much scholarly basis, at around 540. Possible commemorations include Kilbrandon, a place name which occurs on Mull, Islay and Seil, where the remains of a ruined chapel, said to have been built on the site of a cell which he occupied, can be seen from in front of the parish church; Kilbrannan Chapel near Skipness in South Kintyre; and the Kilbrannan Sound, the stretch of water between Arran and Kintyre.

Bride or Bridget (c. 451–525)

Despite there being no evidence that the celebrated Irish abbess of Kildare ever came to Argyll, Graham Ritchie claims that there are more dedications to her in the region than to any other saint.[3] They include the Kilbride chapels just south of Oban, near Garbhallt on Loch Fyne, and at Rhudle near Kilmartin. She is commemorated in both a window and an icon in St Bride's Episcopal Church at Onich, North Ballachulish.

Canice, Cainnech, or Kenneth (c. 525–600)

Founder of the monastery at Aghaboe or Achad Bó, between Leinster and Munster, he was a close friend of Columba. Adomnán mentions him visiting Columba on Hinba and also describes him making a miraculously calm passage to Iona in the midst of a storm. On another occasion, he apparently forgot to take his staff with him when he set sail for Ireland from Iona. Columba somehow miraculously dispatched it to the 'the little island of Aitech', identified by John Marsden as Texa, the islet in Loch Indaal to the south of Islay, where Cainnech found it lying on the shore as he passed by.[4] Possible commemorations include Kilchenzie, south of Campbeltown; Cill Choinnich or Kilchanie on the Isle of Tiree; Kilchanie on Coll; Kilkenneth on Colonsay; and the island of Inchkenneth off the west coast of Mull. He seems to have gone on to evangelise the Picts in North East Fife.

Catan or Cathan (d. 560 or 595?)

There was more than one saint with this name. Martyrologies describe what may be a composite figure from Bangor, County Down, of royal lineage and educated by Patrick. He seems to have come to Argyll before setting up a monastic community at the south end of the island of Bute. Apparent dedications to him across Argyll include a stone called Cruidhe Chattan (Catan's heel) on Colonsay, Cill-Cathain at Kildalton on Islay and Ardchattan Priory by Loch Etive. The name Kilchattan is found associated with churches or chapels on the islands of Gigha, Colonsay and Luing where he supposedly lived for a time as a hermit.

Ciaran – sixth century

There are several Irish saints with this name, two of whom seem to have had strong cults in Argyll. The first (c. 501–530) was Bishop of Saigir in County Offaly and the second (c. 516–546) abbot of Clonmacnoise. John Marsden suggests that the earlier Ciaran may have come to Kintyre around the time of Fergus Mór and the foundation of the kingdom of Scottic Dál Riata and been active around Campbeltown.[5] There are several apparent dedications in this area, including St Ciaran's Cave. Campbeltown itself was originally known as Ceann Loch Cille Chiaran – the Head of the Loch of Ciaran's Chapel – and Kilcherran Church, first mentioned in the thirteenth century, was the parish church for the eastern part of the South Kintyre peninsula. There is also a Loch Ciaran near Clachan a few miles south of Tarbert. Kilchiaran Chapel and Bay on Islay possibly commemorate the later Ciaran of Clonmacnoise.

Colmanella, or Colman Elo (c. 556–611)

Best known as the founder of the church at Llan Elo, or Lynally, near Durrow, he is said to have been the author of an early devotional work, *The Alphabet of Piety*. According to a Medieval Irish life, his mother was said to be Columba's sister. Some later sources suggest that he came to Iona with Columba. Adomnán describes him sailing to Iona through the Coryvreckan whirlpool and being blessed by Columba with a fair wind for a return voyage to Ireland. Kilcalmonell Parish Church at Clachan, Kintyre, possibly commemorated him.

Comgall (d. 602)

Founder of the monastery at Bangor on Belfast Lough, he is associated in a legend of uncertain provenance with establishing a monastery on Tiree which was attacked by the Picts. Comgall called on the Lord in prayer and the Picts were struck with blindness and a storm drove their ship aground. They subsequently released the monks and begged forgiveness. Comgall prayed for them and their sight was restored and the storm abated. Adomnán mentions him visiting Columba on Hinba.

Comgan, Comhghan or Congan – sixth century?

Described in the *Aberdeen Breviary* as an Irish king who was driven from his kingdom and became a monk at Lochalsh in northern Argyll, he appears to be commemorated in the medieval chapel of Kilchoan on the western end of the Ardnamurchan peninsula. Other sources describe a Comgan whose mother was Columba's sister and there also appear to be links with Findoca. There are other possible dedications incorporating the name Comgan on Islay and around the Argyll coast.[6]

Statue of St Conan, south wall of St Conan's Kirk

Conan – seventh century?

Another shadowy figure, he is associated particularly with Lorne and specifically with the area around Loch Awe. There have been suggestions that the island of Innis Chonain was his base and that he may have been buried there. He is commemorated in St Conan's Well, used until relatively recent times for baptisms but now a somewhat unprepossessing swampy spring surrounded by a wooden fence that stands by the side of the main A85 road opposite the police station in the middle of Dalmally. His statue looks down Loch Awe from amidst the flying buttresses of St Conan's Kirk.

Constantine (d. 576?)

This saint, unusual in possibly being British rather than Irish, and associated with the monastery at Govan in Glasgow, is said to have been martyred by a group of pirates. Local legend suggests that his martyrdom took place at Kilchousland a few miles up the east side of the Kintyre peninsula from Campbeltown, where there is now a ruined chapel, but there is no hard evidence to support this story.

Dallán Forgaill – sixth century

A blind poet from Moynehall in Co. Cavan, he almost certainly wrote the *Amra Choluimb Chille*, an account of Columba written shortly after his death. Although there is no evidence that he ever left Ireland, he is possibly commemorated at Kiladalloig in Kintyre.

Domongart – sixth century

This saint, who appears in the Martyrology of Tallaght, may possibly be commemorated in Kildouenegarth, one of the lost churches of the Glassary parish.

Donan, or Donnan (d. 617?)

According to accounts in several Irish annals, he accompanied Columba to Iona and later founded a monastery on Eigg, where he was massacred along with around fifty companions, apparently by pirates. While most dedications to him are in the Western Isles, he is possibly commemorated at Kildonan in Kintyre.

Ernan – sixth century

Confusingly, there are several Ernans associated with Columba, three of whom may conceivably be dedicatees of churches in Argyll. The earliest one, his maternal uncle, supposedly travelled to Iona with him. He was made abbot of the monastery on Hinba but soon afterwards was taken ill and, according to Adomnán, died almost immediately after returning to Iona. He is possibly commemorated in Kilearnadil, the name of the original parish church on Jura and now applied to the burial ground.

Ernan (d. 635)

Adomnán describes this second Ernan who, as a boy, met Columba in Ireland, as 'famous throughout all the churches of Scotia'. There may well have been dedications to him in Argyll.

Ernan (d. c. 640)

The third Ernan, Columba's nephew, is mostly associated with monasteries in Ireland. The burial ground of Cill Mhic Eòghainn on Ulva may conceivably commemorate him. William Watson and Rachel Butter are sceptical about claims that he is also commemorated by the old parish church of Kilvicheon on Mull.

Fillan – sixth century

Once again, the Fillan of the *Aberdeen Breviary* is a composite figure. Most dedications are found in the Loch Earn area, although there are place names possibly commemorating him in Argyll near Tyndrum and at Killinallan on Islay.

Findlugan – sixth century

A contemporary of Columba whose life he apparently saved by interposing his body between the saint and a would-be assassin on the island of Hinba, he seems to have become the first abbot of a monastery established by Columba near Lough Foyle in northern Ireland. It has been suggested that he established and gave his name to the monastery at Finlaggan on Islay.

Finan, or Finnan – seventh century

There were several Irish saints with this name. The one who seems to have the clearest Argyll connections is thought to have come from Leinster and died between 675 and 695. He is said to have landed at Kilchoan from where he walked across the Ardnamurchan peninsula, stopping to rest on the shoulder of a hill between the townships of Ockle and Gortenfern which is known as Suidhe Fhianain (St Finnan's Seat). From there he saw the island on Loch Shiel on which he resolved to establish his cell and where he lived for some time. Known as Eilean Fhianain, and also as the Green Isle, it marks Argyll's northern boundary. On its summit there is a ruined chapel. A bronze bell housed in a recess on the east wall behind the altar was reputedly used by him but is unlikely to date back beyond the tenth century. A spring on the eastern flank of Beinn Resipol, the highest mountain in Sunart, is known as Tobar Fhianain. There are also possible dedications on Islay, Mull, Coll and Tiree and at Kilfinan in Cowal. Some accounts suggest that in order to undergo penitential suffering he deliberately contracted leprosy from a child who came to him. His name has been adopted by a modern Orthodox Christian Community based near Acharacle and its chapel contains two modern icons of him. Much of his missionary work

St Finnan's Bell

seems to have taken place in the area north of Argyll where he is commemorated at Glenfinnan and in other place names.

Findoca

A very shadowy figure of unknown date and provenance who deserves inclusion in this list if only because she is one of very few female saints associated with Argyll. A thirteenth-century land grant refers to 'the church of Findoca of Inchealt', which has led to speculation that she may have been abbess and perhaps even the founder of a nunnery on the island of Inishail in Loch Awe. A document dating from 1433 suggests that Killunaig Church on Coll, which had a link with the nunnery on Iona, was dedicated to her and it is also possible that she was commemorated in the burial ground of Killunaig on Mull.

Fintan Munnu, Mun or Munn (d. 635)

Originally from Leinster, and known as Fintan in Ireland, he was said to be a cousin of Columba and is sometimes described as a leper and a healer of lepers, although this could well be a confusion with Finnan. Adomnán, who describes him as one 'who came to enjoy renown among all the churches of the Scotti', tells of how he arrived as a young man on Iona hoping to join the monastery. He arrived just after Columba had died and Bathán, the new abbot, made it clear that he should not remain there, quoting a prophecy from Columba that God wished him to be an abbot in Ireland. So accordingly he went back there.

Despite this story, the focus of his cult seems to have been Argyll rather than Ireland and there are several dedications to him in the region, including an ancient chapel on the island of Eilean Munde in Loch Leven near Ballachulish where he is said to have lived for a while as a hermit. He is credited with founding the church at Kilmun on the north shore of the Holy Loch, where a recent ground-penetrating radar survey has revealed a circular enclosure suggesting a seventh-or eighth-century monastic settlement, and an early cross-incised stone has been re-discovered. A charter of 1262 mentions a church dedicated to Munn on this site. Medieval lives and legends suggest that the name 'Holy Loch' derived from sand which he brought there in his sandals from either the Holy Land or 'the Land of Promise'. The name Kilmun is also found just north of Loch Avich near the Castle of the Red Haired Maiden, in Glen Aray near Inveraray, and near Dalavich on Loch Awe where there are the remains of a rect-angular building, possibly a chapel. His other name, Fintan, seems to have given rise to the dedication of a chapel and burial ground at Killundine in Morvern, originally known as Cill Fhionntáin.

It is striking that the four places named Kilmun in Argyll were all close to Campbell centres of power. According to local trad-ition, Kilmun Chapel by Loch Awe was used for burials during the Campbells' occupation of the nearby castle on Innis Chonnell. The collegiate church established at Kilmun on the Holy Loch in 1442 by Duncan Campbell has been the main burial place for subsequent Campbell chiefs, including most of the Earls and Dukes of Argyll (see pages 140–1). Indeed, Munn seems effectively to have been

Window depicting St Munn, Kilmun Church

taken up as the patron saint of the Campbells. Rachel Butter writes that 'it is tempting to suppose that the Campbells themselves introduced the cult of Munn to Argyll' but she thinks it goes back earlier and that 'Munnu was a saint with a powerful cult in Argyll possibly from the seventh century – the Campbells may well have appropriated it to reinforce their rootedness in the ancient landscape'.[7] She suggests that Kilmun on Loch Awe may originally have been the most important site associated with the saint and conceivably where he was buried. Somewhat ironically, given Munn's strong Campbell connections, Eilean Munde in Loch Leven became the favoured burial place for several branches of the MacDonald clan.

Both the Church of Scotland and Roman Catholic churches at Ballachulish are dedicated to Munn, as is the Roman Catholic Church at Dunoon. A fine stained-glass window dating from 1924 in Kilmun Church on the Holy Loch portrays him landing from a boat on the Cowal shore and also depicts his meeting with three other monks at which he hears that Columba has died.

Kessog (d. 520?)

Supposedly born into the royal family of Munster, he is said to have sailed from Ireland aged 50 around 510 and established a retreat on the island of Inchtavanach, later known as Monk's Island, on Loch Lomond near Luss. His evangelistic work is associated more with Perthshire and the Trossachs than Argyll but he is said to have been murdered by pagan Picts near his retreat around 520. A significant cult seems to have developed in the Middle Ages, making Luss an important place of pilgrimage.

Kevin – sixth century

Associated with Glendalough in Ireland, there is no record of him coming to Argyll although the old parish church of Kilkivan, three miles west of Campbeltown, may possibly have commemorated him.

Maelrubha (c. 642–722)

Born in Derry, and said to have been a descendant of Niall of the Nine Hostages, a distant cousin of Columba and a pupil of Comgall of Bangor, he apparently came to Iona in 671. According to one story, he first put in to Islay where the old parish church of Kilarrow was dedicated to him. Another story has him sailing up Loch Fyne and landing at Strathlachan on the west coast of Cowal. He is also said to have built chapels at Glenn Barr on Kintyre, at Kilmelford, and on an island in Loch Etive. Places named Kilmory or Kilmorrie possibly commemorate him. They include the Chapel at Kilmory Knap on Loch Sween, the parish church of Craignish and the chapel at Dunstaffnage Castle. He is remembered principally as an evangelist to the Picts and as founder of the ecclesiastical settlement at Applecross in Ross-shire which became the centre of his mission. The majority of dedications to him are found in the north west Highlands.

Marnock (d. 625)

Another Irish saint who is commemorated more outside Argyll, notably in Ayrshire and Banffshire, than within it, he supposedly sailed up Loch Fyne. Dalvernock in Glen Shira east of Inveraray (possibly a corruption of Dalmarnock), Ardmanock Bay off the Cowal peninsula and Kilmarnock Hill near Toward may be named after him. There is overlap between the names Marnock and Ernan.

Martin (316–397)

An anomaly in this list, as someone who came from Continental Europe and never set foot in the British Isles, he was born in Hungary and set up monastic communities in France, becoming Bishop of Tours. He counts as an Argyll saint because of the important commemorations of him in the region, including Kilmartin in mid-Argyll and St Martin's Cross in front of Iona Abbey. Adomnán drew heavily on the Life of Martin by Sulpicius Severus when writing his own Life of Columba, in which he remarks that Martin was often mentioned in the prayers of the Iona monks. Martin serves as a reminder that saints are often immigrants and do not need to have been physically present in an area to have left their mark on its spiritual landscape.

Modan – sixth or seventh century

Edwin Sprott Towill describes him as a Highland Gaidheal and the Laird of Benderloch but it seems much more likely that he was yet another Irish missionary monk.[8] Although principally associated with Falkirk and Stirling, he also seems to have worked intensively around the shores of Loch Etive. His Argyll dedications possibly include Balmahaodhan at Ardchattan and Kilmodan at Clachan of Glendaruel in West Cowal.

Moluag, or Lugadh (c. 520–592)

Possibly from Antrim and educated at Bangor, he is credited with founding the church on Lismore. Although he is not mentioned by Adomnán, legends suggest that he was a friend and rival of Columba and that both men wanted the fertile and strategically placed island of Lismore as their monastic base and raced each other there in their coracles. Moluag, sensing that Columba was going to arrive first, took his axe and sliced off his thumb which he threw ashore to stake his claim, crying 'My flesh and blood have first possession of the island'. Columba responded by cursing the island, prophesying that the rocks would lie with their sharp edges uppermost and that only alder trees would grow there. Moluag responded that the Lord would smooth the jagged ridges and make the alder burn pleasantly. In fact, the rocks on Lismore make for easy walking and the alders on the island, which are found in a copse at a bay known as Port Moluaig, on the north east point where he is said to have stepped ashore, make especially good fire wood.

There are suggestions that Moluag first went to Kintyre where there is a settlement called Killmaluag with a burial ground and carved stones in Glen Barr. Other Argyll dedications include Portcill-Moluaig on Loch Caolisport in Knapdale and Kilmoluag on Mull and Tiree. He seems to have spent the latter part of his life in the north of Scotland with his main base at Rosemarkie in Ross-shire where he supposedly died.

Moluag is one of the best-attested and longest established of Argyll's saints. His supposed crosier, or bachall mòr, is still preserved on the island of Lismore in the charge of its hereditary keepers. It is kept in Bachuil Country House, a large eighteenth-century house which is run as an up-market guest house by the current Baron and Baroness of Bachuil and Coabs of St Moluag, Niall and Anita

Livingstone. Another possible relic of the saint, now in the Museum of Scotland in Edinburgh, is a small iron bell found in a farm in the parish of Kilmichael Glassary in the early nineteenth century. Legend has it that Moluag cast the bell miraculously with a bundle of rushes for fuel. The parish church on Lismore, which is dedicated to him, has a stained-glass window dating from 1926 depicting both Moluag and Columba.

Oran, Odran or Odhrán – sixth century

A native of the Irish midlands, he is said to have been the oldest of the twelve monks who accompanied Columba to Iona in 563. A story found in slightly different versions in a number of medieval manuscripts describes the bizarre circumstances of his death. It recounts how the walls of a chapel that Columba tried to build on Iona were mysteriously destroyed every night. A strange mermaid-like creature emerged from the sea with the message that the chapel could not be built until a living man was buried below its foundations. Oran volunteered for this role and was duly buried alive. Three days after his burial Columba ordered his body to be disinterred. Oran was still alive and announced that there was no God, no judgement, no heaven and no hell. Appalled by this heretical outburst, Columba ordered his body to be re-buried with more earth heaped over it.

This story provides an origin legend for St Oran's Chapel, the oldest extant stone building on Iona which is surrounded by the cemetery known as the Reilig Odhráin. Oran also gave his name to the first of the high-standing crosses erected on Iona. He is commemorated at Kiloran Bay at the north end of Colonsay and in St Oran's Well in the grounds of Colonsay House. It is also possible that the island of Oronsay is named after him, and he is said to have visited Mull and Tiree. The church built in 1888 for the inhabitants of the village of Connel, originally a mission station and from 1910 the parish church, is dedicated to Oran and has a window, installed in 1935, depicting him alongside Columba.

Ronan

There is considerable uncertainty as to the identity of the saint who is apparently the object of two dedications on Iona, at Port Ronan and Tempell Ronan, the name given to the island's medieval parish church, and who also seems to be commemorated at Cill Ronain in Kilchoman parish on Islay and at Kilmaronag in the parish of Ardchattan in Lorne. At least twelve different Ronans appear in Irish martyrologies. Bede mentions an Irish monk of that name who was active in Northumbria around 650. Watson suggests that the Ronan commemorated on Islay was an abbot on Bute who died in 737.

Sléibíne (d. 767)

Abbot of Iona from 752–767, he is possibly commemorated in dedications at Killevin on Loch Fyne and Kilslevan in Kilarrow parish on Islay.

The thirty-seven saints listed above may not all have set foot in Argyll, although it is quite feasible that many of the thirty-five who were originally from Ireland came to or through Dál Riata as missionary monks. Some may have remained there for some time while others moved on to evangelize the Pictish people to the north and east. They have left their mark on its landscape primarily because local people chose to remember and honour them through the naming of churches, chapels, wells, crosses and other sacred places as well as through legends and stories which located them in the region. Their commemoration was part of the wider cult of saints which characterised the whole of the Medieval Christian world. Saints were revered because they linked earth and heaven and were seen as protectors, patrons and intermediaries between this world and the next. Their cults and dedications express a popular fascination with holy and exemplary lives, mission and miracles. As well as contributing so significantly to the toponymy of Argyll, they have been a hugely important part of its imagined spiritual landscape.

6

Early Christian Carved Stones and Crosses

During the early centuries of Christianity in Argyll stone symbols of the new faith appeared across the region, often through the simple device of a cross incised on an existing standing stone or prominent piece of rock. These carved stones provide the most widespread evidence for early Christianity in Argyll and the oldest go back more than 1,350 years. Often found in what now seem very remote places, many are still in their original locations, while others have been gathered into the shelter of churches and museums to protect them from the elements. Altogether, more than 350 early medieval carved Christian stones have been identified in Argyll, by far the biggest concentration anywhere in Scotland. There are over a hundred on the island of Iona alone and significant numbers in Knapdale, notably at Cladh a' Bhile near Ellary, Kilmory Knap and Keills. They range in date from the seventh to the eleventh century and show a progression from crude and simple cross-incised slabs to elaborately carved high crosses.

Fewer than ten per cent of these stones have any written inscription and they seem essentially to have been intended to provide powerful visual pointers to the new faith and pictorial representations of some of its central themes and stories. The distinctive Christian symbol of the cross, initially in its simplest form but later with considerable embellishment, was carved on prehistoric standing stones, on the walls of caves and on everyday objects, such as the quern, used for grinding corn, found at Dunadd. Cross-incised stones were planted in particular places possibly to mark territorial boundaries and sacred enclosures or as visual aids for worship and preaching, but probably most often as grave markers and pilgrim stations in a landscape of the dead, which may in its own way have been as elaborately planned and full of ritual as that of the pre-Christian Kilmartin Valley.

There is considerable debate among historians and archaeologists as to whether some of the earliest carved stones point to a degree of fusion and accommodation between pagan and Christian beliefs or rather emphasize the radical discontinuity between them. A couple of stones found on Colonsay, which could be taken to suggest either syncretism or Christian repudiation of the pagan past, show just how difficult it is to read the message of these enduring monuments to Argyll's early Christian past. The first is housed in the island's square parish church which looks down over the bay where the ferry arrives. Resting on a plinth in front of the communion table, it was discovered covering a natural spring known as Tobar Chattan, which had been filled in towards the end of the nineteenth century. The descriptive label next to it suggests that this stone might originally have been a pagan phallic symbol which 'appears to have been worked into the shape of a cross' and may have marked a pre-Christian sacred spring, later Christianised as a holy well and dedicated to St Catan. I have to say that I find it difficult to discern any clear cross shape in the metre long stone although it has evidently been tapered and carved in a rudimentary way. In its prime position in the church, it speaks of elemental faith and of the importance of water in both pre-Christian and Christian Celtic religion.

The other prominent early carved stone to be found on Colonsay, known as 'Dealbh na Leisge' (The Statue of the Sloth), is even more bizarre and surreal. It originally stood at the east end of the Chapel at Riasg Buidhe on the north east coast of the island, but was moved around 1870 to stand guard over Tobar Odhráin (St Oran's Well) in the gardens of Colonsay House. Probably carved in the eighth or ninth century, the 4½ feet high slab of local Torridian flagstone appears on one side to depict a bearded figure, possibly a cleric, his robes fashioned to form a spiral-decorated cross and with a forked fish-like tail where the feet should be. Viewed from the other side, the stone slab looks for all the world like an erect phallus. It has been suggested that it dates from the period of Viking occupation of Colonsay and may represent either a satirical jibe at Christian monasticism or some kind of syncretistic fusion of pagan and Christian imagery. It is impossible to say. Certainly, in its current position among ferns and bushes, Dealbh na Leisge presents a strange and enigmatic figure, perhaps suggesting more than anything else the abiding presence of the little people and the world of gnomes and goblins.

'Dealbh na Leisg' stone figure, Colonsay

In contrast to these ambiguous symbols, the great majority of Argyll's cross-marked stones display an austere simplicity in their design. This is certainly true of the earliest example that can be dated with reasonable accuracy. Found on Iona and now displayed near the entrance to the newly refurbished museum behind the Abbey, it is very unusual among Argyll stones in having lettering on its

Gravestone of Echoid Buide, Iona

top edge. The Latin inscription LAPIS ECHODI has been taken to indicate that it marked the grave of Echoid Buide, the youngest son of Aédán MacGabráin and ruler of Dál Riata who died in 629.

It is significant that this earliest dateable cross-incised stone, almost certainly carved within a generation of Columba's death, marked a grave. This seems to have been the context for the erection of many of the early Christian carved stones and crosses. They are overwhelmingly found in burial grounds, like Cladh a' Bhile at Ellary on Loch Caolisport. This ancient graveyard, which Mary Donaldson conjectured might have had an association with the royal house of Dál Riata because of its proximity to Castell Tor (see page 53), has sadly reverted to the condition of 'an almost inaccessible bog' described by a visitor in 1869. All but a handful of the twenty-nine cross-incised stones, thought to date from the early eighth century, which were catalogued and fixed in an upright position by Marion Campbell in 1960, are now covered with long grass and bracken and almost impossible to see. Fortunately, a particularly fine dressed slab of chlorite-schist, which displays on its east face an elaborate marigold-like hexafoil design above an equal-armed cross, is still clearly visible. Described as 'the most elaborate monument of its period in western Scotland', its nearest parallel is in a manuscript dating from around 700 in the monastery at Luxeuil in France founded by the Irish monk, Columbanus.[1] A similar marigold design is carved on the wall of St Ciarian's cave in Kintyre.

Further good examples of early cross-marked stones originally situated in burial grounds are now displayed in the chapels at Keills and Kilmory Knap in Knapdale. There is an unusual grave slab now propped up against the wall of the churchyard at Clachan in North

Marigold decorated stone, Cladh a' Bhile

Kintyre, on which is carved both a Latin cross and a ring-cross conjoined on a common stem. Another grave marker, which probably came originally from an early Christian site on Eilean Mòr, the most westerly of the islands off the mouth of Loch Sween, is now in the porch of Tayvallich Church. Stones seem to have been erected to mark the place of death as well as of burial. They were seen as protecting the dead and ensuring their salvation by almost literally making the sign of the cross over their bodies. Adomnán noted that following the death of Columba's uncle, Ernan, while he was visiting Iona, a cross was set up where he had died in front of the door to the corn kiln and another cross was erected where Columba had been standing at the moment of his death.

The significance of carved crosses in the creation of a ritual land-scape of the dead is perhaps most dramatically displayed in what seems to have happened on Iona in the aftermath of the enshrine-ment of Columba's relics in the mid eighth century. Some time between 730 and 753 the saint's original simple underground grave appears to have been opened and his remains re-interred, together with his sacred bell, books, staff and tunic, in an elaborate elevated casket shrine on the site of the chapel to the left of the great west door of Iona Abbey. Peter Yeoman of Historic Scotland has recently suggested that the context for this re-enshrinement may have been the takeover of Dál Riata by the Picts under King Oengus. It was almost certainly also inspired by the broader cult of the saints which swept over Christian Europe in this period, producing a heightened sense of their miraculous powers and the continued corporeal pres-ence exerted through their relics, and greatly stimulating pilgrimage to their shrines.

The enshrinement of Columba's relics seems to have been accom-panied by the development of a processional route designed to lead pilgrims from their landing place near the present ferry terminal on Iona up to Columba's shrine through a ritual landscape and along a street of the dead, modelled perhaps on the route to the Church of the Holy Sepulchre in Jerusalem known as the Via Dolorosa. Rein-forcing the sense of a deliberately planned landscape of death, this route also became the way in which the coffins of those who were buried on Iona were brought to the graveyard at the Reilig Odhráin, which had been established outside the monastic precincts in the previous century.

The creation of this processional way reflected a renewed inter-est in dramatizing and revivifying the faith by encouraging people to walk symbolically in the footsteps of Christ on the way to his crucifixion at Calvary, as shown by the development of the practice of establishing Stations of the Cross in churches. This new emphasis on walking as well as talking the faith also chimed in with the interest in sacred space and holy places aroused by works such as Adomnán's *De Locis Sanctis*, written on Iona at the end of the seventh century. The cult of the saints stimulated among the Christian faithful not just pilgrimages to saints' shrines in a quest to connect with their power through touching their relics, but also a more radical desire to die and to be buried near saints. This became particularly important with respect to Columba and Iona, reinforcing the already strong belief that one should go west to die. Many would have echoed the sentiments of a statement attributed to Adomnán and now stencilled on the wall in the entrance to the cloisters of Iona Abbey: 'If I be destined to die in Iona, it were a merciful leavetaking. I know not under the blue sky a better spot for death.' Even if you did not manage to die there, you could be buried there, especially if you were rich. Being laid to rest near Columba meant that you were already close to God and supposedly made the journey to heaven shorter. In that way, Iona became important and attractive as a gateway to the afterlife. Several Irish kings and princes were recorded as journeying 'in pilgrimage and penance' to spend their last years there in the late eighth century.

This was the context for the laying out of several of the features that can still very clearly be seen by visitors to Iona today – notably the cemetery at the Reilig Odhráin and the Street of the Dead which runs to and through it and on to the site of Columba's shrine. It made Iona in a very conscious way a landscape of the dead, both in terms of the continuing corporeal and spiritual presence of Columba and other holy figures buried there and also in its popularity as a final resting place for many influential and wealthy people. A sign of how powerful this appeal became was the emergence of a legend that Mary Magdalene had been buried in a cave on Iona and an even more far-fetched story that John Martinus, her son by Jesus, had been born on the island.[2]

Equally fanciful is the information still given in many guidebooks that numerous early kings of Scotland were buried on Iona. There is, in fact, no actual evidence that the kings of Dál Riata from the sixth to the ninth century were buried on the island and Dr James Fraser of Edinburgh University has persuasively argued that the notion of Iona as the mausoleum of early Scottish kings was a fiction invented by King Alexander I in the early twelfth century. Wanting to present his immediate antecedents, Margaret and Malcolm, as representatives of a new dynasty buried in Dunfermline, he consigned earlier Scottish monarchs to Iona to suggest that they belonged firmly to the past. Accounts of Scottish and Norwegian kings being buried on Iona first surface in the fourteenth century. When Donald Monro,

Archdeacon of the Isles, visited the island in 1549, he was told that four Irish, eight Scandinavian and forty-eight Scottish kings, including Macbeth, were buried in the Reilig Odhráin and was shown three chapels, each with a marble slab, engraved respectively in Latin 'Grave of the Kings of Scotland', 'Grave of the Kings of Ireland' and 'Grave of the Kings of Norway'. By the time James Boswell got there in 1773 with Samuel Johnson he was disappointed to find 'only some grave-stones flat on the earth and we could see no inscriptions. How far short was this of marble monuments, like those in Westminster Abbey, which I had imagined here.' It is not the first nor the last time that Argyll's spiritual landscape has been manipulated and re-imagined for political purposes. However, even if Iona may not, strictly speaking, deserve its accolade as the burial place of Scotland's early kings, it did undoubtedly become a favourite location for the great and the good to have their final resting place, as the many coffin roads to its shores testify.

The most visible and enduring legacy of Iona's make-over as a ritual landscape are the four high-standing crosses erected along the processional pilgrim way to Columba's shrine and possibly intended as prayer stations. Although only one remains in its entirety and its original location, fragments of the others have been sensitively re-assembled and are now displayed in the recently refurbished museum behind the Abbey. Together they form the finest collection in Britain of these distinctive and elaborate expressions of early medieval Christianity, representing the culmination of the sculptor's art first displayed in the chiselling out of a simple cross design on a block of stone. The earliest to have been erected seems to have been St Oran's Cross, which is thought to date from the mid eighth century. A ringless cross fashioned out of three pieces of coarse mica-shist from Mull fitted together and decorated with bosses and spirals, with a depiction of the Virgin and Child between two angels at the top of its shaft, it was recorded in the nineteenth century as standing in St Oran's Chapel and was probably originally located in the Reilig Odhráin.

The three other crosses seem to have been erected in the later eighth or early ninth century close to the chapel where Columba's relics had been re-enshrined and elevated. Closest to the chapel was St John's Cross, a composite artefact with the main shaft made up of four

St John's Cross casts its shadow over St Columba's shrine Chapel, Iona

pieces of green chlorite-schist from the Argyll mainland and the ring segments fashioned out of mica-shist from the Ross of Mull. Decorated on both sides with bosses and spirals, it had fallen down by 1699, when the first extant drawing was made, and by 1895 was in fragments. The Duke of Argyll's factor collected up the pieces and in 1927 the cross was re-assembled and re-erected in situ. However, it fell down again in 1957 and in 1970 a concrete replica was installed in its base. Close by stood St Matthew's Cross, which depicted on its shaft the temptation of Adam and Eve standing below the fruit-laden branches of a tree with a serpent coiled round its trunk. Its broken shaft was removed to the Abbey Museum in 1994.

St Martin's Cross, which still stands in its original position, is both the most elaborately carved and the best preserved of the four Iona crosses. It remains an iconic feature of Iona's spiritual landscape and is the gathering point for the weekly pilgrimage around the island organised by the Iona Community. Carved from a single block of grey epidorite (granite) rock, probably from the Argyll mainland, it stands 16 feet 8 inches high in its stepped box. Most of the east face is covered with carved bosses surrounded by interlacing snakes. There has been much speculation about the significance of this motif which is found on several other Argyll crosses. Are the serpents sloughing off their skins to symbolise the new life of Christian conversion and baptism, or do they rather symbolise evil which is being vanquished by the power of the Cross? Various Biblical verses have been proposed to explain their presence, including Exodus 7:12, which describes the magicians of Egypt throwing down their staffs which turned into serpents before being swallowed up by Aaron's staff, and John 3:14 with its message: 'Just as Moses lifted up the serpent in the desert, so also must the Son of man be lifted up'. Ian Fisher is inclined to think that the ubiquitous snake and boss motif may rather be associated with Columba who was well known for taking on monsters and is said to have banished snakes from Iona.[3]

There are more bosses and intertwined serpents at the bottom of the west face of St Martin's Cross. Above them are four pictorial panels. The lowest features four figures who have been identified either as David and Goliath with David and Saul or the four evangelists. Above them is a figure playing a harp, generally taken to be King David, seated with outstretched legs and facing a kneeling man playing a triple pipe. The next panel up shows Abraham sacrificing Isaac whose arms are extended above a rect-angular altar with the small winged figure of an angel looking on. Above them is a seated figure between two rearing lion-like creatures, usually thought to be Dan-iel in the lions' den although also interpreted as Jesus with the wild beasts during his temptation in the wilderness. This theme is continued in the side-arms of the cross, where two passant leonine beasts flank a central roun-del with a seated Virgin and Child between four small angels, and in the top arm where there are three pairs of back-to-back lion-like beasts with intertwined tails.

Tasha Gefreh, an art histo-rian at Edinburgh University, has suggested that these images on St Martin's Cross were deliberately designed to be viewed sequentially through the day as the sun struck different features. Noting that the first part to

St Martin's Cross, Iona – west face

be highlighted in the morning is the bottom of the east face and the last in the late afternoon the top of the west face, she has proposed that the Cross tells the story of salvation beginning with the ser-pent's curse and ending with the birth of Christ. The interplay of sun and shadow on the other Iona crosses through the day is beautifully illustrated through highly effective lighting in the museum where they are now displayed.

Although the best known of Argyll's high crosses are to be found on Iona, there are several others worthy of note. They include the free-standing cross covered on both faces with interlacing knot-work and diagonal key patterns which now stands at the back of Kilmartin Parish Church; the rather eroded Kilnave Cross, still in its original position on the west shore of Loch Gruinart on Islay; and the Keills Cross which depicts a man surrounded by lions similar to that found on St Martin's Cross and usually thought to be Daniel, as well as a winged figure, tentatively identified as either St Michael or St John, at the centre of its top arm. The most outstanding example is the Kildalton Cross on Islay. If, as several archaeologists believe, St Martin's Cross originally had wooden arms which have long since disintegrated, the Kildalton Cross is the only free-standing ring cross to have survived entirely intact in Scotland. Standing 8 feet 8 inches high and carved from grey-green chlorite schist, it is certainly the most imposing. The west face of the shaft is largely covered by the familiar snake and boss decoration with four lions looking towards the central boss of the cross-head. At the top of the east face of the shaft is a depiction of the Virgin and Child with angels, which appears to be modelled on the carving in the same position on St Oran's Cross. The arms of the cross head contain depictions of Cain slaying Abel, Abraham sacrificing Isaac and what appear to be peacocks feasting on grapes, an image which is also found in the Book of Kells. Within the top arm two angels stand above a figure gripping the jaws of a rearing beast, possibly David killing the lion as described in 1 Samuel 17, although also identified as Daniel or Jesus among the wild beasts.

Alexander Ewing, the first bishop of the Episcopal Diocese of Argyll and the Isles, is one of many to have enthused about these iconic features of Argyll's Christian landscape:

> On those sweet lochs and dreamy shores, which are characteristic of this diocese, where the islands lie asleep, as it were, upon the main, there is, indeed, more than one Iona. More than one green bosom is surmounted by that memorial and monument of the past, the round-headed cross, with its mysterious interlacing and Runic

knots – a mixture of commemoration; emblems of religion, of war-fare, and of the chase, of priest and people, of prey and its captor, of Pagan and Christian, strangely mixed together.[4]

Whatever their function, whether to mark graves or boundaries, to delineate sacred space where criminals and others could find sanctuary, or to stop pilgrims in their tracks and turn their minds to eternal thoughts, these high crosses point to the evangelical simplicity of Argyll's early Christianity. It is striking that the episodes that they depict – Daniel in the lion's den, Abraham's sacrifice of Isaac, Cain's slaughter of Abel – are amongst the most forbidding stories in the Scriptures with their emphasis on struggle and sacrifice.

It is perhaps no coincidence that these high-standing crosses were erected during the period when the Christian Gaels of Argyll were being attacked by the pagan Vikings. The first Viking attack on Iona was in 795 and there were increasingly ferocious raids thereafter, with sixty-eight members of the monastic community being killed in 806 and a monk called Blathmac being put to death in 825 for refusing to divulge the whereabouts of the precious casket containing Columba's relics, which he had hidden under a mound. It is possible that one of these massacres is commemorated in the Gaelic name for the bay to the south of Iona's main pier, Port nam Mairtear. It could suggest martyrdom, as its English translation, Martyrs Bay, suggests, but it could also simply mean 'Bay of the Dead' and indicate that this was where coffins were landed for burial on the island. Around the middle of the ninth century the centre of operations of the Columban monastic family was moved from Iona to Kells in Ireland and some of Columba's relics were taken there, others being moved to Dunkeld. It is tempting to see the high crosses erected on Iona and Islay during this period of Viking raids as symbols of Christian Gaelic defiance against the pagan Norse invaders.

For much of the ninth, tenth and eleventh centuries the islands and much of the western seaboard of Argyll were effectively under Norse control. These are often seen as the 'Dark Ages' and it is certainly the case that there was less Christian art produced in this period than previously. However, Christianity did not disappear and the practice of erecting cross-inscribed stones continued through the period of Viking occupation. In time, many of the Norse settlers themselves converted to Christianity and there are distinct signs of Viking influence in some of the grave slabs dating from the late tenth and eleventh centuries, like the distinctive hogback stone in Luss churchyard.

Early Christian carved stones and crosses were a key element in Argyll's physical and spiritual landscape for around five hundred years. Archaeologists have demonstrated how they spread from Argyll to the rest of Scotland via a clear trail reaching through the Perthshire glens into Angus and Aberdeenshire. Several remain today in the graveyards and monastic enclosures where they were first planted and which are often now sadly overgrown and abandoned. Others have turned up embedded in the walls of farms and cottages as well as in the foundations of churches and chapels. Were they seen simply as handy building blocks or rather as sacred stones which might bring good fortune to a new byre or dwelling place? Who can say? We are back to Argyll's intimate but ambiguous relationship with stone, and in this case with stones that were at once both sacred and mundane, which marked death and could also be used for new life. Re-used and re-evaluated, they belong to Argyll's spiritual landscape as surely as the chapels that were built out of them around the ancient burial grounds where they once rested, alone and undisturbed.

Hogback stone, Luss churchyard

7

Cells, Caves and Chapels

Among the most ubiquitous and evocative legacies of Argyll's medieval spiritual landscape are the 170 or so small rectangular chapels, now nearly all ruined and roofless, which seem disproportionately located in the remotest parts of the region. Ancient maps and records show that the great majority were named after an Irish saint. Often sited close to a burial ground containing early carved Christian stones and crosses and with a well or stream nearby, their romantic lure was well captured over 150 years ago by Alexander Ewing:

> He who sails along the shores of Argyll, and lands in any of its mountain coves in the stillness of an Autumn morning, and finds, as he may in almost every bay, the ruins of an ancient chapel, sees that which he will not see elsewhere, and that which it is probable he will never forget. Small and weather-worn and unroofed as it is, it is yet the church of one of those Celtic Fathers, and his cell is close at hand. They were solitaries, those saints, Brandon, Finian, Fillan, whose names now mark their church, or the well beside it of that clear water peculiar to Argyll. There, among the grassy knolls, or under the cairn, overgrown with ferns and ivy, and through which the foxglove and wild rose lift their heads, sleeps, and for a thousand years has slept, a Christian Apostle and his congregation.[1]

A good many antiquarians and local historians have followed Ewing in suggesting that these remote ruins were once the haunts of the early Celtic saints and mark the places where they lived out their solitary lives as hermits or came to pray. In fact, as we have already noted, dedications to saints, together with the 'Kil' prefix that usually accompanied them, often came many centuries after they had died and cannot be taken as evidence of the actual physical presence of the individual commemorated. The great majority of Argyll's medieval chapels date from between the twelfth and fourteenth centuries, 600 years or more after the golden age of the Celtic saints. Undoubtedly many of them were built on the site of earlier ecclesiastical settlements. This is clear from the fact that they are so often surrounded by graveyards containing carved stones from the seventh, eighth and ninth centuries. Presumably the stone chapels replaced earlier wooden buildings. Whether they were erected on the sites of ancient monastic cells is much more difficult to say.

We know that early Irish monks and missionaries sought out remote and inaccessible places in which they lived for periods as hermits to be near to God. They often called these their 'desert' places, using the Gaelic word 'diseart' and drawing their inspiration from the Desert Fathers whose retreat into caves in Egypt and Sinai is often taken to be the origin of Christian monasticism. Glenorchy Parish Church at Dalmally was originally called Clachan an Diseart and there are early references to a monk named Mealog having a retreat there. Curiously, there are very few other 'diseart' place names in Argyll (although there is one associated with a burial ground 400 metres north east of Iona Abbey) and the evidence for other possible hermit settlements is largely archaeological rather than linguistic. It is on this basis that Ian Fisher has proposed enclosed sites at Sgòr nam Ban-naomha on Canna, Ceann a'Mhara on Tiree, Nave Island to the north of Islay, Cladh a'Bhearnaig on Kerrera, and Eilean Mór in the mouth of Loch Sween as likely locations for occupation by anchorites, perhaps accompanied by lay-penitents living under the kind of strict discipline portrayed in Adomnán's Life of Columba. Significantly, all of these are relatively inhospitable island sites and all have medieval chapels close by.[2]

The most striking evidence of monastic or ascetic retreat to 'a desert place' in the early Christian period is provided by the beehive cells on Eileach an Naoimh, the southernmost of the Garvellach islands which lie in the Firth of Lorne, south of Mull and north of Jura. Also known as Holy Isle, its Gaelic name means 'rocky place of the saint'. The monastery there is said to have been established around 540 by Brendan and the island has been proposed as the location for Columba's Hinba retreat as well as the burial place of his mother Eithne. Contained within walled enclosures in a hollow on the island's summit are a burial ground with early Christian grave markers, an underground cell with two chambers and other ruined buildings including two roofless chapels or churches dating from the eleventh or twelfth century. Closer to the shore, immediately above the rocky landing place, are the restored remains of a double beehive cell made out of local sandstone slabs and consisting of two round inter-connecting chambers with thick walls. If these ruined cells do date from the time of Brendan, which is far from proven, then they are among the oldest extant church buildings in the British Isles. There is no written record of their existence before the ninth century when the monastery apparently fell victim to Viking raiders.

There does seem to be a direct link between the distinctive beehive cells occupied by ascetics and hermits on Eileach an Naoimh and the two chapels built there many hundreds of years later, perhaps to cater for pilgrims coming to what was seen as a holy place. There is evidence that pilgrims came in the later Middle Ages to another site which has been identified as a likely location for anchorite cells, Sgòr nam Ban-naomha on Canna. The ruined hermits' huts which stood on a rock platform at the foot of steep cliffs there seem to have been used as beds on which the sick were laid, with offerings of round stones being placed on an altar fashioned from an eighth-century grave slab in a characteristic merging of pagan and Christian ritual practices.

Another focus for medieval pilgrimage were the coastal caves that were believed to have served as the 'desert places' or solitary retreats of Celtic saints. The history of the best-known of these, St Columba's cave near Ellary on Loch Caolisport, has already been recounted (pages 52–54). Whether Columba himself ever stayed there, the cave does seem to have been used by Christian hermits or itinerant preachers in the seventh and eighth centuries when the crosses on the back wall were probably carved. There is further evidence of Christian occupation in the twelfth century when the chapel, which is now a romantic overgrown ruin beside the path leading to the cave, was built perhaps for use by pilgrims coming to venerate what had become a sacred site. A cave in the cliffs on the south side of Eilean Mór similarly associated with a saint also became a place of pilgrimage. Originally entered through a narrow tunnel and thought to have been used as a solitary retreat for ascetic meditation by St Abbán, this cave has two early rock-cut crosses on its east wall, one with a hexafoil marigold design and the other an unusual cross of arcs resembling flower petals and apparently incorporating the early Christian 'Chi-Rho' symbol. Among the late medieval pilgrims who came here was one who described himself on a cross erected around 1400 as 'John, priest and hermit of this island' suggesting a continuation of the solitary eremetical tradition supposedly established by Abbán. Close to the Eilean Mór cave are the substantial remains of a chapel that is thought to date from the early thirteenth century and is one of the best preserved of Argyll's medieval church buildings. Other coastal caves with a tradition of occupation by hermits or anchorites include the Nun's Cave, near Carsaig on the Ross of Mull, the west wall of which has numerous incised cross carvings thought to date from the late sixth century onwards; a cave at Scoor, also on the Ross of Mull, where there are eighteen linear incised crosses on the walls; and St Ciaran's Cave near Achinhoan Head on the south east coast of Kintyre, which contains a boulder carved with an elaborate marigold design similar to that found at the burial ground at Cladh a' Bhile.

The remote location of so many of Argyll's medieval chapels certainly makes it tempting to suggest that they were established on the sites of early monastic settlements and hermits' cells. A disproportionate number of them were built on islands – a map of 1654 shows eleven on Colonsay, and thirty-one have been identified on Islay. Local place names may provide a clue as to their origins. As well as the occasional 'diseart' or 'disirt', and the ubiquitous 'Kil' prefix before a saint's name, these include 'cladh' and reilig', suggesting a burial place, 'teampull', denoting a church and 'annaid' or 'annat', a somewhat mysterious term which has been variously understood to mean a church containing the relics of its founder or a church abandoned, possibly during the Viking attacks of the ninth and tenth centuries, and subsequently rebuilt on the same site.[3] Dedications may yield further clues although they need to be treated with caution. There are chapels dedicated to Columba close to the supposed footprints which bear his name near Southend in Kintyre and near Locahline in Morvern, but there is no knowing which came first or whether, indeed, both chapels and footprints received their names at the same time.

It seems likely that chapels were built in the later Middle Ages at sites which were already regarded in some senses as holy and sacred. This may simply be because they had long been used for burials and were part of the ritual landscape of the dead, although some undoubtedly had associations with early saints, hermits and holy men and others may have been pre-Christian sacred sites. In an interesting recent book entitled *Contextual Landscape Study of the Early Christian Churches of Argyll*, and subtitled 'The Persistence of Memory', Megan Meredith-Lobay locates Argyll's early churches and chapels in a rich spiritual landscape built out of memories and associations. She argues that they were not part of monastic families but rather set up around existing places of ritual and power. All-important here was the collective memory of places already in the landscape. It is certainly striking how many of the medieval chapels in Argyll, and the burial grounds and monastic settlements which preceded them, are sited close to iron age settlements such as forts, duns, crannogs and hut circles, and to neolithic or bronze age ritual centres like standing stones, cairns, burial cists and barrows. Noting this very close relationship between the early Christian landscape of Argyll and the prehistoric ritual landscape, Megan Meredith-Lobay suggests that the church utilised the landscapes of memory, such as bronze or iron age burial sites and prehistoric settlements that had been the focus of ritual activities. The built monuments of the Christian faith interacted deliberately with these visual reminders of the past.[4]

Desire for physical interaction with places of ritual importance in both the pre-Christian and Christian past may well have motivated those who built the chapels which appeared across Argyll from the early twelfth century onwards. This period saw a romantic revival of interest in the Celtic saints expressed in the appearance of a spate of *Vitae*, which in many cases chronicled their supposed lives and activities for the first time. It was part of a broader intellectual movement, dubbed the twelfth century renaissance, which also manifested itself in a new interest in pilgrimage and spirituality and in the stories of the Holy Grail and the Arthurian legends. In addition to the power of spiritual memory filtered through this newly enhanced romantic imagination, secular politics may also have made an important contribution to the chapel-building movement. This was the period when a new political aristocracy was flexing its muscles and achieving ascendancy in Argyll, notably the MacDonald Lords of the Isles, who were directly responsible for the erection of several chapels, including that on Eilean Mór. Their influence is particularly obvious in those chapels built near castles, like Dunstaffnage, erected by Duncan MacDougall, Lord of Lorne, and Finlaggan by John, Lord of the Isles, both in the mid fourteenth century. Although they were still some way off achieving their ascendancy over Argyll, the Campbells were also church builders, with the Campbells of Craignish constructing the medieval parish church at Kilmarie around 1200.

It is difficult to determine the exact purpose for which many of these medieval churches and chapels were built. They are generally plain single-chamber rectangular structures with little embellishment and adornment and relatively small in size, rarely exceeding forty feet in length and twenty feet in width. Were these embodiments of Argyll's evangelical simplicity designed, as some have suggested, primarily for private prayer and meditation, catering predominantly for pilgrims and for those seeking to emulate the ascetic spirituality of the early monks and saints? It is possible that several of the chapels built by wealthy and influential clan chiefs were rather intended to be family mausoleums and burial chambers, as in the cases of St Oran's Chapel on Iona, probably built as a mortuary chapel by Somerled or his son Reginald in the late 12th century, and the collegiate church erected by Duncan Campbell at Kilmun in 1441 (pages 139–41). In his extensive recent study of the Diocese of Argyll in the Middle Ages Iain MacDonald concludes that, while it is impossible to determine the exact purpose of Argyll's many chapels, they were unquestionably an important element of the sacred landscape and contributed considerably to both worship and pastoral care, especially in the larger upland parishes.[5]

The internal architecture of the chapels suggests that they were used for worship and for the sacraments of baptism and communion. Although the predominant single-chambered structure seems to indicate that there was no separation between clergy and laity during services, there is evidence in some cases, as at Kilchiaran chapel on Islay, of a raised chancel or sanctuary at the east end reached by stone steps from the nave. Few interior furnishings have survived but here and there a stone font can be found, as again at Kilchiaran. The medieval font from Kilneuair Church, said to have been removed in 1914, has been re-erected at the west end of the ruined nave where it sits on a recycled millstone. South Knapdale Parish Church at Achahoish contains a font which is said to have come from St Columba's cave. An unusual altar frontal possibly dating from the early sixteenth century lying in the graveyard on Inishail presumably originally comes from the old parish church there. In the centre is a Crucifix flanked by two figures, one of whom holds a chalice and the other a cup to catch blood dripping from Christ's wounds. To the left are two men-at-arms and to the right a heraldic group comprising two more armed men supporting a crown which is held over a shield displaying a galley with furled sail.

Many of the chapels probably contained a bell, not hung in a tower as in later practice but portable so that it could be rung by hand either inside or outside the church. As well as being used to summon people to worship and possibly for liturgical purposes during Mass, such bells seem also to have been rung by a priest or some other person walking round the parish to mark its boundaries. There are several stories about the homing instincts of these medieval bells. The bell of Baile Bhaodáin at Ardchattan, which was often taken out to heal the sick in the surrounding countryside, had to be returned to the church immediately or it would fly back home of its own accord, ringing out the most melodious music ever heard by the human ear. Bells associated with

Font in the ruined nave of Kilneuair Church

saints were treated as relics or shrines and, like the pastoral staffs or bachals, often had their own hereditary keepers or dewars. The most ornate surviving bell shrine from Argyll, known as the Torbhlaren Bell, was discovered in 1814 by workers removing stones for the construction of a dyke at a farm about a mile from Kilmichael Glassary. Wrapped in a woollen cloth, it had probably been hidden during the Reformation. The corroded iron bell is contained in an elaborately decorated and perfectly preserved shrine depicting the hand of God reaching down from a cloud towards the crucified Christ. This bell, which has been associated with St Moluag, is now on display in the National Museum of Scotland.[6]

Many of Argyll's medieval chapels functioned as parish churches, whether they were originally designed for the purpose or not, and fulfilled that role up to and, in several cases, beyond the Reformation, often being rebuilt and extended. The chapel at Kilneuair on the south east shore of Loch Awe, which may possibly occupy the site of Columba's monastery of Cella Diuni, served as the principal place of worship for the extensive Glassary parish until the late sixteenth century. St Columba's Church in Southend went on being used for worship until the late seventeenth century. St Cathan's Chapel on Gigha served as the island's parish church until the early eighteenth century and Kilbrannan Chapel at Skipness seems only to have stopped being used when Claonaig Church was built in 1756. The chapel on Eilean Mór was used for worship until 1734, when the new parish of South Knapdale was created. Parishioners rowed out every Sunday to attend worship in the thirteenth-century chapel on the island of Inishail in Loch Awe until 1736, when a new church was built near Cladich. Killean old parish church in Kintyre, which dated back at least as far as the early thirteenth century, was only finally abandoned in 1770 on the grounds that it had become structurally unsafe. Only ocassionally, as at Lochgoilhead, was an old medieval chapel incorporated into a later building that is still in use as the parish church today. The alternative of building a brand new church, often on a very different site, was probably preferred because of the remote location of so many of the chapels, their small size and poor structural state. In some cases, as at Kilneuair, the townships which they served had disappeared.

Although they gradually fell out of regular use for worship, Argyll's numerous medieval churches remained important as vessels for community memory and, even in a ruined state, kept their spiritual associations. Abandoned for regular Presbyterian services, they still attracted local people for less official liturgical observances. In 1764 John Walker noted of the inhabitants of Iona that 'having no opportunity of public worship above three or four times a year, when visited by their minister, it is their custom to repair on the Sabbath to their devotions in the ruined Abbey, to Columba's tomb and to the Chapells of several different saints'. Several Catholic artefacts remained undisturbed. Visiting Inchkenneth Chapel off the Isle of Mull in 1772, Dr Samuel Johnson was intrigued to find that 'On one side of the altar is a bas relief of the blessed Virgin, and by it lies a little bell; which, though cracked, and without a clapper, has remained there for ages, guarded only by the venerableness of the place.' He also noted that 'The ground round the chapel is covered with gravestones of chiefs and ladies'.[7] The practice of burying local people around the abandoned chapels went on through the nineteenth and into the twentieth century. Extensive burial enclosures were often erected next to them – there is a particularly ornate example dating from the late eighteenth or early nineteenth century at Kilneuair.

Eighteenth-century burial enclosure, Kilneuair Church

In recent decades some of Argyll's medieval chapels have taken on a new lease of life as museums, preserving and displaying early Christian and late medieval carved stones and grave slabs. Those at Kilmory Knap and Keills have been roofed over for this purpose. Others are in a parlous state. The main wall of Kilneuair Chapel is propped up by wooden shafts and a notice on the old parish church at Kilchattan on Luing, unusual in being built largely of local slate flagstones, warns 'Keep Out – Dangerous Ruin'. Dangerous they may be but with trees and bushes growing up out of their crumbling stonework and ferns and bracken carpeting their floors, they are also eloquent testaments to the region's Christian past.

Kilchattan Chapel, Luing

8

Monasteries and Abbeys – The MacDonalds' Contribution

The golden age of medieval monasticism in the British Isles is perhaps most vividly evoked and certainly most dramatically preserved in the great abbeys of the Scottish Borders and North Yorkshire. Argyll may lack anything on the scale of Melrose, Jedburgh, Rievaulx and Fountains, but it does contain five significant medieval monastic sites – the abbey and nunnery on Iona, Saddell Abbey on the eastern coast of Kintyre, and the priories at Ardchattan on the north shore of Loch Etive and on the island of Oronsay. With the exception of Iona Abbey, all are now ruins, adding to their atmosphere as poignant monuments of a long vanished era of spiritual calm and contemplation.

These five monastic communities have one important feature in common. All were founded by direct descendants of Somerled (c. 1126–1164), who was arguably second only to Columba in terms of his importance in the spiritual as well as the political history of medieval Argyll. He himself may have been responsible for the initial foundation of the Cistercian house at Saddell around 1160. His son Reginald founded the Benedictine Abbey on Iona around 1203 and his daughter Bethoc was the first prioress of the nunnery established there at the same time. Somerled's grandson, Duncan, founded the Valiscaullian monastery at Ardchattan in 1230 and his great-great-great grandson, John, Lord of the Isles, established the Augustinian priory on Oronsay some time between 1325 and 1353.

To understand the significance of Somerled's contribution to Argyll's religious and political life we need to remember that for much of the ninth, tenth and eleventh centuries many of the islands and coastal areas of the mainland were occupied and dominated by the pagan Norse. Somerled was himself of mixed Norse and Gaelic descent – his mother was Norse and his father claimed descent from the ancient kings of Dál Riata. His own name Sumar-lidi, Somhairle in Gaelic, meant summer traveller. He is often portrayed as the fearless warrior who ousted the Norse from Argyll in a stunning naval battle off Islay in 1156 in which he deployed over eighty galleys, and thereafter established his rule both over the islands and over much of the mainland. This paved the way for the ascendancy of his direct descendants the MacDonalds, later Lords of the Isles, and the MacDougalls. In fact, most historians now agree that although he did preserve the language and culture of Gaeldom in Argyll when Norse might otherwise have prevailed, his achievements were as much to fuse Norse and Gaelic culture as to replace one completely with the other. Although naval superiority and military might may have played a part in his consolidation of power, equally important was his marriage to Ragnhilde, daughter of Olaf, King of Man, from whom he acquired the title Rex Insularum, rendered in Gaelic Ri lnnse Gall and Ceann Tir (literally the Strangers' Isles and Kintyre). It was an accurate description in that his power was largely confined to the islands and Kintyre and did not extend deep into mid or north Argyll. The Norse hold over the Western Isles remained – it was not until the Treaty of Perth in 1266 that Norway gave up all claims to them – and the churches on the islands of Argyll remained in the province of Nidaros (Trondheim) until 1472.[1]

Perhaps Somerled's most enduring contribution to Argyll's religious life lay in founding a dynasty, the Clan Somhairle, which was to be deeply involved in supporting Christianity and endowing churches and monasteries. Effectively, Argyll was split between his three surviving sons. Dugald, the eldest, who gave his name to the Clan MacDougall, held sway over Lorne, Morvern, Ardnamurchan and possibly the isles of Mull, Lismore, Kerrera, Jura, Tiree and Col – he and his MacDougall descendants styled themselves Kings of the South Isles and Lords of Lorne and built the great castles of Dunstaffnage, Dunollie and Duntrune. The second son, Reginald or Ranald, who inherited parts of Kintyre and Islay, which he seems to have shared with the third son, Angus, was, through his son Donald, the founder of the Clan Donald which came to be the dominant power across much of Argyll for the rest of the Middle Ages, assuming the titles King of the Hebrides (ri Innse Gall) and later Lord of the Isles (Dominus Insularum). Both the MacDougalls and the MacDonalds were huge patrons of the church in Argyll and especially of its monasteries.

Somerled and his descendants expressed their support for the church, which was doubtless in part inspired by a desire to consolidate and legitimize their power as well as by more pious and altruistic motives, primarily through establishing monasteries. Their foundations in Argyll came at a time of monastic revival across Europe fuelled by a wave of asceticism and a longing to return to the simplicity of the primitive church and the communal life of the apostles as recorded in the Book of Acts. There was a particular reaction against the increased wealth and worldliness of the great Benedictine Abbeys and a feeling that they had departed far from the precepts of their saintly founder, Benedict. Among the new monastic orders were the Cistercians, formed in 1098 when a group of Benedictine monks withdrew from the abbey of Molesmc, led by their abbot, Robert, seeking seclusion and poverty. Their settlement at Citeaux in the Burgundian forest was hardly more than an obscure hermitage until the arrival of Bernard of Clairvaux with thirty recruits in 1112. Thereafter the community underwent rapid expansion and planted numerous colonies.

It was the Cistercians who provided Argyll with the earliest of its medieval monastic communites, Saddell Abbey. The story goes that Malachy, Bishop of Armagh, came to Kintyre in the middle of the twelfth century seeking a site for a monastery and found the perfect place in a quiet glen on the east side of the Kintyre peninsula about eight miles north east of Campbeltown. Land was granted by either Somerled or his son, Reginald, and monks came over from Mellifont in County Louth, the first Cistercian monastery in Ireland, which Malachy had founded in 1142. Building began at Saddell around 1160 on a slightly raised promontory immediately above the confluence of Saddell Water and a stream subsequently known as Allt nam Manach, or Water of the Monks. Three main ranges of conventual buildings were grouped around a cloister on the south side of a cruciform church. There is a tradition that Somerled's body was brought for burial at the newly founded monastery after he had been killed at Renfrew in 1164. Some versions of the story say that his heart was buried at Saddell and the rest of his corpse interred in St Oran's Chapel on Iona.

Saddell had a relatively peaceful and uneventful existence for the next three hundred or more years with the Cistercian monks keeping largely to themselves. The end of the community came in the late fifteenth century and coincided with the collapse of the power of its MacDonald protectors and patrons. From around 1470 there seem to have been no monks left at the Abbey. In a letter written in 1507 King James IV observed that the monastery had seen no monastic life within living memory and had fallen into the hands of laymen, a fate which befell several other foundations. He sought to unite the Abbey with the Bishopric of Argyll at Lismore and gave Saddell and all its lands as a barony to David Hamilton, the Bishop of Argyll, who built a castle by the shore using the stones from the deserted monastery. A rather bleak tower which looks more like a fort than an episcopal palace, it is now owned by the Landmark Trust and can be rented for the week by those seeking to get a taste of the austere life of a sixteenth century bishop. James IV subsequently wrote to Pope Julius II proposing that the see of Argyll and its Cathedral be moved from Lismore to Saddell but this did not happen.

Saddell Abbey was the biggest ecclesiastical building in Kintyre prior to the Reformation and in its heyday had extensive lands stretching into mid-Argyll. It is difficult to sense its prestige and importance now when it seems a small, quiet backwater, tucked away and surrounded by yew trees and rhododendrons. Most of the stones were removed from the buildings during the eighteenth and nineteenth centuries for use on the Saddell Castle estate. All that is left now is part of the chancel and north transept of the Abbey church and a small portion of the centre of the south claustral range, possibly the undercroft of the refectory, which, when I visited, was largely covered by a fallen tree. As so often in Argyll, it is a landscape of the dead. The abbey ruins were used as a graveyard in post-Reformation times and the area is full of tombstones. Standing guard over the whole site at its highest and most westerly point, although somewhat obscured by dense shrubs and trees, is an imposing inscribed marble panel flanked by Doric pilasters commemorating Colonel Donald Campbell of Glensaddell who died in 1784. Twelve carved stone monuments dating from the 1300s and 1400s, consisting of six grave slabs, five effigies and part of a standing cross, are housed in a functional modern shelter erected by Historic Scotland near the entrance to the site.

Saddell Abbey

It is difficult for a visitor today to gain much sense of the monastic life that once flourished at Saddell. Perhaps the most evocative feature is the nearby holy well, which was probably attached to the Abbey and may have provided water for drinking or baptisms. A muddy path at the south side of the road bridge leads beside the Allt nam Mannach to a well covered with lichens and ferns. The water flows into a bowl with a large Latin cross carved below which is clearly the work of a nineteenth-century romantic. For me this dark, dank, green corner with its reminder of the religious associations of running water has a more powerful spiritual atmosphere than the monastic ruins.

Next in chronological order after Saddell comes the best-known and most instantly recognizable of all Argyll's ecclesiastical buildings, the Benedictine Abbey on Iona. It was deliberately built on the site of Columba's monastery, which had remained a place of pilgrimage despite successive Viking raids that continued until 986 and the removal of the saint's relics to Dunkeld and Kells in Ireland. By the eleventh century the monastic community was a shadow of its former self, with no abbot and just a handful of monks. However, nobles and some kings continued to be buried there and several of the Norse rulers of the Hebrides, who increasingly converted to Christianity, venerated Iona. In 980 Olaf Sihtriccson, the Viking King of Dublin, retired there 'in penitence and pilgrimage'. A hundred years later when Magnus Barelegs, King of Norway, raided both the Outer and Inner Hebrides, he spared Iona, apparently halting at the doorway to Columba's shrine chapel, locking the door and ordering his men not to touch it.

It is not clear what happened to the fabric of the monastery, which presumably continued to consist largely of wooden or wattle and daub huts, during this long period of decline. There is a tradition that Queen Margaret of Scotland initiated and paid for new building work but this cannot be proved. It was Somerled and his heirs who brought about a significant and lasting change in Iona's fortunes. He was determined that there should be a resident abbot once again and tried unsuccessfully, just before his death in 1164, to persuade Flaithbertach Ó Brolchain, Abbot of Derry and a descendant of Columba, to come over from Ireland and fulfil the role. Around 1203 Somerled's son, Reginald, founded the Benedictine Abbey on Iona, which was placed under the direct protection of the Pope. The monks seem to have been recruited from Ireland, maintaining the Celtic tradition, and in papal bulls and other official documents the Abbey retained its name of 'the monastery of St Columba', underlining the continuity with its sixth-century predecessor.

Benedictine monks continued to work and worship on Iona for over 350 years although it never had the influence nor the prestige of Columba's community. There were considerable problems with the fabric of the stone Abbey. By the early fifteenth century it seems to have been in ruins thanks to the combined effect of winter gales, rain and neglect. It was re-built thanks to the support of the MacDonald Lords of the Isles whose patronage was central to the Abbey's survival. The key period of re-building was between 1450 and 1476 under the supervision of Lord John the Second of the Isles, assisted by his cousin Bishop Angus MacDonald and the reforming abbots, Dominic Mackenzie and John MacKinnon. Much of what visitors see today dates from this period, including the decorative carvings on the pillars inside the Abbey showing Biblical scenes. In 1498

King James IV asked the Pope to make Iona, rather than Snizort on Skye, the seat of the Bishop of the Isles. His request was granted and in 1499 Iona Abbey was granted *in commendam* to Bishop John Campbell. Subsequent Bishops of the Isles held the Abbey on a similar basis. The practice of appointing either episcopal or lay commendators to run monasteries was common in this period. It allowed the Crown to gain access to their considerable lands and wealth. The monastic community on Iona dwindled in the early sixteenth century – a charter of 1532 mentions the bishop-commendator, the prior and just six monks. It is not clear how many monks were left by the time of the Scottish Reformation in 1560, nor what happened to them then.

Visitors to Iona Abbey today see it much as it was in its late medieval heyday with some parts surviving from the original early thirteenth-century building and the rest from the mid fifteenth-century reconstruction, albeit with much late nineteenth- and early twentieth-century restoration. The Abbey church was laid out in a traditional cruciform shape with a long narrow nave, a square chancel and north and south transepts forming the arms of the cross. A niche in the east wall of the north transept contains the feet of a statue, possibly of Columba, and this may have been where the pilgrims who flocked to Iona throughout the Middle Ages to venerate him were first received. The cloisters are unusually on the north rather than the south side of the church. On the eastern side a range includes the chapter house and, above it, the dormitory with stairs leading straight down to the north transept of the church, allowing the monks, who slept with their habits on, to come down for Nocturnes at 2am. The north range contains the refectory, with its pulpit from which the Bible or rule would be read during meal times, and behind it the abbot's house, the Michael Chapel and the Infirmary, which is now a museum. Most of these buildings are still much as they were when the medieval monks lived, worked and prayed in them, although the dormitory is now divided into a warren of smaller rooms. Guests staying for a week with the Iona Community live in the monastic quarters and experience the rhythms and routines of a religious community.

The oldest surviving building on Iona is not the Abbey but St Oran's Chapel, the small rectangular building that stands in the graveyard

St Oran's Chapel with Iona Abbey behind

known as the Reilig Odhráin to the south west of the Abbey. It is thought to date from the mid to late twelfth century and to have been established as a mortuary chapel to house the remains of the Clan Somhairle, and specifically the MacDonald Lords of the Isles. It may be that Somerled himself built it around 1150. In his recent book on *Clan Donald and Iona Abbey* Ian MacDonnell suggests that Somerled is buried on one side of the altar in the Chapel and his son Reginald on the other. He goes on to suggest that seven subsequent MacDonald Lords of the Isles are buried in the Chapel. This may be a slight exaggeration but given the huge number of Campbell mausoleums dotted across Argyll, we can surely allow their great rivals a little embellishment in respect of this sacred MacDonald site. There is certainly a strong likelihood that St Oran's Chapel was the burial place of John, the first Lord of the Isles, after his death at Ardtornish Castle in Morvern in 1386. It is said that abbot Fingon Mackinnon and his monks came out to meet the body when it arrived at Martyrs' Bay, escorted it along the Street of the Dead and conducted funeral services over the following eight days and nights.

Perhaps even more haunting than the restored Abbey is the ruined nunnery through which many visitors to Iona walk on their way between the ferry jetty and the Abbey. It was probably founded by Reginald around the same time as the Abbey, and his sister Bethoc

Nunnery, Iona

seems to have been the first prioress. There are conflicting accounts as to whether the nuns were Benedictines, like the monks in the Abbey, or belonged to the Augustinian order. Either way, they led a secluded life of contemplation and prayer. This appears to have been the only religious house for women established in Argyll in this period although there is an unattested tradition that there was a Benedictine nunnery at Balnahard on the north side of Colonsay. Prioresses continued to be appointed until the Reformation but there are indications that, as with the monastic community in the Abbey, the nunnery was in a severely depleted state by the early sixteenth century. A memorial to Prioress Anna MacLean, who died in 1543, was badly damaged when the roof of the church collapsed in 1830 and now survives only in very fragmented form. In its heyday, the nunnery was an extensive complex consisting of a large church with side aisle, chapel and cloisters surrounded by ranges housing the chapter house, dormitory and guest accommodation. The walls of the church and the south range survive. The foundations of the cloisters between them are now planted as a garden which serves as an eloquent if silent reminder of the often forgotten and neglected role played by women in the history of the church. Reflections on this theme at this site are an important part of the weekly pilgrimage around the island led by staff members of the Iona Community.

Argyll's third monastic site, Ardchattan Priory, was founded by Somerled's grandson, Duncan MacDougall, Lord of Lorne and the builder of Dunstaffnage Castle, in 1230 for the Valliscaulian order, an offshoot of the Cistercians who took their name from their mother house at Val des Choux in Burgundy. It seems to have been deliberately located near to a much earlier Christian site. On the hillside above are the remains of an early chapel and well dedicated to St Modan. Ardchattan was not a large community and there were never more than twenty brothers pursuing the austere lifestyle required of the Valliscaulians, which included maintaining a vow of silence, wearing hair shirts, sleeping fully clothed and worshipping seven times a day. Like Iona Abbey, there was extensive re-building in the fifteenth century when the choir was extended and a new refectory constructed. The MacDougalls continued to be patrons and strong supporters of the Priory throughout its history and, indeed, became effectively hereditary priors during the fifteenth century. Perhaps the outstanding artefact surviving on the site is the MacDougall Cross commissioned by Prior Eugenius MacDougall in 1500. It is one of the few pieces of West Highland sculpture to record the sculptor's name, in this case John Ó Brolchán, who was responsible for carving the Crucifixion on one side and the Virgin and Child on the other.

As elsewhere, the community at Ardchattan dwindled during the sixteenth century. In 1538 there were just six monks and by 1560 only three. Around 1545, John Campbell, later Bishop of the Isles, became Commendator Prior and appropriated the buildings and endowments. His son, Alexander, was appointed the last prior in 1580. In 1600, on the death of the last monk, he was granted the Priory lands and rights by James VI and became the first laird of Ardchattan. He began the process of converting parts of the priory into a private house, turning the old refectory into a dining room. The house remained in Campbell hands for 400 years. The monastic church was used as the parish church until 1732, when a new parish church was built using stones from the priory.

The priory ruins are open to the public between April and October and are well worth visiting. They are reached by taking the single track road which forks off the A828 immediately north of the Connel Bridge and hugs the north shore of Loch Etive. Park just inside the gates of the house and walk up the drive and through a cobbled farmyard to gain access to the ruins. Cows graze in the nearby fields and spreading oak trees shade the collection of nine sculptured stones dating from between the tenth and sixteenth centuries propped against one of the old walls. As so often in Argyll, Ardchattan Priory is more than anything else a landscape of the dead. Its ruined buildings have become a sprawling burial ground filled with gravestones and monuments, especially for Campbells of various hues. Private burial aisles established in the seventeenth century contain the bodies of Campbells of Lochnell, Lochawe and Barcaldine. Also buried there is Colin Campbell of Glenure, victim of the famous Appin murder. Contained in the Ardchattan Aisle, with forbidding skull and crossbones carvings on either side of the entrance, are huge, grim granite memorials to four late-nineteenth-century Campbells of Ardchattan. A more cheerful prospect awaits those who wander through the grounds of the adjoining house, which are also open to the public. At the end of the wild garden to the north, a stone bears the inscription 'I To the Hills Will Lift Mine Eyes From Whence Doth Come Mine Aid'. If ever there was an excuse for misquoting the start of Psalm 121 (there should, of course, be a full stop after 'Eyes' and a question mark after 'Aid'), this place affords it, looking out as it does on to the hills above where, amid the trees, are the ruined chapel and well dedicated to Modan.

The last of the major medieval monasteries of Argyll, Oronsay Priory, seems to have been founded as a house for Augustinian canons some time between 1325 and 1353 by John I, Lord of the Isles. According to one story, this was in gratitude for a divorce granted him so that he could marry Margaret, daughter of King Robert II. This priory too was built deliberately on the site of an early Christian settlement, in this case a monastic community established possibly as early as the sixth century by either Columba or Oran, who may have given his name to the island, which can be accessed by a causeway from neighbouring Colonsay at low tide. Some eighteenth- and nineteenth-century sources suggest that there was also an abbey established on Colonsay around the same time on the site later occupied by Kiloran House but this seems incorrect. Dedicated to Columba, Oronsay Priory continued to house Augustinian canons, regular clergy who lived in community according to the Rule of St Augustine, until 1560, with the last known prior, Robert Lamont, being elected in 1555. Its lands and property were then given *in commendam* to Maol Choluim MacDubhthaich and subsequently granted to the Bishops of the Isles by King James VI.

Perhaps because of its comparative remoteness, and also thanks to some sensitive restoration work, a considerable part of the roofless Priory buildings, mostly dating from the fourteenth and sixteenth centuries, still survive. The cloisters, reconstructed in 1883, are particularly evocative and, as I can personally testify, lend themselves well to hide and seek games with children. The east range includes the Chapter House, which was divided in the late eighteenth century to create the McNeil Burial Aisle. The north range, which probably housed the kitchen and refectory, is adjoined by a Chapel. On the south side of the cloisters are the remains of the Priory Church, an aiseless nave dating from the fourteenth century, the walls of which are largely intact. The separate Prior's House was roofed and refurbished in 1927 to house a fine collection of tapered grave slabs, dating from the fourteenth to the sixteenth centuries. There are also many medieval grave markers in the adjacent burial ground.

Oronsay's founder, who was Somerled's great-great-great grandson and chief of the Clan Donald, was known as 'John of Islay' and 'Good Lord John' because of his considerable support for the church. He refurbished the chapels on Eilean Mór and at Finlaggan on Islay and contributed substantially to the maintenance of Iona Abbey. He was also the first to style himself *Dominus Insularum*, or Lord of the Isles, in 1336 and kept the title until his death in 1386. In fact, the MacDonald Lords of the Isles effectively dominated Argyll, and especially its islands and western seaboard, from the twelfth until the end of the fifteenth century and had a considerable and benign impact on its religion and culture. As the title implies, their base was maritime rather than on the mainland, underlining the importance of sea travel in this period. Somerled had established his headquarters on Islay and it was on that green and fertile island that the Lords of the Isles continued to make their base. While their military headquarters was at Dunivaig on the south east coast, their political and administrative centre was at Finlaggan in the north east of the island. It was a place of religious ritual centred on the seven-feet-square Stone of Inauguration. When a chief of the Clan Donald was installed as Lord or King of the Isles, he stood barefoot in the footprints cut into the stone, and was anointed by the Bishop of Argyll and seven priests.

The Lordship of the Isles was forfeited by the Crown in 1493 and the last holder of the title died in 1503. So ended the sway over Argyll exerted by Somerled's MacDonald and MacDougall successors over three centuries. They were substantial patrons of the church and were directly responsible for the great monastic foundations which were such an important feature of Argyll's medieval spiritual landscape. Without them, the region would lack its most iconic religious landmark, Iona Abbey. It would almost certainly also be without its magnificent concentration of sculptured grave slabs and crosses, many of which they commissioned. It is important not to romanticise the motives that led the MacDonalds and their kinsmen to support the church. Politics was as important a factor as piety. Somerled's descendants used Iona to underpin their authority in their Hebridean kingdom, just as he had done. Throughout the fourteenth century, the Abbey was controlled, with MacDonald approval, by the MacKinnons who ran it as much as a secular lordship as a religious community. On Oronsay similarly, the MacDuffies held the office of prior as a hereditary fiefdom. That said, however, the Lords of the Isles and their allies were substantial and generous patrons of church and culture.

Wandering round Argyll's monastic ruins today, it is easy to idealise the depth of spirituality and religious fervour that they once encompassed and to see them as shining beacons of Medieval Christian faith and learning, which were summarily snuffed out at the Reformation. In fact, all four seem to have been languishing long before 1560, run by lay or episcopal commendators and with just a handful of monks left in the community. Their decline came about as a result of changing patterns of belief and political power as much as at the hands of brutish Puritan iconoclasts. In their heyday they were undoubtedly places of contemplation, detachment from the values and preoccupations of the world, and what we now call mindfulness. As well as having an atmosphere of deep prayer and devotion, which still pervades them today, they were centres of culture and craftsmanship, producing in their workshops the exquisitely carved stones now displayed within their ruined walls.

9

Muscular Christianity in the West Highland Sculptured Stones

Argyll's ruined medieval chapels, monasteries and priories are now visited largely because of their superb collections of carved grave slabs and crosses dating from the fourteenth to the sixteenth centuries. Altogether, there are around 800 of these West Highland sculptured stones, as they are often known, the great majority of which are located in Argyll and its islands. Iona alone has over 170, many of which are displayed in the newly refurbished museum behind the Abbey. There are also particular concentrations in Knapdale at Kilmory Knap, Keills, Kilberry and in the churchyard at Kilmartin where twenty-three carved stones slabs are housed in the burial aisle built for Bishop Neil Campbell of Argyll and his wife in 1627. There are good collections at Lochaline in Morvern, where seventeen stones are displayed in the Old Session House next to the parish church, at Oronsay Priory, where thirty grave slabs have been gathered in the restored byre, and at Saddell Abbey and Ardchattan Priory.

The West Highland grave slabs and crosses were produced in a number of workshops across Argyll, each with its own distinctive style and constituting a distinct and recognisable 'school' of sculpture. Iona was probably the most prolific, producing most of the surviving standing crosses as well as many gravestones. Its hallmark is a prevalence of animal and leaf motifs, technically, if rather dauntingly described, as 'trilobate foliaceous ornament'. The Kintyre school, represented by stones at Kilmory and Killean, which may conceivably have had its workshop at Saddell, used similar ornamentation but in a less rhythmic and more cluttered form. The third distinct school, that of Loch Awe, was artistically the least gifted and produced more haphazard designs. Its stones are found in mid-Argyll, Lorne and Loch Fyneside. Kilmartin seems to have stones from both the Iona and Loch Awe schools. Stones at Kilmory and Keills with a distinctive style that do not conform to any of these three schools have led archaeologists to suggest that there was a fourth, Loch Sween, school which possibly drew on the other traditions. In the first half of the sixteenth century Oronsay Priory seems to have become an important centre for monumental sculpture, with characteristic patterns of leaves, animals and galleys, perhaps forming a fifth school.

These striking and beautifully worked artefacts tell us much about both the spiritual and political landscape of Iona in the late medieval and early modern period. Many of these stones were probably commissioned by the MacDonald Lords of the Isles and other prominent noble families, including the rising Campbells, and they reflect the outlook and ethos of a warrior aristocracy, imbued with the values of knightly chivalry. The images that recur again and again on the grave slabs are those of a male-dominated culture of military elites and muscular Christianity. There are few representations of women, among the exceptions being the grave slab for Prioress Anna MacLean in the Nunnery on Iona and an effigy of what appears to be a laywoman with a book and rosary on Oronsay. There are some depictions of abbots, bishops and clerics, including a striking sixteenth-century Oronsay effigy of a prior clad in cassock and cope, with the base of his pastoral staff pushed into the mouth of a small devil's head. The great majority of the grave slabs and effigies depict warriors clad in full armour, often brandishing axes or swords. On those stones where there are no human figures, the most common design is a huge two-handed longsword, or claymore, which often runs right down the length of the stone. Much use is made of the interlacing floral and vine-like motifs found on the earlier high-standing crosses but the overall emphasis of these later medieval sculptured stones is much more macho and militant. A typical effigy of a man in armour from Oronsay, thought to date from the late fourteenth or early fifteenth century, shows the tip of his scabbard resting on the back of a small leering devil with the hindquarters of an animal. The popularity of this theme of the militant vanquishing of the forces of evil is evident in the numerous depictions of the sword-wielding

Grave slabs of warriors, Kilmartin Churchyard

warrior archangel Michael, often with a slaughtered dragon at his feet.

Another popular symbol on the West Highland sculptured stones is the sea-going galley known as the birlinn or lymphan, and specifically the Galley of Lorne, that badge of maritime supremacy adopted by the MacDonald Lords of the Isles and their kinsmen the MacDougalls, and taken over by the Campbells in the later fifteenth century. There are over eighty representations of galleys on West Highland grave slabs. Sometimes they are in full sail – this seems to be a characteristic motif of the Oronsay school – and sometimes the sails are furled. There is a particularly fine depiction of a galley flying a large pennant towards the bottom of one of the faces of the shaft of a free-standing cross preserved in the Iona museum identified by an inscription as having been made in 1489 for John MacKinnon, Abbot of Iona from 1467 until around 1499, and his father who was chief of the MacKinnon clan.

Free-standing disc-headed crosses were almost certainly sculpted in the same workshops that produced the grave slabs, with the majority of those that have survived thought to have come from Iona. Several still stand in or close to the site where they were originally erected. There are relatively early examples, dating from the late fourteenth or early fifteenth century, in the grounds of Keil Church, Lochaline and at Kilchoman on Islay. Macmillan's Cross at Kilmory, which is thought to date from the late fifteenth century, stood until 1981 in

*Macmillan's Cross,
Kilmory:
Cross Head
Sword on shaft
Hunting scene*

its original socket hole in the churchyard and is now housed inside the roofed chapel. An inscription associates it with Alexander Macmillan, believed to have been keeper of Castle Sween for the Lords of the Isles before 1481. The west face shows the Crucified Saviour flanked by Mary and John on the Cross Head, with a single sword occupying most of the shaft, while the east shaft shows a huntsman with an axe observing three hounds attacking a deer. MacLean's Cross on Iona (page 22) also dates from this period, as does the Oronsay Cross which stands close to the west wall of the priory and is almost certainly the work of an Irish master mason, Mael-Sachlainn ó Cuinn, who seems to have left Iona when it was languishing and come to Oronsay. A slightly later free-standing ringed cross, thought to date from the early sixteenth century, now stands at the back of Kilmartin Church. Its shaft was recorded as lying in the churchyard around 1860. The top arm was recovered from a culvert in 1973 and the reconstructed cross erected in the church in 1977. The front shows the crucified Saviour, with an angel above, and on the back a similar angel stands over the figure of Christ in majesty.

These late medieval crosses have a similar muscular Christian feel to the grave slabs. The figures of the Virgin and Child have been ousted from the central place that they occupied on the earlier high-standing crosses from the ninth and tenth centuries and replaced by the stark and contorted torso of the crucified Jesus, naked except for a loin cloth. This portrayal of a muscular, if suffering, Saviour is a striking feature of all the crosses mentioned above, except that at Keil Church, Lochaline, which is decorated only by plant scrolls and dragons' heads. There is a particularly grotesque and harrowing portrayal of the Crucified Christ, his body writhing in agony, on a cross head displayed at Kilberry. Thought to date from the early sixteenth century, it was found in 1851 by a boy digging a garden and subsequently re-united with its shaft which appears to come out of the mouth of a dragon, possibly representing Satan.

Cross at the back of Kilmartin Church

Three carved crosses were moved from their

original location and show signs of mutilation. The earliest is the Kilmichael Cross, probably dating from the thirteenth century, which displays a naked figure of the Crucified Christ similar to those already described. Originally sited at Kilmichael Glassary, it was commandeered for use as a door lintel in the post-Reformation church built there in the late seventeenth or early eighteenth century. Discovered when this church was demolished in 1827, it was removed to Bellanoch where a blacksmith repaired it with iron clamps. For a time it served as the market cross at Kilmichael and was then moved in the early 1850s to the grounds of the newly built private chapel of the Malcolm family of Poltalloch, dedicated to St Columba. It remained there for over 150 years until concern about its deterioration led to a further move to the Kilmartin Museum where it currently stands in the entrance porch.

The Campbeltown Cross is thought to have been carved around 1380 and originally sited in the graveyard at Kilkivan, near Machrihanish. An inscription records that it was made for Andrew MacEachern, a parson who is known to have transferred from Kilkivan to the benefice of Kilchoman on Islay around that time. At some point after the Reformation the image of the crucified Saviour, which occupied the central position on the head, was removed and two other figures, one of whom has been identified from a surviving Bible and chalice as a cleric, were chiselled away. Figures of Mary, John and two other saints, the archangel Michael vanquishing a dragon, a mermaid and the head of a sea monster together with sundry animals were left untouched by the Protestant iconoclasts. Purged of its Catholic excrescences, the cross was erected in the Main Street of Campbeltown soon after its foundation as a burgh in 1609 to serve as the market cross. Taken down for safe keeping during the Second World War, when Campbeltown was a major naval base, it was re-erected in the 1940s at the Old Quay Head, where it sits somewhat uncomfortably today in the middle of a very busy roundabout.

The Inveraray Cross, which possibly came originally from the medieval chapel at Kilmalieu, has a similar date and history. An inscription indicates that three generations of noblemen 'caused it to be made'. With the central cross-head depiction of the Crucified Saviour and another panel carefully removed, it was erected as the market cross in Inveraray in the mid seventeenth century and re-located to its present site, on the loch shore at the bottom of Main Street, in 1839. Images of a hound pursuing a boar and a horseman with a hawk on his wrist adorn the lower part of the front face of the shaft. These symbols of secular manliness were apparently more acceptable to Protestant sensibilities than the graphic depictions of the naked Christ on the Cross.

The ending of the political power of key noble clans spelt the death knell for the West Highland sculptured stones. It is significant that their main flowering was in the century or so before the forfeiture of the Lordship of the Isles in 1493. It was probably the loss of noble patronage more than anything else that led to the decline and the loss of this great artistic tradition. The Reformation also had an impact on this aspect of Argyll's spiritual landscape. Many of the subjects and figures which had previously been portrayed on grave slabs were regarded as Popish or pagan. Gravestones continued to be carved long after Protestantism had taken hold in Argyll but they lacked the intricate detail, originality and exuberance of design which character-ised those produced in the great late-mediaeval monastic workshops. Instead, they were for the most part decorated simply and sometimes rather crudely with a skull and crossbones, an hourglass, a coffin or other stark reminders of human mortality. Burials were no longer allowed inside churches and various acts were passed in Parliament and by the General Assembly of the Church of Scotland to 'raise, demolish, abolish, cast down or deface all idolatrous images, pic-tures and other idolatrous monuments'. Several of the great West Highland sculptured stones were smashed, like the headless Kilberry Cross, and others were purged of their more Catholic elements, like the Campbeltown and Inveraray crosses. A good number were spared and survived, however, and some were recycled. Two medie-val grave slabs at Keil Churchyard, Lochaline, were re-appropriated in the eighteenth century with new names carved on them and simi-lar re-use was made of stones at Kilmartin. We are back once again to the familiar theme of adapting rather than destroying the religious landscape of the past.

10

Bishops and Books –
Lismore and Carnasserie Castle

Argyll lacks a great medieval cathedral on the scale of Glasgow, Dunkeld, Dunblane or St Andrews. This is a reflection partly of its relative poverty and partly of the fact that, for much of the Middle Ages, mainland Argyll was part of the vast diocese of Dunkeld and most of its islands part of the see of Sodor, which took in the Isle of Man, the Outer Hebrides and all the Inner Isles except Lismore, Kerrera, Seil, Luing and the Cumbraes and had its cathedral at Snizort on Skye.

Argyll did gain its own diocese and cathedral during the later Middle Ages. It was centred on the island of Lismore at the mouth of Loch Linnhe. To those who sail past it today on their way to Mull, this ten-mile-long island, which is reached either via car ferry from Oban or on the short passenger crossing from Port Appin, may seem a rather peripheral place. Yet it has been an important feature in Argyll's spiritual landscape, not just as the seat of its bishop and site of its only cathedral, traces of which can still be found in the architecture of the small simple parish church in the middle of the island, but also as the location of a seminary and through giving its name to the greatest treasury of medieval Gaelic literature.

There are conflicting accounts as to precisely why and when the bishopric of Argyll was carved out of the see of Dunkeld. The fullest, but probably not the most accurate, is to be found in the *Scotichron-icon*, written in the mid fifteenth century by Walter Bower, Abbot of Inchcolm. He suggests it happened in the 1180s or 1190s when John, Bishop of Dunkeld, who did not know 'the Scottish or Irish Gaelic tongue' and could not provide pastoral care 'for the ferocious and savage people', sent his chaplain Harald, who knew Gaelic, to

Rome with a letter requesting that the Pope divide the diocese into two. The Pope agreed and consecrated Harald as bishop of the new diocese of Argyll.

While Bower's chronology is probably right – the first mention of the Diocese of Argyll in Papal documents is in 1193 – other aspects of his account are probably erroneous. Iain MacDonald, who has done much research on this subject, is inclined to think that the origins of the bishopric lie in the political sphere, and specifically in the desire of Somerled's descendants to consolidate their hold over the church in their territories. It has been suggested that the first bishop, Harald, whose name is Norwegian, was actually sent from Nidaros, or indeed that he may already have been Bishop of Sodor.[1]

The new diocese effectively established the boundaries of mainland Argyll as they remained until local government reorganisation in the late twentieth century. It encompassed forty-eight parishes extending from Glenelg in the north to Kilcolmkill on the tip of Kintyre in the south and from Kilchoan in Ardnamurchan in the west to Lochgoilhead in the east. Some sources suggest that the first seat of the Bishopric of Argyll was at Muckairn (now Taynuilt) on the south shore of Loch Etive. Its early name, Killespickerill, is said to mean the church of Bishop Harald, whose Norse name was rendered into Gaelic as Erailt. Muckairn would certainly have provided a central location but if, indeed, it was chosen it seems to have been only an interim arrangement. A list of Scottish sees compiled before 1272 describes it as 'the smallest of our cathedrals, fifty-six feet long by thirty feet broad, perhaps the humblest in Britain. It had no aisles and seems to have had neither transepts nor nave'. No traces remain of this building.

It may be that when Bishop Harald died the bishopric of Argyll was temporarily placed under the charge of the Bishop of Sodor and that this was when the see was transferred from Killespickerill to Lismore. The first clear reference to a bishop of Lismore is found in a document of 1225. Lismore was the only island included within the new diocese, which was otherwise made up entirely of mainland parishes. The decision to make it the seat of the bishop and the site of the cathedral, whether taken by the Bishop of Sodor or Somerled's descendants, may well have been partly political. Lismore also had clear geographical advantages with good sea links north to Ardnamurchan and Morvern and south to Kintyre as well as to Lorne and mid-Argyll. The main reason for its choice, however, was probably its strong past religious traditions and the familiar desire to build on an existing spiritual landscape. Thanks to the impact and influence of Moluag, Lismore was probably second only to Iona in terms of its significance as a monastic centre in the 'golden age' of Celtic Christianity in the sixth and seventh centuries. Although his relics were translated to Rosemarkie in the mid ninth century, much the same time that Columba's went to Dunkeld and probably for the same reason of danger of Viking attack, it remained an import-ant ecclesiastical centre with a resident monastic community. There appears to have been a revived cult of Moluag in the twelfth century – his *Bachull Mòr* or staff may date from this period – and the Clan Somhairle seems to have capitalised on this to promote Lismore as the episcopal centre for Argyll and the Hebrides.

The first mention of a Dean of Lismore does not come until 1240. Significantly, he was called Gillemoluoc, or servant of Moluag. Although the first reference to the Cathedral is in 1314, building may have begun in the mid thirteenth century, under the patronage of the MacDougall Lords of the Isles, who were building Ardchat-tan Priory and the chapel at Dunstaffnage Castle around the same time. Lismore Cathedral was almost certainly erected on the site of the monastery which Moluag had founded. Excavations in the area around it suggest a circular vallum similar to those which sur-rounded early monastic sites. It was a simple structure consisting of an aisleless choir and nave with a small tower. Although smaller than Iona Abbey, it was bigger than the Cathedral of the diocese of Sodor at Snizort. The small chapter was made up of a Dean, Precen-tor, Chancellor and Treasurer. There were also three rural deans, covering Glassary, Lorne and Kintyre.

Lismore Cathedral did not have a very long or glorious history. Although the Cathedral was endowed with lands on the adjacent mainland, providing the origin for the name Appin (Apuin in Gaelic means abbey lands), the diocese of Argyll as a whole struggled finan-cially. Much of the episcopal revenue came from tithes 'in kind' from the forty-eight parishes, which were often affected by bad harvests, the poor quality of land and bad weather. Substantial building work was undertaken in the late thirteenth and early fourteenth centuries, but a Papal letter of 1411 noted that on account of wars, famines and plagues, the Cathedral was lacking in 'jewels, ecclesiastical ornaments, books or other necessities'.[2] While remaining the *de jure* Cathedral of the diocese, Lismore ceased to function as the principal seat of governance for bishops of Argyll, which transferred to Dunoon from the mid fifteenth century. Dunoon Castle became the main episcopal residence and its parish church took on the function of a pro-Cathedral, reflecting the shift of power in Argyll from the Clan Dougall in Lorne to the Clan Campbell in Cowal. There also seems to have been a growing disenchantment with bishops on the part of the natives of Lismore, which made the island an uncomfortable place for them to reside. In 1452 Bishop Lauder and his followers were ambushed and assaulted by a group of islanders in what was possibly part of on-going protests against the imposition of Lowland, non-Gaelic-speaking clergy in the parishes of Argyll. From 1470 onwards patronage of the offices of the Cathedral dignitaries was in the hands of the earls of Argyll and the chiefs of the Campbells of Glen Orchy. Non-residence was rife and very few of the Cathedral Chapter whom they appointed seem to have lived on the island.

In 1512 King James IV, keen to consolidate his hold over Kintyre, sought to transfer the see of Argyll from Lismore to Saddell. He noted that the Cathedral had fallen into ruin and pointed out that the new location would be much more fertile. Although his attempt was unsuccessful, Lismore Cathedral went into further decline. None of those who held the bishopric of Argyll after 1525 had themselves consecrated there or showed any interest in it as the episcopal seat. In a letter to the Pope in 1539, noting that the see was vacant yet again, James V complained: 'The land is mountainous and sterile, the rents small, and the people uncivilised, so that very few desire to hold the bishopric'.[3] On another occasion, he described Lismore as being 'at the very back of the realm'. The cathedral effectively operated from the sixteenth century as a rural parish church. A massive stone pulpit was built to equip it for this role but by the end of the century the nave had fallen into ruin and worship was concentrated in the small choir. By 1679 much of the building was roofless and in 1749 dressed stone from the ruined nave was used to build the Manse and barn. Restoration in 1900 turned the choir of the old Cathedral into a parish church. Visitors now see what, from the outside, looks like a typical simple West Highland kirk, white painted with a little bird-cage belfry. Inside there are traces of its medieval Cathedral origins in the form of a piscina, or holy-water stoup, triple sedilia (seats) on the south wall, dating from the early fourteenth century, and a doorway on the north wall with a carved head, one of which is mitred, on each side. A window erected in 1926 above the gallery shows Moluag with his crozier and Bible, and Columba with his hand raised in blessing, his servant Bathán behind him and the opening words of Psalm 100 inscribed below.

For those who look carefully around the island, there are other reminders of Lismore's former ecclesiastical glories. The ruins of the bishops' residence at Achadun sit imposingly on the summit of a limestone ridge on the west coast opposite the tiny island of Bernera. It was occupied by bishops of Argyll from the mid thirteenth century until David Hamilton's decision to build Saddell Castle, in which he lived from 1508 to 1512, effectively ended its use as an episcopal residence. More recently, Lismore briefly boasted a Roman Catholic seminary. In 1803 the seminary for the Highland district was transferred from Moidart to Kilcheran, a newly erected house towards the southern end of the island. A chapel was built there in 1815 but in 1828 the seminary was moved to Aquhorthies and thereafter to Blairs near Aberdeen. The chapel was subsequently used in the 1840s by a United Succession congregation. A small burial enclosure behind the house contains the graves of two brothers who were both Catholic priests.

For many scholars, Lismore is important not for its religious history but for a collection of poems which bears its name. The Book of the Dean of Lismore, the most important manuscript in the history of Gaelic verse in Scotland, was compiled between 1512 and 1542 by James Macgregor. Although he held the office of Dean of Lismore, he was, like many of his colleagues, an absentee cleric, based at Fortingall in Glen Lyon in Highland Perthshire. While his work was supported by both MacDonald and Campbell patrons in a rare example of co-operation between these two rival clans, recent research by Martin MacGregor has demonstrated that it was principally a Campbell inspired and sponsored venture, with a particular connection to Duncan Campbell of Glenorchy.[4] Many of the poems in the book, which date from between 1200 to 1520, are dedicated to either the first or second Earl of Argyll and clearly have an Argyll provenance. They provide an interesting if not always very edifying commentary on the religious life of the region in the late Middle Ages. Several describe priests lusting after women, bearing out Iain MacDonald's findings that clerical celibacy was often flouted and that a good number of illegitimate sons of priests followed their fathers into Argyll parishes. A poem allegedly composed by Isabel Campbell, Countess of Argyll, who died in 1510, praises the rigidity and girth of her personal chaplain's penis. There is also much heroic verse describing the life and last days of Ossian, the last of the Fiana. This includes a lament for the loss of the old heathen spirit of Argyll with the take-over of Christianity, put into the mouth of Ossian:

> I grieve that the Hill of the Fiana is in bondage to the clerics...Once, O Fort of Cruachan, I spent my time joyfully around thy banks. I once found shields and spears, dogs and beagles beneath thy walls. But today the Hill of the Fiana is under clerics and croziers.[5]

Carnasserie Castle, the roofless but otherwise well-preserved fortified mansion that stands just off the A816 road north of Kilmartin may seem an odd place to pair with Lismore, but there are several reasons for bracketing them together in this chapter. They link the themes of bishops, books, Campbells and Gaelic culture. There is also a more direct link. John Carswell, who re-built and lived in Carnasserie Castle in the 1560s, counted among his many ecclesiastical titles the Treasurership of Lismore Cathedral, an office to which he was appointed by the fourth Earl of Argyll in 1550.

Carswell was the most important Protestant minister in the whole of the Highlands in the years following the Reformation. Probably born in Kilmartin in 1522, following an early flirtation with the MacDonalds he became a strong supporter of the Earls of Argyll, and a key promoter of the new Reformed faith which they espoused so strongly. He combined the role of parson at Kilmartin with that of the fifth Earl's personal chaplain and in 1559 was given the lands and title of Carnasserie, a site which contained standing stones and cairns as well as a dwelling house. In 1560 he was appointed Superintendent of Argyll, effectively making him the equivalent of a bishop in the Reformed Kirk. He went on to acquire lands and titles across the region, leasing the bishopric of Argyll and the abbacy of

Carnasserie Castle

Saddell in 1563 and accepting from the Catholic Queen Mary in 1565 the bishopric of the Isles and the Abbacy of Iona, an action which caused some consternation among his Reformed brethren. Known locally as Carsualach Mór Chàrn-Àsaraidh, or Big Carswell of Carnasserie, he stood nearly seven feet tall and was undoubtedly very ambitious, although Marion Campbell is perhaps right to suggest that he accumulated so many ecclesiastical titles partly because they unlocked the rents and funds which enabled him to put Protestant clergy into Argyll's empty parishes and forward the Reformation. He died in 1572 and was buried in the midst of a great storm in a stone coffin at Ardchattan Priory.

Carnasserie was central to Carswell's project of making Argyll Protestant without destroying its Gaelic culture and language. The castle which he created with the help of builders from Stirling Castle reflects his humanistic and Renaissance values as well as his staunch Protestantism. It is spacious and elegant but also has a distinctly militaristic character and slightly austere atmosphere. Like Saddell Castle, there is more than a hint of muscular Christianity about it. A five-storey tower is combined with a three storey house to create the effect of something between a fort and a mansion. As a fortified Protestant stronghold in Campbell ownership, it went on to play a significant role in the bitter religious struggles of the seventeenth century, being garrisoned during the Civil War and becoming a base for supporters of the ninth Earl of Argyll's rising against King James VII and II in 1685, when it was besieged and burned down by pro-Royalist forces.

Carnasserie's main claim to fame is not its role in these bloody conflicts, however. Like Lismore, it is remembered chiefly for a book. It was in the Castle's drawing room that Carswell carried out his most famous project, the translation into Gaelic of John Knox's Book of Common Order, the directory of worship of the new Reformed Scottish Kirk. Published in 1567, it was the first ever printed book in Gaelic, and, as Donald Meek has shown, reflected Carswell's vision of a Celtic Protestant west, embracing Scotland and Ireland.[6] His Gaelic version of this classic Presbyterian liturgical text was an adaptation as much as a translation, informed by his own deep immersion in Argyll's distinctive spiritual traditions. He added a reference to 'the saints and archangels' in acknowledgement of the region's strong lingering attachment to the cults of local saints and the figure of St Michael, and introduced a special liturgy for blessing a ship.

Carswell wanted to follow up his translation of the Book of Common Order with a Gaelic Bible. In 1567 the new Protestant Synod of Argyll, which was already engaged in translating the catechisms and metrical psalter, resolved to bring out a Gaelic Old Testament. The Synod of Argyll remained at the forefront of promoting Gaelic versions of key Christian texts. The second printed Gaelic book to appear in Scotland was the Synod's translation of Calvin's Geneva Cathecism, published in 1631. It was followed in 1653 by a translation of the Shorter Westminster Cathecism. The Synod of Argyll was also responsible for the first Gaelic Psalter, which was published in 1659. Around the same time it initiated a project to produce a complete Gaelic translation of the Bible. Dugald Campbell, minister of Knapdale, had completed a translation of the Old Testament by the time of his death in 1673 but it was never published. Argyll ministers had an important hand in the first Gaelic Bible which was eventually published in the late eighteenth century – the Old Testament was translated largely by John Stuart, minister of Luss, and John Smith, assistant minister of the parish of Kilbrandon and Kilchattan and subsequently minister at Campbeltown.[7]

Carswell deeply respected and wished to preserve and perpetuate the Gaelic language and culture of Argyll but he was concerned that its inhabitants were more focused on ancient pagan legends than on the truths of the Reformed Christian faith. He wrote in the preface to his book, 'great is the sin of those who prefer vain lying tales of the People of the goddess Danu, or Milesian heroes and Fionn mac Coull and his Féinn, and many others I shall not name, to the faithful Word of God and the perfect way of truth'. This was to be a recurrent theme of Argyll ecclesiastics – Andrew Boyd, appointed Bishop of Argyll in 1613, found the region full of ignorance and disorder and 'in many places the name of the Saviour unknown'. Yet for all his concerns, Carswell was himself steeped in Argyll's pre-Christian myths and legends. Above Carnasserie Castle's elegant doorway, under a shield displaying the Argyll coat of arms, the Galley of Lorne with furled sail on one side and the Lion Rampant of the Royal Arms of Scotland on the other, marking the fifth Earl of Argyll's marriage to Jean Stewart the natural daughter of James V, is carved the Gaelic inscription 'Dia Le Ua NDuibh[n]e' (God be with O'Duine), a reference to the Campbells' legendary descent from Fionn's Diarmaid. Carswell used the same invocation in the dedication of his translation of the Book of Common Order to the fifth Earl. He may have been uneasy with the lingering popular preference for the pagan tales of Fianna over the Christian Gospel but he was enough of an Argyll man to harbour his own romantic attachment to Fionn, especially when it came to his Campbell patrons.

Jane Dawson has observed that the text over the doorway at Carnasserie, the first post-Reformation Gaelic inscription anywhere in Scotland, brings together Highland and Lowland, Gael and Scot, Celtic and Protestant. She argues that Carswell promoted his patron the fifth Earl of Argyll as a godly Gael in the heroic mould of the ancient Celtic warrior chieftains and that together the two men 'established the "Gaelic Calvinism" which characterized the Kirk in the Highlands in the first 150 years of its life'.[8] In its somewhat austere grandeur, Carnasserie Castle stands today as a reminder of the amalgam of Renaissance humanism, evangelical Protestantism and Gaelic culture which has helped shape Argyll's spiritual landscape and created its distinctive quality. It also points very clearly to the importance of the Campbells and their chiefs in that landscape.

11

The Campbells are Coming – Kilmun, Campbeltown and Inveraray

It is impossible to over-exaggerate the impact of the Campbells in general, and their clan chiefs the Earls and Dukes of Argyll in particular, on the spiritual landscape of Argyll over the last five and a half centuries. Their legacy is all around: in two of the region's most important towns, the eponymous Campbeltown and Inveraray, and also in the smaller townships of Bowmore and Port Ellen on Islay, consciously planned expressions of ordered Protestant values; in the churches which they built and the many more with Campbell memorials in the form of monument tablets, busts and stained-glass windows and surrounded by Campbell gravestones, burial enclosures and mausoleums. As Frank Walker reflects in his architectural guide to Argyll and the Islands, 'no other family has left its mark so clearly on the man-made landscape of Argyll'.[1]

It is not just these tangible physical remains that testify to the Campbells' dominating presence in Argyll's religious history. Campbell influence has been a major reason for the presence and persistence of Argyll's distinctive theological and spiritual tradition, at once Presbyterian, liberal and intellectual and at the same time romantic, mystical and liturgical. With a few exceptions, the chiefs of the clan Campbell, and many of their followers, have been passionately Presbyterian – indeed they were among the first to espouse Reformation principles in Scotland. They have also for the most part been liberal and open in their theological outlook. Campbells have been prominent in the long list of Argyll born and raised moderate and cultured Presbyterian divines. The loyalty of the Earls and Dukes of Argyll to the Kirk, their support for scholarly, moderate, open-minded ministers, their patronage of Gaelic learning, their interest in folklore and their strongly mystical bent have played a significant role in making Argyll Presbyterianism very different from the more hard-edged and rigidly Calvinist faith to the north and west, and the drier, more rational religion to the east and south.

Although they did not originate in the West Highlands, the Campbells have more associations with Argyll than any other clan. Their badge is the gale or bog myrtle found throughout the boggy region. Their rallying cry 'Cruachan' invokes the name of a former farming township on the north bank of Loch Awe, opposite Innis Chonnell Castle, which was the gathering place of the clan. Their coat of arms features the Galley of Lorne. They claim Gaelic ancestry through the Fianna. These Argyll associations and credentials were established as the Campbells built up their power base and political dominance from their first arrival in the area in the thirteenth century on the basis of shrewd alliances with the Crown, strong ambition and considerable intellectual capacity.

The Campbells have not had a good press. They have had their share of black sheep and have sometimes shown arrogance and insensitivity. The unpopularity of the Campbell lairds of Jura, whose long hold over the island from 1666 to 1938 is commemorated by a plaque in the parish church and a now-crumbling mausoleum at the edge of Kilearnadil cemetery, is perpetuated in the name of the most expensive and long-matured Jura single malt. It is called Prophecy after the prediction of an elderly woman, evicted in the early 1700s, that the line would eventually come to an end with a one-eyed man leaving the island on a white horse. In the event, the last laird, Charles Campbell, who had a glass eye, sold Ardfin House and its contents in 1938 and his personal possessions were carried to the pier at Craighouse in a cart drawn by a white horse.

If anti-Campbell sentiment is now used to sell whisky, it has a long pedigree. Historians have sniped at the clan and its leaders for their slippery duplicity, helped by the fact that the Gaelic word Cambeul means a wry or twisted mouth. In his monumental 1837 study of the Highlanders of Scotland, W.F. Skene wrote that the Clan Campbell was built on 'a policy characterised by cunning and perfidy'. In 1938 Hector MacKechnie castigated 'the sleekit Campbells, who combined claymore and parchment as never Celts before and encroached on all their neighbours.'[2] Dislike of the Campbells has, of course, been especially prevalent among the MacDonalds, whose long animosity against the clan that ousted them from their dominant position in the West Highlands and islands reached its height in the aftermath of the infamous massacre of Glencoe. A recent booklet on Iona Abbey, written by an Australian based member of the Clan Donald, accuses the Campbells of seeking to play down, and indeed obliterate, the MacDonalds' contribution to the religious life of Argyll in the later Middle Ages.[3] The cover of another recent book about the struggle between the two clans in the mid seventeenth century, Ronald Williams' *The Heather and the Gale*, blames the Campbells for 'that fatal confrontation wherein Gaeldom, Catholicism and the King were eventually overwhelmed by Calvinism and bloody revolution'. These are just two examples among many where the Campbells are portrayed as inimical to and destructive of the culture and religion of the Gaels and too attached to the court and to Lowland ways.

The Campbells were undoubtedly ambitious but they made a hugely positive contribution to the spiritual, ecclesiastical and cultural life of Argyll, not least in its Gaelic aspects. This contribution has recently been emphasized by a number of scholars who have defended them against their many critics. They include Stephen Boardman, whose book on the clan in the Middle Ages was published in 2006, Jane Dawson, who has argued that the Campbells played a notably positive role in the Scottish Reformation, and Martin MacGregor who has demonstrated how the Campbells were imbued with both principle and a deeply felt Scottish patriotism in their project to fuse Gaelic and British identity.[4]

Like so much of Argyll's history, the origins of the Campbells are shrouded in misty legend and romance. Genealogies produced in the seventeenth century, by which time the clan was firmly ensconced in its ascendancy over the area, trace its origins to Diarmaid O'Duibne, a companion of Finn MacCoull, giving it Irish Gaelic ancestry. In Fingalian legend, Diarmaid eloped with Finn's wife, Gráinne. He died after slaying a wild boar and standing barefoot on its bristles which had been poisoned by Finn. Among the place names possibly commemorating this episode are Ben Tuirc, the Hill of the Boar in Kintyre, and Diarmid's Pillar, a solitary monolith at the north end of Loch Nell in Lorne. The legend may explain why a boar's head features prominently on the Campbell coat of arms – there is a fine example of this symbol among the funeral accoutrements of the ninth Duke of Argyll, which have recently gone on display in Kilmun Church. The Campbell family name originally seems to have been MacDuibne or O'Duibne, as picked up by John Carswell in his dedications to Archibald, fifth Earl of Argyll (page 133). As the Campbells developed their hold on Argyll, the ancient Gaelic heartland of Dál Riata, and sought to establish their claim to headship of the Gaels in succession to the MacDonald Lords of the Isles, they further emphasized their Irish/Gaelic roots. By 1887 the eighth Duke of Argyll could confidently write of 'the purely Celtic family from which I descended – a family of Scoto-Irish origin – that is to say, belonging to that Celtic colony from Ireland which founded the Dalriadic kingdom, and to whom the name of Scots originally belonged'.[5]

Boar's Head recovered from Argyll Mausoleum

Seventeenth-century genealogies additionally claim British and Norman descent for the Campbells. Several begin with the British King Arthur, and one starts with Constantine, King of Britain and Arthur's grandfather. W.D.H. Sellar, who has done considerable research in this area, is inclined to think that the Campbells were British in origin, with their roots in the old kingdom of Strathclyde.[6] Alastair Campbell of Airds, author of the superb three volume history of the clan, broadly agrees with this thesis although he suggests that the Arthur referred to in several genealogies is not the British king of Round Table fame but rather the son of King Aédán, founder of the Scottish Dál Riata, whose death at the hands of the Picts in 596 was foretold by Columba. He suggests that the Campbells can claim both British and Scoto/Irish ancestry.

The earliest Campbell of whom there is a clear and authentic historical record is Gillespic Cambell (the p did not come in until the 1460s), recorded as being the recipient of lands near Stirling in the mid 1240s. He married Effric, daughter of Colin, Lord of Carrick, making him the first cousin once removed of Robert the Bruce. The name Gillespic, Anglicised as 'Archibald' which became a favourite Campbell name, means 'servant of a bishop' and possibly gives substance to stories that the Campbells first entered Argyll as followers of a thirteenth century bishop from Ayrshire. His son Colin, known as Cailean Mór, is the first of the family who can definitely be associated with Argyll, and specifically with the area around Loch Awe which was the earliest Campbell stronghold. In the mid 1290s he appears to have been granted the title of bailie of Loch Awe and Ardscotnish by King Edward I who was seeking to impose his authority on Scotland. A cairn by the side of the ancient drove road from the north shore of Loch Avich to Loch Scammadale via the Streang of Lorne marks the place where he was killed around 1296 in an ambush by the MacDougalls, who were strong opponents of the English crown. He was buried in Kilchrenan churchyard where, in 1866, the eighth Duke of Argyll erected a huge pink granite tombstone decorated with a carved sword in his memory. Subsequent Campbell clan chiefs have styled themselves MacCailean Mór to signify their descent from him.

Some accounts suggest that this Colin acquired the castle of Innis Chonnell in Loch Awe through marriage. Alistair Campbell is sceptical about this claim and thinks that the original Campbell base in Argyll may rather have been Caisteal na Nighinn Ruaidh (the Castle of the Red Haired Maiden) on Loch Avich. Innis Chonnell Castle, which had probably been built by the MacDougall Lords of Lorn in the early 1200s, does, however, seem to have become the main Campbell stronghold from the early 1300s. This was the period when the Campbells really began to acquire land and power, thanks largely to their association with Robert the Bruce, who gave up his loyalty to the English Crown in 1306 in a successful bid to win the Scottish throne. Colin's son, Neil, raised a fleet of galleys in 1306 in the Firth of Clyde in support of King Robert and seems to have been rewarded with a grant of land. His son, another Colin, received a further grant from the king of the lands of Lochawe and Ardscotnish in a free barony, in return for the provision of a fully manned and equipped galley of forty oars for forty days whenever required. His son, Dugald, was made Sheriff of Argyll, a new post based in Tarbert on Loch Fyne, in 1326. Through the fourteenth and fifteenth centuries the Campbells of Lochawe continued to grow in power and prestige, extending their influence and land holdings through Cowal, Knapdale and Lorne as a result of their close association with, and support for, Bruce's successors. Appointed hereditary royal lieutenants with vice-regal powers, they became the principal agents of royal authority in the Western Highlands and Islands, and to an extent unequalled by any other clan, managed to combine the roles of Gaelic potentates and major figures at the Lowland Scottish Court.

The Campbells of Lochawe, the senior branch of the family that went on to spawn several cadet branches, the most important being the Campbells of Glenorchy (and later of Breadalbane), strongly supported the church in late medieval Argyll. Perhaps the first significant ecclesiastical patron among the clan chiefs was Duncan Campbell, who around 1440 was either granted or simply adopted the title of Lord Campbell of Lochawe. As well as giving financial support to the mendicant orders of the Dominicans and the Carmelites across Western Scotland, he bestowed lands in Knapdale to the Cistercian Abbey at Saddell in Kintyre. Most importantly, he founded a collegiate church at Kilmun on the shore of the Holy Loch in 1441. It was to become the clan's ecclesiastical centre and the burial place of its chiefs for the next 500 years.

Kilmun was the most westerly collegiate church in late medieval Scotland. The main function of such churches, which housed a settled religious community of the kind that might be found in a small monastery or cathedral, was to say masses for the souls of the founder and provide a family burial place. Several reasons have been put forward as to why Duncan Campbell chose to extend the small church on the north shore of the Holy Loch to fulfil this purpose. It may have been that it was already a holy place to which pilgrims were coming because of its association with St Munn and also possibly because of its proximity to an earlier Christian settlement on the other side of the loch at Ardanadam. The closeness of other ecclesiastical sites dedicated to Munn to earlier Campbell centres of power has already been pointed out (page 74). The choice of this particular location probably also reflected the southward shift in the Campbells' sphere of power and influence from the Loch Awe area to mid-Argyll and Cowal, which also led to the increasing use of Dunoon Castle as a stronghold and the establishment of Inveraray as the main clan base. It may be significant that Duncan Campbell also founded a chapel dedicated to St Catherine on the south east shore of Loch Fyne overlooking the ferry crossing to Inveraray.

Duncan Campbell's decision to turn the small parish church on Holy Loch into a much bigger establishment with a Provost and five or six perpetual chaplains conformed to a pattern which was developing across medieval Scotland, reflecting the wealth of the new aristocratic elite. It may also have been part of a wider campaign against the intrusion by bishops of non-Gaelic-speaking Lowland incumbents into Argyll parishes. A collegiate church by-passed episcopal authority and allowed Duncan Campbell to bring Gaelic-speaking clergy into the region. This was an important aspect of the Campbells' broader support for Gaelic culture and learning, as evidenced by their later patronage of the Book of the Dean of Lismore. The Campbells' close connection with royalty is reflected in Duncan's triple dedication of the church to the late King James I of Scotland, the reigning King James II and his own son Celestine 'in honour of God, Saint Mund and all the saints' and its decoration with the royal arms. [7]

All that now remains of the mid fifteenth-century Collegiate Church is the tower, which is thought to be where the Provost and chaplains lived. Recent surveys suggest that its ground floor dates from the twelfth century. The church was badly damaged during the Covenanting wars in 1646 by the pro-royalist Lamonts, traditional enemies of the Campbells, who laid siege to the tower in which around a hundred local inhabitants had taken refuge. After enticing out those huddled inside with a promise that they would be allowed to leave in safety, the Lamonts slaughtered over thirty-five men, women and children on the loch shore and set light to the building. The scorch marks and cracked stones resulting from this action can still be seen on the inside of the tower, which now stands in a semi-ruined state adjacent to Kilmun Parish Church.

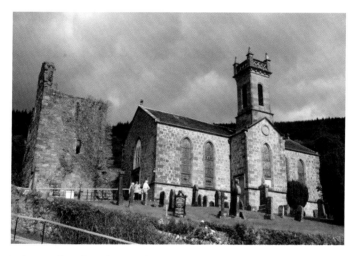

Kilmun Church with ruined tower to the left

For two hundred years or so Campbell chiefs were buried under the floor of the collegiate church. By the early seventeenth century, however, there were reports of an unpleasant stench from their decomposing bodies and in 1669 the ninth Earl of Argyll built a private burial chapel adjoining the north wall of the church. In 1795 it was re-built and extended as a mausoleum, being further refurbished and given an unusual cast iron domed roof by the Marquess of Lorne in 1892 (page 193).The Argyll Mausoleum, as it is known, has recently been restored and opened to the public. Beneath its stone floor lie the remains of the earls of Argyll who were originally buried under the church floor. The beautifully carved effigies of Duncan Campbell, dressed in full armour, and his wife Marjory, which originally stood to the north of the altar of the collegiate church, are housed within the mausoleum together with two rows of burial chambers containing the coffins of nine Dukes of Argyll, who died between 1703 and 1949. A museum constructed out of the entrance lobby to the adjoining parish church, which was rebuilt first in 1688 and then again in 1841, tells the story of the Campbells and displays funeral insignia, which for long languished in the mausoleum.

As well as establishing the family's ecclesiastical base at Kilmun, Duncan Campbell may well have been responsible for planning and initiating work on its secular counterpart, Inveraray Castle, to replace Innis Chonnell as the principal clan seat and stronghold, a role that it has fulfilled ever since. Most of the building work on the first castle, which stood about 80 metres north east of the present castle, was done soon after his death in 1453. Its site on Loch Fyne gave direct maritime links to the Campbells' newly acquired estates in Cowal, and access to the Firth of Clyde and the sea lanes to Ireland. The small town that grew up around the castle acquired considerable importance with the rise of the herring industry and was granted the status of a burgh in 1474.

By the latter part of the fifteenth century the Campbells were in a dominant and confident position in Argyll. The addition of the 'p' in their name seems to have been part of an attempt to expand their genealogical profile to suggest Norman ancestry (from an invented family called de Campo Bello) in addition to their Arthurian and Gaelic/Finnian origins. Duncan's grandson and successor, Colin, clan chief from 1453 to 1493, was created Earl of Argyll by King James II in 1457 and in 1469 he acquired through marriage the Lordship of Lorne, a title which brought the Galley of Lorne into the Campbell coat of arms. Like his predecessors, he was appointed Royal Lieutenant with vice-regal authority over much of mainland Argyll and its adjacent islands. The appointment of his son, Archibald, as Lieutenant of the Isles gave official sanction to the Campbells' triumph over the MacDonalds who forfeited their title and power as Lords of the Isles in 1493. Thereafter the Campbells effectively assumed the headship of the Gaels throughout the West Highlands and islands.

There was considerable Campbell involvement in the church in Argyll through the late Middle Ages. The Campbells of Auchinellan were known as 'The Race of Bishops' because of the number of senior churchmen they produced, their progenitor being Neil Campbell, Dean of Argyll around 1400. There were two Campbell bishops of Argyll and five Campbell bishops of the Isles between 1487 and 1638. Four priors of Iona Abbey from one clan commemorated on a sixteenth-century grave slab formerly in the Reilig Odhráin are thought to be Campbells. There were also several Campbell Deans of Lismore.

By the late fifteenth century the Earls of Argyll, along with the heads of other cadet branches of the Campbell clan, had achieved a virtual monopoly over lay patronage of ecclesiastical appointments in Argyll, including the offices of cathedral dignitaries. They took their responsibilities seriously and maintained an active and benign interest in church affairs. James IV's request to the Pope in 1499 to make Iona Abbey the seat of the Diocese of the Isles was made at the suggestion of Archibald, second Earl of Argyll. It was in that year that the Abbey was granted for life *in commendam* to John Campbell, Bishop of the Isles and a half-brother of Duncan Campbell of Glenorchy. He seems to have maintained a close relationship with the Abbey and was buried there in 1510. On the basis of his considerable research on the clan in this period, Stephen Boardman concludes that the Campbells did much to preserve the Gaelic literature and culture of Argyll, and the legacy and reputation of Iona and other monastic foundations that had previously been nurtured by the MacDonalds, as well as supporting broader intellectual endeavour. Colin, third Earl of Argyll from 1513 to 1529, was a close friend and patron of the humanist scholar, Hector Boece, for whom he procured books from Iona Abbey library, and also a significant supporter of the Book of the Dean of Lismore.

The Campbell chiefs enthusiastically espoused the doctrines of the Protestant Reformers which swept across Scotland in the mid sixteenth century. Archibald, fourth Earl of Argyll, was the first of the Scottish nobility to embrace the Reformation. His domestic chaplain, John Douglas, a former Carmelite friar, read common prayers in Inveraray taken from the second Prayer Book of Edward VI in what was probably the first use of a reformed English-language liturgy in Argyll. The fourth Earl was prominent among the lords of the congregation who signed the first open declaration in support of the Protestant cause in 1557. On his deathbed the following year he solemnly charged his son and heir, another Archibald, to forward the cause of Reformed religion. The fifth Earl, who was a close friend and supporter of John Knox as well as of John Carswell, duly put himself at the head of the Protestant movement in Scotland and was in no small measure responsible for its triumph in 1560. He also used the educational facilities within his household to offer training for prospective ministers. Among his most important protegées was Neil Campbell, his personal page, who went on to pursue a distinguished ecclesiastical career, eventually becoming Bishop of Argyll in 1606. He married the daughter of John Carswell and together they produced a large family of Campbell clerics. The sixth Earl personally carried out an ecclesiastical visitation throughout Argyll in 1574 to ensure that each parish had a Protestant minister in receipt of an adequate stipend and that prayers, sacraments and discipline followed the forms set out in Carswell's Gaelic translation of the Book of Common Order.

The Campbell clan played a crucial role in establishing the Protestant Kirk throughout Argyll on the basis of a formidable patronage network, and ties of kinship and family allegiance. In the early 1600s Campbell lairds brought Protestantism to several outlying areas, formerly MacDonald strongholds, including Kintyre, Ardnamurchan and Islay. With the notable exception of the seventh Earl, who converted to Roman Catholicism, Campbell chiefs remained loyal to the Protestant, and more specifically the Presbyterian, cause throughout the rest of the turbulent seventeenth century. Indeed, two of them were prompted by this loyalty to lead armed rebellions against the Crown, provoking bloodshed and disruption in Argyll and their own executions for treason. Archibald, eighth Earl and first Marquess of Argyll was a leading figure in the ultra-Presbyterian Covenanting movement that fiercely opposed Charles I's efforts to impose bishops and Anglican liturgy on the Scottish Kirk. A classic exemplar of the strain of Evangelical simplicity that I have identified as a key component of the spiritual make-up of Argyll, he devoted many hours to private prayer and family worship. He also led the Covenanting forces in the so-called Bishops' Wars of 1639 to 1640 and subsequently in the early stages of the British Civil War.

The Covenanters' armed struggle against the High Church tendencies of the Stuart monarchy exacerbated long-standing animosity in Argyll between the Presbyterian Campbells and the still Roman Catholic MacDonalds. Throughout 1644 and 1645 MacDonalds took advantage of the absence of the eighth Earl and his supporters in the Covenanting army to wreak revenge on the Campbells in their newly acquired territories. They laid waste much of Lorne, Knapdale and Kintyre, burning, pillaging and killing as they rampaged through the countryside. The level of destruction increased after the main Covenanting Army was defeated at Kilsyth in 1645, and by 1647 the Campbells had effectively been pushed back to their strongholds in Kilberry, Duntroon, Craignish and Dunstaffnage castles, where they were trapped. Charles I's surrender to the Scottish army at Newark in 1647 reversed the fortunes of the war and led to all royalist forces being ordered to disband. Alasdair MacDonald, leader of the 1,000 strong band which had ravaged Argyll, retreated to Islay but left around 400 of his supporters to hold the fort at Dunaverty. Led by David Leslie, the Covenanting forces marched through Kintyre and besieged the castle, eventually killing around 300 of its defenders, most of whom were MacDougalls.

Following the restoration of Charles II, the eighth Earl of Argyll was beheaded in 1661 and hailed as a Presbyterian martyr. His skeleton and severed head, which was stuck on a spike and put on public display, lie under the floor of the Kilmun Mausoleum, marked by a simple cross. A rather macabre exhibit in the new Kilmun Church museum invites visitors to put a coin in the slot and watch an eerie apparition of his grisly remains. His son, the ninth Earl, also called Archibald, was equally committed to the defence of Protestantism against absolutist monarchy. Exiled to Holland in 1681, he set sail from there in 1685 with three heavily armed ships to raise a rebellion in Scotland against the staunchly Catholic King James VII and II. Timed to coincide with the Duke of Monmouth's rising in the south west of England, it led to skirmishes across Argyll before petering out. The ninth Earl sailed his flotilla to Tobermory, Port Askaig and then down the Kintyre coast to Campbletown, gathering supporters en route. He mustered nearly 2,000 at Tarbert, Loch Fyne, under the banner 'For the Protestant Religion and Against Popery, Prelacy and Erastianism'. A force twice that size under the Marquess of Atholl was sent into Argyll to check them and there were skirmishes on the shores of Loch Fyne. The ninth Earl's followers gradually deserted as he marched to the Lowlands via Loch Fyne, Loch Long, Loch Striven and Gareloch. Eventually, at a battle on the south bank of the Clyde, he gave himself up and was subsequently beheaded like his father in Edinburgh. Atholl went through Argyll dealing with the remaining pockets of resistance, the last of which was a Campbell garrison at Carnasserie Castle where, after sporadic fighting and an attempt to blow up the walls, the rebels surrendered on 23 June. It was the last military engagement on Argyll soil. The inhabitants of Kilmartin suffered for their support for Argyll's rebellion – in the reprisals that followed forty-three of them lost the animals and goods that provided their livelihood.

These events provide a grim reminder of the darker side of Argyll's spiritual landscape and the terrible effects of Scotland's religious wars and the feuding between the Campbells and their Lamont and MacDonald foes. They have seared themselves into the landscape – the ghosts of the Dunaverty massacre haunt and disturb the peace of Columba's footsteps and well on to which so many bodies were hurled from the cliff above, while the walls of Carnasserie Castle still bear the marks of the explosion and siege. Not even the house of God was exempt from the effects of this period of terror, as the scorch marks on the tower adjoining Kilmun Church testify.

The Campbells' unswerving loyalty to the Protestant cause in the sixteenth and seventeenth centuries had another lasting effect on both the physical and the spiritual landscape of Argyll. They undoubtedly played a leading part in the destruction and desecration of many of the region's medieval Christian crosses and sculptured stones. Removal of idolatrous monuments was demanded in a series of measures passed by the Privy Council and the Scottish Parliament from 1560 onwards. The fifth Earl of Argyll seems to have taken up this task promptly and vigorously and was praised by John Carswell for 'destroying the false faith and false worship, burning images and idols, and casting down and smashing altars and places where false sacrifices were offered'.[8] The eighth Earl and first Marquess responded with similar alacrity to a resolution passed by the Synod of Argyll in 1642 against idolatrous monuments by making an expedition through the islands destroying carved crosses and other objects associated with medieval Catholic devotion.

It is difficult to be certain exactly how many of Argyll's medieval religious monuments were deliberately destroyed in the aftermath of the Reformation and how instrumental the Campbell chiefs were in the iconoclasm. An account written in 1693 suggests that 360 crosses on Iona alone were smashed or hurled into the sea but this is generally agreed to be an exaggeration. A report to the Vatican described the first Marquess of Argyll personally overthrowing some of the finest monuments in Iona monastery, including several altars, and the recently published book on the Clan Donald and Iona accuses him of destroying the chapel roof, dispersing the irreplaceable library and overthrowing St Oran's Cross because of its Clan Donald associations.[9] The report of the Royal Commission on the Ancient and Historical Monuments of Scotland is more circumspect. While conceding that he did destroy various crosses, it notes that he spared MacLean's and St Martin's crosses as well as the marble altar slab and that 'his main effort was apparently devoted to the attempt to remove the great bell of the Abbey to his new church in Campbeltown'.[10]

Some accounts of the removal of this bell suggest that it had been hanging there since the days of St Columba. In fact, it bore the arms and initials of King Charles I and Neil Campbell, Bishop of the Isles, and was only seven years old, having been cast in Middleburg, Holland, in 1638 as part of the restoration of the Abbey church on Iona as the Cathedral of the Isles, which had begun in 1635 on the king's instructions. There is a story that the Marquess's efforts to carry away an older medieval bell were thwarted by the protestations and curses hurled at him by a nonagenarian former nun of the MacLean family.

This is an area where passion, quite understandably, tends to over-ride historical accuracy. There is no doubt that reforming Protestants, and few were more zealous in this cause than the Campbells, did see it as their Godly duty to remove what they saw as symbols of religious idolatory. Whether they went on frenzied orgies of destruction, hurling delicately carved crosses into the sea, is more questionable. The destruction of medieval churches and monuments seems on the whole to have been a gradual process taking place over the 300 years or so after the Reformation rather than a sudden assault in its immediate aftermath. As well as the depredations of the weather and the forces of nature, the key factor behind their gradual ruin and disappearance seems to have been the enthusiasm on the part of both local people and visitors for removing stones either as souvenirs or to use in building, something probably inspired more by superstition or indifference than by iconoclastic Protestant zeal. There appears to have been a preference, where feasible, for re-using the monuments of the old Roman Catholic faith in the new Reformed forms of worship rather than destroying them. When the chancel of Iona Abbey was turned into a Protestant place of worship in 1635, the plinth on which the new pulpit rested was made out of the base of a late medieval cross.

Recent historians have tended to downplay the nature and extent of the iconoclasm perpetrated by the Campbells in general and the earls of Argyll in particular and suggest that it was, in Jane Dawson's words, 'gentle and considerate'. Rather than totally destroying medieval sacred stones, they removed offending elements, such as carvings of the virgin, the saints and the crucified Christ. Such was the fate that befell the market crosses in Campbeltown and Inveraray. Stephen Boardman regards Clan Donald propaganda from the seventeenth century onwards, which portrayed the Campbells as deliberately destroying the spiritual icons of the Gaels and the relics of medieval Catholic faith, as 'deceptive'. Marian Pallister suggests that the particularly destructive iconoclasm which took place in southern Kintyre, where carved stones at Saddell were mutilated and one cross apparently hurled into the sea off Southend, may have represented an understandable backlash on the part of poor farmers and fishermen against the savagery of the MacDonald reprisals in the area and the greed of landlords and priests.[11]

Having removed some of the great stone symbols of medieval Christianity from Argyll, the Campbells built new monuments to the Protestant faith. A pillar was erected in Church Square in the centre of Inveraray in 1754 by Duncan Campbell to commemorate his grandfather Colin and other Covenanting ancestors, 'adherents of evangelical religion and the liberty of the people', who were executed in 1685 for supporting the ninth Earl of Argyll's rebellion. It was moved to its present site near the Garden Bridge in the grounds of Inveraray Castle in 1983. More significant as lasting monuments to Argyll's new Protestant identity are the planned towns of Campbeltown, Inveraray, Bowmore and Port Ellen which remain today striking symbols of Presbyterian virtues – ordered, unostentatious, white-painted and severely symmetrical with a prominent and solidly built church at their centre.

Campbeltown was the earliest and largest of the planned Campbell Protestant settlements in Argyll. In the aftermath of the 1603 Union of the crowns of England and Scotland, James VI and I requested the seventh Earl of Argyll to settle Protestants from the supposedly civilised and loyal Lowlands amid the unruly Gaels of Kintyre, which was still largely Catholic and under MacDonald dominance. So began a project very similar to the better known plantations in Ulster. A 1609 Act of Parliament gave the seventh Earl authority to plant a burgh in what had previously been known as Leann Loch Cille Chiaran, the Head of the Loch of Ciaran's Chapel, near the southern tip of Kintyre. He called it Campbeltown and invited Lowland farmers and traders to settle there, although he proved to be rather diffident in the matter of enforcing the Reformed religion in the peninsula over which he had been given charge by the king. His wife was a Catholic and he himself converted to Catholicism in 1618, renouncing his Argyll estates in favour of his son. His successors were rather more enthusiastic about the Protestant plantation of Kintyre and the development of Campeltown. There was an influx of Covenanting families from Ayrshire and Renfrewshire fleeing the 'killing times' of the mid seventeenth century. In 1642 the town's first stone-built church was built near the shore in what became known as Kirk Street and was furnished with the bell which the First Marquess of Argyll had appropriated from Iona Abbey. Later known as the old Gaelic church, it remained in use until around 1770.

In 1700 Campbeltown was made a royal burgh by William III at the request of the tenth Earl of Argyll. The monarch's action signalled the rehabilitation of the Campbells and their return to royal favour after the exiles and executions of the previous century. They were once again close to the Crown thanks to the fall of the Stuarts and the 1689 Glorious Revolution, which brought William and Mary to the throne and secured the Protestant succession and in which they had taken a major hand. The tenth Earl of Argyll was one of those who went to Holland to offer the Scottish crown to William and Mary. He was rewarded for his support by being created the first Duke of Argyll in 1701. Throughout the eighteenth century the Campbells were staunchly loyal to the Hanoverians and opposed to the Jacobite Pretenders to the throne.

Campbeltown flourished with the growth of farming, herring fishing, mining and shipping in the eighteenth century and remained a Presbyterian stronghold. In 1706 a T-shaped church was built in Kirk Street for use by Lowland (i.e. English speaking) worshippers. It was replaced in 1778 by the austerely classical Castlehill Church erected on the prominent, elevated site at the top of the town, which the seventh Earl of Argyll had chosen for his own House of Lochead in 1610. Converted in 1983 into residential use, it still dominates the townscape. In the first decade of the nineteenth century the equally austerely classical Highland Parish Church, with a five-bay mansion house façade and approached up a flight of steps, was built for Gaelic-speaking worshippers. English-speaking members of the United Presbyterian Church were given an even grander place of worship with the building of what is now known as Lorn and Lowland Church in 1869–72. An ungainly structure with a huge, top-heavy square steeple, it was seemingly designed to tower over every other church spire and distillery stack in the town. Both buildings, still in use by Church of Scotland congregations, reinforce Campbeltown's solidly Protestant identity.

The planning and development of Inveraray was even more firmly under Campbell control. Chosen as the seat of the clan chiefs in the fifteenth century, it began as little more than a castle surrounded by a few houses but grew steadily as a trading and market centre with the growing prosperity of herring fishing in Loch Fyne and was made a royal burgh by Charles I in 1648. What visitors see today is the planned new town first envisaged in the 1740s by the third Duke of Argyll. The old town, by all accounts a sprawling, dilapidated and dissolute settlement with forty-three taverns, was razed to the ground in 1745 to make way for the gardens and policies of the new castle, a plain classical structure lacking the Gothic fairytale effect created when conical roofs were put on the towers after a fire in 1877 (and restored after a further fire in 1975). The new town was built under the direction of the fourth and fifth Dukes of Argyll between 1753 and 1776 a discrete half mile south of the castle on the shores of Loch Fyne. Its white-painted facades, wide arches and symmetrical grid structure exude a sense of classical order and Presbyterian restraint. As in Campbletown a medieval cross, purged of its idolatrous excrescences, was erected at a focal point at the bottom of the main street near the loch shore. In the light of their reputation for destroying Argyll's medieval monuments it is interesting that the Campbells should have been so keen to install carved crosses, albeit with their more Catholic features carefully chiselled away, in central locations in their two planned Protestant towns.

Inveraray parish church, designed by Robert Mylne and completed in 1802, stands in a dominant position in the town at the head of Main Street in the middle of a square with the old court house and prison on one side and the town's former grammar school and two main banks on the other – a perfect picture of Presbyterian order and probity with law and order, education and commerce all gathered together and watched over by the Kirk. Designed to resemble Solomon's Temple in Jerusalem, it has identically pedimented and pilastered classical façades looking out in two directions over the town. It is, in fact, one of the supreme architectural expressions of Argyll's hybrid spiritual landscape, half Highland Gaelic and half English-speaking Lowland, and also of its dominance by the Campbells. The church is divided into two discrete places of worship – a Highland half looking north to the Gaelic heartlands and a Lowland half looking south. In 1957 the Gaelic end was turned into a church hall and is now used for jumble sales and also to house a rather good exhibition on the building's history. Worship is focused on the English end which was extensively remodelled in 1898 according to the principles of the romantic Celtic Presbyterianism espoused by the eighth Duke of Argyll and his third wife, Ina (pages 191–2).

Inveraray's whitewashed order was replicated by Campbell lairds on the island of Islay. It was most obviously imitated at Bowmore, a planned settlement in the late 1760s by Daniel Campbell, a direct descendant of the second Earl of Argyll whose ancestors came from Skipness in Kintyre. At its heart, in a commanding position at the top of the town, is the distinctive circular structure of Kilarrow Parish Church, now better known as 'the Round Church', on which building began in 1768. While on a Grand Tour of Europe before he became laird of Islay, young Daniel met and befriended the future fifth Duke of Argyll. There is a tradition that Bowmore's round church was based on a design by a French architect whom Daniel also encountered on this tour, but in fact it seems that he took over John Adam's design for a round church at Inveraray that had been shelved because it did not provide separate buildings for Gaelic- and English-speaking worshippers. A sandstone tablet above the main entrance door records in Latin the building of Bowmore Church at Daniel Campbell's own expense 'with pious intent and to promote truth and honour' and its dedication to 'Deo Optimo Maximo', a suitably Deistic phrase for the broad theology of the Campbells. The porch contains marble monuments to two later Campbells of Islay, and a huge twin-chambered sarcophogus inside the church commemorates Walter Frederick Campbell, grandson of the fifth Duke of Argyll, and his first wife, Lady Elinor Campbell, in whose memory he built and named Port Ellen in 1821. Many other Campbell lairds and heritors built and supported churches across Argyll during the eighteenth and nineteenth centuries.

The Campbells provided a disproportionate number of ministers to the parish kirks of Argyll. There were Campbell ministers in Southend continuously from 1696 to 1798 and from 1833 to 1880, and in the linked parishes of Kilmelford and Kilninver for 120 of the 200 years between 1700 and 1900. Kilmichael Glassary had two long-serving Campbell ministers, both called Donald, who were in post respectively from 1691 to 1722 and from 1852 to 1904. Jura's longest-serving minister, Neil Campbell, occupied the charge from 1703 to 1759. As well as being blessed with remarkable longevity, Campbell ministers often displayed considerable intellectual gifts. The combined parish of Ardchattan and Muckairn counts two outstandingly clever Campbells among its incumbents: Colin Campbell, who occupied the charge from 1667 to 1726, was a renowned mathematician and pioneer of natural theology and George Campbell, minister from 1796 to 1817, a distinguished classical scholar. Alexander Campbell, born in Kilchrenan and minister of Kilberry from 1781 to 1823, who was described as being 'of eccentric habits', produced a prospectus for linking Loch Awe with the Crinan canal and received a Highland Society Gold Medal for adapting Small's plough for use in hilly country. Several Campbells with strong Argyll connections became distinguished academic theologians, like George Campbell from Inveraray who became Professor of Divinity at Edinburgh University in 1690. Archibald Campbell, Professor of Divinity and Church History at the University of St Andrews in the 1730s, whose family came from Succoth near Inveraray, was in many respects the founding father of the Moderate movement that brought the broad open-minded philosophy of the Scottish Enlightenment into the Church of Scotland.

Campbell patronage undoubtedly helped to spread liberal theology in the eighteenth-century Church of Scotland. Archibald Campbell, the third Duke of Argyll, was especially influential in this regard. His namesake, the St Andrews professor mentioned above, dedicated his important work, *An Enquiry into the Original of Moral Virtue* (1733), which attacked Calvinist notions of original sin and total depravity and argued rather that virtue stood at the very heart of human nature, to him, using his title of 'Earl of Islay, Lord Oronsay, Dunoon and Aros' which had been granted in 1701. The third Duke strongly championed George Campbell, Principal and Professor of Divinity at Marischal College, Aberdeen, through the 1760s, who was a leading apologist and representative for the broad, latitudinarian stance of the Moderates. There is room for a doctoral thesis on the extent to which Campbell heritors and patrons favoured liberal and Moderate ministers and placed them in the pulpits of the churches of Argyll. My strong sense is that this was a key influence in promoting Argyll's distinctive blend of open-minded, liturgical, liberal Presbyterianism.

It is surely no coincidence that the best-known and most liberal minister-theologian in the nineteenth century Church of Scotland should have been a Campbell. John McLeod Campbell, born and brought up in Kilninver where his father, Donald, was parish minister from 1798 to 1838, and presented to the living of Rhu on Gare Loch by the sixth Duke of Argyll, was arraigned for heresy and deposed from the ministry in 1831 for preaching the doctrine of universal rather than limited atonement and emphasizing God's love and forgiveness in contrast to the prevailing notion of penal substitution. He lived with his father in Kilninver for some years after his deposition, continuing to preach about God as a kind and loving father seeking to restore his lost children rather than a stern judge demanding punishment. A window installed in Rhu and Shandon Church in 1925 in his memory depicts a procession of saints walking up the steps of light. Another prominent nineteenth-century Scottish 'heretic', Alexander Robinson, who was deposed from the ministry of the Church of Scotland in 1897 for supposedly denying the truthfulness of the Gospels and the divinity, miracles and resurrection of Christ, was incumbent at the Campbell 'cathedral' of Kilmun, having been presented to the charge by the eighth Duke of Argyll. He is commemorated in a stained-glass window in Kilmun Church by Stephen Adam depicting St John with the text 'God is Love'.

Although the predominant note struck by Campbell patrons, ministers and theologians was one of moderate, enlightened liberalism, there were still lingering echoes of the narrower and more intolerant Covenanting zeal that had animated many Campbells in the seventeenth century. Colin Campbell, minister of Ardchattan, appeared at the door of Kilchoan Church with a sword and a pistol in 1697 to bar the entrance of Alexander MacDonald, the popular minister of Ardnamurchan who had been deposed by the Presbytery of Lorne for his Episcopalian tendencies. Among the last and most stalwart adherents to the Covenanting creed was Alexander Campbell of Luing, who led a secession from the Church of Scotland in 1787 of latter day Covenanters. Although 'The Covenanters of Lorne', as they were known, grew to around 200 in the linked parish of Kilbrandon and Kilchattan, by the time of his death in 1829 he was the only one left. Before he died, he erected several gravestones in Kilchattan graveyard expounding his beliefs in some detail and annoying some islanders who overturned them. He retaliated by putting up a tablet on the outer wall of the cemetery with the message 'If any person take authority to meddle with this stone again, see what judgment came upon Jehoiahim that burnt the roll' and erecting a substantial table tomb bearing in large lettering the words: 'I protest that none be buried after me in this grave which I have dug for myself as Jacob did (Gen.50.5) having adhered till death to the whole work of the second reformation in Scotland between the year 1638 and 1649 and died in full assurance of the heavenly inheritance.' These stones, and others erected on both the inner and outer walls of the graveyard extolling 'pure Presbyterian religion, the covenanted cause of Christ and Church government' and fulminating against all other forms of religion, are still there today although the elements, rather than his theological opponents, have worn and cracked them and made them difficult to read. The note of narrow, bitter, hectoring Calvinism that still sounds from these stones in this distant corner of the region serves as a reminder that not all has been eirenic, gentle sweetness and light in Argyll's spiritual landscape.

How do we sum up the Campbells' contribution to the spiritual landscape of Argyll? In many ways, they made it more Protestant, more Presbyterian and more British by linking it more firmly to the Crown and to the Lowlands. This is certainly how they have been seen, as representatives of the Court and the Anglicising establishment. There was undoubtedly a Campbell project from the sixteenth century onwards to civilise and enlighten the region over which the clan held such sway. This agenda, alongside Campbell ambition and political cunning, initiative and innovation, underlay the legacy of ordered, planned towns and kirks staffed by ministers of liberal Enlightenment views. If Argyll was distinctly more Protestant and civilised than the rest of the Highlands, and most contemporaries and historians agree that it was, the Campbells had a lot to do with that. John Buchan indirectly acknowledged as much when he reflected on the state of the Highlands in the late seventeenth century that 'such discipline as the old Church had given them had more or less broken down and the general creed – except for Argyll, where Presbyterianism had made some progress – was a mixture of ill-understood Catholic doctrines and ancestral superstitions'.[12]

Yet alongside their Anglophile Whiggism, their strong Unionism and antipathy to the Jacobite cause and their Presbyterian unease with some of the remnants of medieval piety and devotion, the Campbells also had considerable sympathy for those 'ill-understood Catholic doctrines and ancestral superstitions' that Buchan mentions. They were significant patrons of Gaelic culture and literature. For all their formidable intellect powers and liberal rationalism, they were also deeply imbued with Argyll's mysticism and attachment to the supernatural. At the end of the first volume of his history of the clan, Alistair Campbell points to the surprisingly large number of crystal balls and brooches possessing supposedly magical properties held by the Campbells of Argyll, far more than were owned by most Highland families. They included St Columba's curing stone and other objects believed to have curative and protective powers and to secure good fortune. As we shall see, at least one Duke of Argyll communed with fairies and experienced supernatural visions, while other Campbells were among the leading collectors of Argyll folklore (pages 196–8 and 206). Like the spiritual landscape of the region that they dominated, the Campbells have blended evangelical simplicity with liberal mysticism.

It is perhaps in death that the Campbells have left their greatest mark on that landscape. Visiting Glenorchy Church in 1819 the poet Robert Southey noted that 'a great proportion of the gravestones bear the name Campbell'.[13] The same could be said about most of the graveyards across Argyll. You are never far from a Campbell tombstone. Often, as in the case of the inscribed marble panel flanked by Doric pilasters commemorating Colonel Donald Campbell in the grounds of Saddell Abbey, they stand imposingly and importantly slightly apart from the other gravestones and dominate the surrounding area. Aside from Kilmun, there are prominent and elaborate Campbell mausoleums or burial enclosures at Kilmartin (seventeenth century); Glendaruel (eighteenth century); Ardchattan (various dates); Killevin by Crarae on the shores of Loch Fyne (1727); Kilberry Castle (1733); Dunstaffnage (1740); Kilbrannan, near Skipness (1756); Sonachan (1779); Kilchrenan by Loch Awe (1779); Kilearnadil on Jura (1838); and in woods near Inverneill (1883). Here, more than anywhere, perhaps, the echoes of Campbell confidence can still be felt today. The monument to Captain Dugald Campbell of Kilberry, half hidden in woods near Kilberry Castle, is decorated by a shield, a six-oared galley, cannons, trumpets, drums, sabres, banners and, at its base, two trumpeting angels holding palms. In death as in life the Campbells continue to dominate and haunt Argyll.

12

Parish Churches

Thanks partly to the dominance of the Campbells, Argyll's spiritual landscape for three hundred years and more after the Scottish Reformation of 1560 was overwhelmingly Presbyterian. Roman Catholics, subject to penal laws for much of the period, maintained their heartlands over the Inverness border in Arisaig and Moidart while Episcopalianism also had a stronger presence just beyond Argyll in Glencoe and Perthshire. Within Presbyterianism, notoriously given to splits and splintering, Argyll remained considerably more loyal than the rest of the Highlands to the established church, or Auld Kirk as it came to be known.

This adherence to established Presbyterianism expressed itself in the building, throughout the eighteenth and nineteenth centuries, of a large number of parish churches, many of which are still in use today. They range from sizeable and architecturally sophisticated buildings in the main urban centres and increasingly fashionable coastal resorts to small, simple country kirks. It is these rural churches that are among the most ubiquitous and perhaps also most characteristic features of Argyll's post-Reformation religious landscape. They are well worth visiting today and, for the most part, unlike nearly all the urban parish churches, they are kept unlocked and open. Many, especially those erected in the first wave of building, are simple hall-like structures, much like the medieval chapels which they often replaced, either of a simple oblong shape or conforming to a T plan to allow a centrally placed pulpit to be flanked by galleries round the side. They are often painted white outside and breathe an air of clean evangelical simplicity with the only concession to external adornment being a small birdcage belfry. Their internal furnishings are not always quite so plain as their external appearance might suggest with stained-glass windows, often added like the belfries later in the nineteenth century, pointing to the more romantic and mystical elements in Argyll's spiritual make-up. This brief chapter, which focuses largely on these small rural and village parish churches, is selective and illustrative. It is not intended to provide anything approaching a complete gazetteer and history of Argyll's churches – for that readers should turn to Frank Walker's volume on Argyll and Bute in *The Buildings of Scotland* series and John Hume's introduction to the 'Sacred Argyll and the Clyde' volume in the *Sacred Places* series produced by Scotland's Churches Scheme and published by St Andrew Press in 2011.

Aside from those in the planned settlement of Campbeltown, very few churches were built in Argyll in the 150 years after the Reformation. There were a number of reasons for this. In several places the old medieval chapels went on being used as parish churches but probably around two thirds of them fell into disuse, leading to a serious shortage of places of worship. The unsettled state of church affairs and politics throughout the seventeenth century, which affected Argyll more than many parts of Scotland, was inimical to long-term planning. It was not until 1640, sixty years after the Scottish Reformation, that the Synod of Argyll was created to bring together the four Presbyteries in the region – Inveraray, Kintyre, Dunoon and Lorn. The Presbytery of Skye, which encompassed the Western Isles, was also included but became part of the Synod of Glenelg when it was created in 1724. There were other obstacles to contend with, as Dubhghall MacDubhghaill, minister of Lochgoilhead, observed in 1791:

> After the Reformation, owing to the scarcity of the Protestant preachers, and to the avarice of the Reformers (particularly the laymen who conducted that revolution), so few places of worship were permitted, and these consequently so distant from one another, and so divided by mountains, rivers, and arms of the sea, as to render it extremely difficult, and sometimes impossible, for the ministers to perform the duties of their office, or for the people to attend on their instructions. This was particularly the case in the province of Argyle.[1]

Surviving early post-Reformation churches: a) Kilchrenan Church; b) South Knapdale Church; c) Kilmodan Church

The problem was that the legal obligation to provide, furnish and maintain a parish church and manse fell upon the heritors, or local landowners, who in many instances showed no inclination to fulfil their responsibilities. Their dilatoriness is shown in the example of Knapdale where a rising population and the huge extent of the parish led to a proposal, in 1715, for its division into two. This eventually happened in 1734 but the first two ministers of the new parish of South Knapdale had to perform their duties without a church building or a manse and it was only in 1772, when a newly ordained minister, finding that he had to 'preach in the fields', instigated legal proceedings to compel the heritors to carry out their obligations, that a church was at last built in Achahoish in 1775. The manse was not provided until 1808.

Along with two other churches built in the 1770s, Kilchrenan (1771) and Jura (1776), South Knapdale is one of the oldest surviving post-Reformation parish churches to be built in Argyll. Although all have been altered, they replicate the simplicity and oblong layout of the medieval chapels. None of the churches built earlier in the eighteenth century, which include Kilbrandon Church on Seil (1735), Cladich on Loch Aweside (1736) and Claonaig near Skipness (1756), survive in their present form. Other survivors from this first wave of church building include Southend (1773), Kilmodan at Clachan of Glendaruel (1783), a classic T-plan church, Kilmelford (1785) and Strachur (1789). The early nineteenth century brought a more classical influence and a move away from the rectangular medieval chapel style in favour of a square design, as in Inveraray (1795–1802), Colonsay (1802–4) and Kilberry (1821), which looks for all the world like a respectable bourgeois dwelling. A more daring octagonal design was commissioned by Lord Breadalbane for Glenorchy Parish Church, Dalmally (1810–11), perhaps the first church in Argyll to exhibit some of the features of the Gothic revival.

Argyll had eleven of the thirty-two so-called Parliamentary churches which were built across the Highlands and Islands with Government money as a result of an act of the UK Parliament in 1824. This state-sponsored church building project had its origins in lobbying by Evangelical MPs concerned about the dearth of places of worship in the remoter parts of Scotland. They persuaded the Government to release part of the funds voted for good causes as a thank offering for peace after the Napoleonic Wars. Thomas Telford, the civil engineer famous for bridge and canal building, was put in overall charge of the project and used both the classic T-plan and oblong designs. The architect directly responsible for the new churches in Argyll was William Thomson, who had been involved in the construction of the Crinan Canal. Argyll's Parliamentary churches, built between 1827 and 1829, were at Duror (the first one to be built in Scotland), Acharacle, Ardgour, Strontian, Iona, Portnahaven and The Oa on Islay, Kinlochspelvie on Mull, Ulva, Tobermory on Mull and Kilmichael Glassary. The first five listed are still regularly used for worship and Ulva has services at Easter and Harvest. Their large, clear glass windows give them a light and airy character – no dim religious light here – and they blend Presbyterian plainness with restrained classical and Gothic motifs to create an unostentatious but gracious atmosphere.

The next wave of church building, much more boldly Gothic in style, encompassed Ardchattan (1836), Furnace and Kilmartin (both 1841), Innellan (1852), Ardrishaig (1860) and Luss (1875). Their steep crow-stepped gables and pointed arches are perhaps a touch heavy for their rural village settings. Perhaps more successful were three later nineteenth-century churches built in a more restrained

Kilmartin Church

and solid Gothic style. Tarbert Parish Church (1885), dominating the small town from its hilltop site, has an imposing tower, framed by angled buttresses which recede to reach the four corners of a bold crown-and-lantern Scots Gothic spire. St Oran's Church, Connel (1887–8), supposedly modelled on Iona Abbey, is built to a cruciform plan with a square tower over its crossing. Appin (1889) also has a less pretentious feel than some of the earlier Gothic churches.

The end of the nineteenth and first decade of the twentieth century saw a wonderful flowering of parish church architecture, predominantly in the Romanesque style. Much of it was the work of Peter MacGregor Chalmers (1859–1922), the Glasgow-born architect who was a strong medievalist and closely associated with the Scoto-Catholic movement that sought to make the Church of Scotland more liturgically focused. His work in Argyll includes the churches at Lochaline (1899), Port Charlotte on Islay (1897), Strone (1907), Kilmore, Dervaig on Mull (1904), Kirn (1906), perhaps the finest Romanesque church in Argyll, and Canna (1913). He also re-designed the interiors of several churches, notably Kilmun (1898–9) and Kilmichael Glassary (1908), re-creating a more medieval atmosphere with distinct sanctuaries and more prominence being given to the communion table. His extensive work in Iona Abbey (1908–10) involved re-building the nave and installing the altar-like communion table of Iona marble. Overall, Chalmers made a notable contribution to enhancing the liturgical and spiritual atmosphere of Argyll's churches.

The more general movement of liturgical reform in the later nineteenth century, which removed the central pulpit and galleries favoured in the post-Reformation period and replaced them with a central communion table and side pulpit, went further in Argyll than many other parts of Scotland, and certainly further than elsewhere in the Highland and Islands. It was not just a more sacramental approach to worship that changed the face of Argyll's churches. Many were also subjected to constant re-ordering and re-building simply to accommodate more worshippers. Sometimes this involved complete demolition and new building – several current parish churches are the third or even the fourth buildings to have been erected on the same site between the mid eighteenth and early twentieth centuries. In other cases enlargements were made, as in the case of Dunoon's

High Kirk, which was extended four times between 1770 and 1909, most dramatically in 1834 when the nave was lengthened to accommodate another 300 people.

Despite these changes, there are still many parish churches across Argyll which reflect the architectural principles of the Reformation. Several have high central pulpits drawing the eyes of all the congregation to the preacher and emphasizing the importance of expounding the Word in Presbyterian worship. Striking examples are still to be found in Ardchattan, where there are pulpits for both preacher and precentor with an impressive sounding board above, and also in Kilchoan, Kilberry, Kilmodan and Glenorchy. The Gaelic poet Duncan Ban MacIntyre graphically described the preaching in Glenorchy Kirk during the incumbency of Joseph MacIntyre, which lasted from 1765 to 1823:

And in Clachan of Dysart
It was fine to be today
Seated in a marvellous church,
In a pew of splendid setting,
Hearkening to all that he
Of the gentlest voice would tell us
As he gave the bible story
And the moral derived therefrom.

MacIntyre, who is commemorated in a marble tablet erected close to the pulpit which he filled so worthily and so long, often made reference to the local landscape to illustrate a point. Preaching on one occasion on the immensity of the ocean, he caused something of a sensation among his parishioners, who lived on the shores of Loch Awe, by telling them that their loch was in comparison but Liih an diinain, the midden pool.

Many of Argyll's churches still retain the galleries which allowed the ministers in their high pulpits to look straight into the eyes of the better-off worshippers. Lairds and heritors often had special galleries built with their own separate entrances via outside stairways and a sitting or retiring room at the back. Jura is a case in point, where the laird's retiring room has been put to good use to house a superb collection of photographs telling the history of the island. Galleries were also erected to provide more accommodation in church without the expense of substantial re-building work. Although virtually all the churches now have small communion tables, either in front of a big central pulpit or in a central position with a pulpit to the side, Ardchattan still retains its long central communion table running up the middle of the nave, a reminder of how communion used to be celebrated across Scotland.

Many of Argyll's churches have an air of Presbyterian order and openness that comes in part from the large, clear windows, the whitewashed walls, the light-coloured furniture and the uncluttered simplicity of the interiors. This atmosphere is perhaps most clearly felt in Lochgoilhead Church where eighteenth-century galleries and pews remain, painted beautifully but soberly in white and grey. It is clean, light and airy with something of a Scandinavian feel, but also reminiscent of a courtroom. Other churches exhibit quirkier features while still having a similar feeling of clean, unencumbered simplicity. Kilchattan Church on Luing, built in 1936 and one of several twentieth-century Argyll churches which keep to the simple dignified style of their predecessors (Gigha Parish Church, built in 1932, is another, albeit in a more Romanesque style), feels like a ship inside. The wooden panelling is painted bright blue with light blue walls above and a white wooden roof. The nautical theme is enhanced by the lectern, inscribed with the text 'O hear us when we cry to Thee for those in peril on the sea' and presented by the owners of a Latvian ship wrecked off Culipool in 1936 in thankfulness for the help given by local people to the survivors and for their careful tending of the graves of those who were drowned and are buried in Kilchattan graveyard.

Several familiar themes that we have already encountered crop up in the interior layouts of Argyll's parish churches. The dominance of the Campbells is an almost omni-present one, most obviously reflected in countless memorial tablets. In Lochgoilhead Church virtually the entire east wall, where one might have expected to find an altar, is covered with a huge monument to James Campbell of Ardkinglas, dating from around 1660. Adjoining it at the east end of the north wall is a late medieval arched monument to an earlier Campbell laird decorated with heraldic shields. Kilmodan Church at Clachan of Glendaruel in West Cowal has three separate galleries, which served as lairds' lofts for different Campbell families, each with their own individual staircases and entrances. It is known as 'the Kirk of the Three Doors' as a result and has prompted the observation that the Campbells talked to God but not to each other. Among the many stained-glass windows commemorating Campbells, perhaps the most imposing is the one in St Blaan's Church, Southend, installed by Ina, Dowager Duchess of Argyll in memory of her husband, the eighth Duke.

Their stained-glass windows are, indeed, one of the joys of Argyll's churches. Often installed in the late nineteenth or early twentieth centuries, they greatly enhance the liturgical and mystical aspects of even the simplest churches and provide an element of colour largely lacking in the parish churches of the Western Isles. Ford, at the southern end of Loch Awe, is a good example of a very simple church transformed by the most exquisite windows. A three-lancet

Interior of Lochgoilhead Church
Above: The Gallery
Below: Monument to James Campbell of Ardkinglas

East Window there depicts Faith, Hope and Charity as portrayed by Pre-Raphaelite females in browns and reds, with Temperance similarly depicted in a side window. There are six fine windows by Stephen Adam in Kilmun Church. In Innellan his 'Christ at the Door' (1906), based on Holman Hunt's famous painting, 'The

Light of the World', depicts Jesus holding a lantern which emits an extraordinary rich and almost supernatural glow whatever time of day it is viewed. The remote Kilbrandon Church on Seil has five windows by Scotland's other pre-eminent early-twentieth-century stained-glass artist, Douglas Strachan. Especially striking are three on the east wall depicting Jesus walking on water, stilling the storm and preaching from a boat, appropriately watery themes for Argyll. There is another impressive window by Strachan in Inverchaolain Church depicting St Michael and there are good Nativity lancets by Henry Holiday in Lochgilphead Parish Church.

There are, of course, churches of other Presbyterian denominations aside from the Established or Auld Kirk in Argyll, several of which are not without interest. The Free Church, which originated in a split from the Church of Scotland in 1843 over the issue of patronage, was a less significant presence in Argyll than in other parts of the Highlands. Of the fifty-two ministers in the Argyll Synod in 1843, just seventeen left to join the Free Church. In the much smaller Highland Synod of Caithness and Sutherland, which numbered twenty-nine ministers, nineteen joined the Free Church, while in Ross, also twenty-nine strong, the figure was twenty-two. I suspect both Campbell influence and Argyll's prevailing liberal theological temper were contributory factors in keeping most of its ministers loyal to the Established Church. Where Free Church congregations did form, they often met with considerable opposition from local lairds. The Free Church congregation in Ardnamurchan, denied land on which to build a church by Sir James Riddell, resourcefully had a floating place of worship built at Fairlie's Shipyard on the Clyde. The iron vessel, equipped with pulpit and pews which could accommodate over 500 worshippers, was anchored 150 yards off the Morvern coast near Strontian and served as a place of worship from 1846 until 1868 when a Free Chuch was built in Acharacle. The Floating Church of Loch Sunart, as it was known, was surely the Free Church's most striking contribution to Argyll's spiritual landscape. This denomination was also responsible for two of the region's most ornate ecclesiastical buildings: St John's Church in Dunoon, built in 1876 in French Gothic style, and the Gaelic Free Church in Campbeltown, later Lorne Street Church (1867–68), a polychromatic Gothic extravanganza supposedly based on an

Anglo-Catholic church in Manchester designed by Pugin and long known as the Tartan Church, which since 1995 has housed the Campbeltown Heritage Centre.

Other, more evangelical denominations also had a presence in Argyll, notably the Baptists who were particularly strong on Tiree. Argyll experienced religious revivals in the nineteenth century, although never on the scale of those experienced in the Outer Isles. Baptist membership on Tiree reached a peak in 1859 and in the same year there was a revival in Campbeltown and across South Kintyre with numerous conversions, 'awakenings', supernatural visions and considerably enhanced church attendances – the Highland Church in Campbeltown was kept open all night throughout the winter and the *Glasgow Herald* reported that Gigha had become 'an island of prayer'. Campbeltown retained its reputation for religiosity. Visiting from London in 1887, Alfred Barnard noted 'Sunday in Campbeltown is carried to its Jewish lengths and is quite a day of gloom and penance ... There are nearly as many places of worship as distilleries in the town'.[2] Given that there were thirty-six of the latter, this was quite a claim!

Essentially, though, what characterized Argyll's spiritual landscape through the eighteenth and nineteenth centuries were its simple parish churches quietly engaged in the worship of God without undue fuss or puritanical fervour. Most remain fulfilling that role today, though they are now for the most part grouped into large linked parishes and welcome a diminishing number of worshippers to their sometimes infrequent services. They do, however, welcome a growing number of visitors who come to enjoy their calm and peace as well as the unexpected gems often contained inside them. Long may their doors remain open to host strangers and turn tourists into pilgrims.

13

Morvern Manse – The MacLeod Dynasty

They may not have the visual impact and appeal of churches, but manses have their own important place in Argyll's spiritual landscape. Often the largest dwelling houses in a village and set a little apart from the rest in their own glebe lands, they reflect the traditional status of ministers and their slight distance from their parishioners. Nowadays the great majority of manses have been sold and ministers decanted into bungalows in a cramped corner of the glebe, but some are still in church ownership. The manse on Jura which my great-great-great grandfather, Alexander Kennedy, was the first to occupy stands proud and defiant on its own in a commanding position just outside the village of Craighouse.

Jura Manse

No Argyll manse has played such a significant role in the spiritual life of the region, or indeed, the nation as that at Fiunary on the south coast of Morvern. Located up a narrow track and surrounded by tall trees, it served the linked churches of Fernish in Drimnin and Keil in Lochaline (the former parishes of Killintaig and Kilcolmkiel) in a charge that stretched over 142 square miles. For 107 years it was occupied by members of the same family, the MacLeods, that extraordinary dynasty which has given more than 550 years of service to the church and produced six Moderators of the General Assembly of the Church of Scotland.

The first of the family to occupy Fiunary Manse, Norman MacLeod, arrived from Skye aged 30 in 1775, having been appointed by the Duke of Argyll to reconcile the many Jacobites in this northernmost part of Argyll to the final collapse of the Stewart cause and woo them from Episcopalianism to Presbyterianism and the Established Church. His command of Gaelic and strong pastoral and preaching skills won over many of his 2,000 parishioners and when he died in 1824, after forty-nine years in the parish, he was remembered, in the words of his memorial in Kiel Church, as 'noble in appearance, excelling in scholarship, an eloquent preacher and a genial and faithful pastor'. He was succeeded as minister by his youngest son, John, who remained in the charge for fifty-eight years until his death in 1882. Known as 'the High Priest of Morvern' partly because of his commanding physical presence – he was six feet, nine inches tall – he chose to remain in his parish throughout the period of the Clearances rather than quit for one of the many richer charges which sought to call him or emigrate with the many hundreds of his parishioners who were evicted from their crofts. In the words of his nephew, Donald:

> His later years were spent in pathetic loneliness. He had seen his parish almost emptied of its people. Glen after glen had been turned into sheep-walks, and the cottages in which generations of gallant Highlanders had lived and died were unroofed, their tall walls and gables left standing like mourners beside the grave, and the little plots of garden or of cultivated enclosure allowed to merge into the moorland pasture.[1]

Together father and son achieved what the Duke of Argyll had hoped for and turned Morvern from a Catholic and Episcopalian stronghold into a bastion of Presbyterianism. A census conducted in 1843 revealed that out of 391 families in the parish, 370 were connected with the Established Church of Scotland, eight were Roman Catholic and two Episcopalian. The other eleven families may well have left the Established Church in the Disruption of that year and would later worship at the Free Church built in Lochaline in 1852. This huge Presbyterian preponderance was almost certainly replicated, if not exceeded, in parishes across the rest of Argyll where there was, for the most part, less traditional antipathy towards the Kirk.

Fiunary Manse became something of a nursery for ministers during the 107 years of MacLeod occupancy. Two of Norman MacLeod's twelve children became ministers: John, who followed his father, and Norman (1783–1862) who ministered at the Highland Church at Campbeltown from 1808–25 before going on to Campsie and then St Columba's Glasgow. Norman did much to help West Highlanders during the period of potato famine and clearances in the 1830s and 1840s. A notable champion of Gaelic culture, literacy and education, he persuaded the Church of Scotland to set up Gaelic schools and started the first successful Gaelic periodical. A bust in the entrance porch to the Highland Church in Campbeltown commemorates him as Caraid nan Gaidheal, or 'Friend of the Gaels'. John's two sons, Norman (1838–1911) and John (1840–1898) became ministers in Inverness and Govan respectively.

The best-known and most influential of the MacLeod dynasty in the nineteenth century was yet another Norman (1812–1872), son of Norman, Caraid nan Gaidheal. Born in his father's manse in Campbeltown, he was largely raised at his grandfather's manse at Fiunary. He went on to serve for twenty years in the inner-city Barony Church in Glasgow, where he championed the cause of working men and initiated many social reforms, setting up loan funds and savings banks, soup kitchens and education classes. He also became Queen Victoria's confidant and her favourite chaplain. Like the rest of the MacLeod ministers – and there were several more – he combined a broad evangelical simplicity with a strong liturgical sense and an open-minded, liberal theology. In 1867 he wrote a book about the parish in which his uncle and grandfather had served and where he had spent much of his childhood. *Reminiscences of A Highland Parish*, republished in 2002 as *Morvern, A Highland Parish*, superbly edited by Iain Thornber, is one of the great texts on the spiritual landscape of Argyll.

The book begins with a birdseye view of the parish from its highest point, the top of Sithean na Rapleich, 1,806 feet above sea level. What strikes MacLeod as he surveys the landscape below is the number of ruins, and not just of homes abandoned during the Clearances:

> Ruins there are, too, which show us that whatever defects the Church before the Reformation had accumulated, she excelled the Church of the present in the greater number and the greater beauty of her parish churches. There are few sights which more rebuke the vulgar church parsimony of these later days, or which imbue us with more grateful and generous feelings towards the missionaries of an earlier and more difficult time, than the faith and love which reared so many chapels on distant islands, and so many beautiful and costly fabrics in savage wildernesses.[2]

This opening preamble, reminiscent of Alexander Ewing's musings just two years earlier (page 95), is followed by a lyrical chapter about the Fiunary manse. Norman MacLeod describes it and the associated glebe, on which cottages had been built by his grandfather and uncle for local labourers and shepherds as well as for those destitute and in need of charity, as 'a colony which ever preached sermons, on week days as well as on Sundays, of industry and frugality, and the domestic peace, contentment and cheerfulness of a holy Christian home.'[3] What he recalled particularly from his own childhood days in the Manse was its 'constant cheerfulness'. Throughout their ministries, both Norman and John MacLeod encouraged music making and regularly gave up half of the Manse to be used for dancing on New Year's eve. This was just one of many ways in which it played a key role in the life of the parish:

> The manse was the grand centre to which all the inhabitants of the parish gravitated for help and comfort. Medicines for the sick were weighed out from the chest yearly replenished in Glasgow. The poor, as a matter of course, visited the manse, not for an order on public charity, but for aid from private charity, and it was never refused in kind, such as meal, wool, or potatoes. As there were no lawyers in the parish, lawsuits were adjusted in the manse; and

so were marriages not a few. The distressed came there for comfort, and the perplexed for advice; and there was always something material as well as spiritual to share with them all. No one went away empty in body or soul. Yet the barrel of meal was never empty, nor the cruise of oil extinguished.[4]

During their ministries in Morvern, both Norman and John MacLeod farmed the 68-acre glebe adjacent to the Manse to supplement their £89 stipend and rented Fiunary Farm from the Duke of Argyll. Reminiscing about his own boyhood involvement in farming activities there, 'young' Norman was led into a more general reflection on the Highland manse and its role in inculcating what I have already identified as a distinctive Argyll virtue:

If ever 'muscular Christianity' was taught to the rising generation, the Highland manse of these days was its gymnasium. After school hours, and on 'play-days' and Saturdays, there was no want of employment calculated to develop physical energy. The glebe and farm made a constant demand for labour which it was joy to the boys to afford. Every season brought its own appropriate and interesting work.[5]

Norman MacLeod superbly expressed the straightforward muscular Christianity of his native Argyll in his great hymn 'Courage, brother, do not stumble', written for the working men of Glasgow at a time when he was battling against the dour puritanism and narrow Calvinism of fellow-members of Glasgow Presbytery who were maintaining a steadfast opposition to the running of trams and trains and the opening of parks and museums on a Sunday, the only day which many people had free from work. With its heartfelt plea, 'Perish policy and cunning, perish all that fears the light', and its simple stirring injunction, 'Trust in God and do the right', it was memorably sung at the funeral of another great son of Argyll, the Labour Party leader, John Smith, in 1994.

Perhaps the most moving passage in *Reminiscences of A Highland Parish*, is this lyrical description of Kiel churchyard near Lochaline:

It is situated on a green plateau of table-land which forms a ledge between the low seashore and mountain background. A beautiful tall stone cross from Iona adorns it; a single gothic arch of an old church remains as a witness for the once consecrated ground.

The view from that churchyard of all God's glorious architecture above and below makes one forget those paltry attempts of man to be a fellow-worker with Him in the rearing and adorning of the fitting and the beautiful. There is not in the Highlands a finer expanse of inland seas, of castled promontories, of hills beyond hills, until cloudland and highland mingle, of precipice and waterfall, with all the varied lights and shadows which heathy hillsides, endless hilltops, dark corries, ample bays and rocky shores, can create at morn, noonday, or evening from sun and cloud – a glorious panorama extending from the far west beyond the giant point of Ardnamurchan, 'the height of the great ocean', to the far east, where Ben Cruachan and 'the Shepherds of Etive Glen' stand sentinels in the sky.

No sea king could select a more appropriate resting place than this, from whence to catch a glimpse, as his spirit walked abroad beneath the moonlight, of galleys coming from the Northland of his early home; nor could an old saint find a better resting place, if he desired that after death the mariners, struggling with stormy winds and waves, might see his cross from afar, and thence snatch comfort from this symbol of faith and hope 'in extremis'; nor could any man, who in the frailty of his human nature shrunk from burial in lonely vault, and who wished rather to lie where birds might sing, and summer's sun shine, and winter's storms lift their

MacLeod Memorial, Keil Churchyard, Lochaline

voices to God, and the beautiful world be ever above and around him, find a spot more congenial to his feelings than the kirkyard of 'the Parish'.[6]

Kiel churchyard remains today much as Norman MacLeod described it 150 years ago with its ruined medieval chapel and early-fourteenth-century carved cross. Among the many tombstones and monuments is an imposing railed-off memorial to the two MacLeod ministers of Morvern and their many offspring. It is now in a somewhat shabby state. Not as shabby and forlorn, though, as Fiunary Manse, once the scene of so much activity, merriment and practical Christian charity, which now stands deserted and derelict. It continued to house successive ministers of Morvern until 1957 when it was sold by the General Trustees of the Church of Scotland to George MacLeod, later Lord Macleod of Fiunary, the grandson of Norman MacLeod of the Barony and great-great-grandson of Norman, the first MacLeod minister of Morvern. He came there regularly, often accompanied by groups of borstal boys, but since his death in 1991 it has fallen into disuse and now presents a mournful and melancholy aspect, its roof fallen in and the once-immaculate lawn overgrown with brambles. A particularly poignant example of Argyll's landscape of ghosts and ruins, for all its dank dereliction it still carries the lingering echoes of a great age of evangelical outreach, liberal mysticism and muscular Christianity.

Fiunary Manse today

14

Episcopal Argyll – Alexander Ewing

Although Argyll is an overwhelmingly Presbyterian spiritual land-scape, there have been pockets of Episcopalianism, especially in the north of the county. A visitor to Ardnamurchan in the early eighteenth century noted that 'many of the inhabitants are Camerons and McLachlans and violently Episcopal'. The Episcopal Church received a considerable boost in 1846 when Argyll and the Isles were disjoined from the diocese of Moray and Ross and given their own new united diocese. Its first Bishop, Alexander Ewing, whose family roots were in Loch Fyneside, was both shaped by and representative of Argyll's distinctive spirituality.

Ewing was the ideal figure to forge the identity of the new diocese which he headed from 1847 to 1873. He combined a romantic attachment to Gaeldom and the Celtic tradition with a passionate Protestantism. Holding that the Celtic heritage of the church was 'simple, fervent and evangelical', he disliked the High Church Tractarianism sweeping through the Scottish Episcopal Church, which he felt was overdosing on ritual, and instead espoused a muscular liberal Protestantism. He wrote to a friend, 'Perhaps you will think I am as daft about Protestantism as I am about the Highlands and the Highland scenery. Only remember that in one form of mania I have the companionship of William Wordsworth, and in the other of Martin Luther'. He championed McLeod Campbell's heretical views, which he described as expressing 'the fullness of the Christian Gospel' and expressed the hope that 'one-day or other the more liberal Presbyterians and Episcopalians may find themselves in one Northern Establishment'.[1]

Alongside liberal Protestantism, Ewing's abiding passion was Argyll's Celtic past and Gaelic spirituality. As part of his first Diocesan Synod he led the clergy on a pilgrimage to Iona, perhaps the first since the Reformation. Celebrating Eucharist in the ruined Cathedral, he told them 'we are now in what was the cradle and nursing-mother of Christianity in the west. Here, where for so long a time and from so remote a period the Gospel sounded forth, it is sad to hear but the wild bird's cry and the moan of the sullen wave. Coming as we do on a pilgrimage to the graves of our spiritual fathers, we cannot but mourn the silence and solitude of the tombs'.[2] As well as being one of the first clerics to bemoan the ruined state of Iona Abbey and perhaps sow the seeds for its revival as an active place of worship, as he did in a book published in 1865, he was also among the earliest to invoke the concept of Celtic Christianity that has been so potent in our own age. He suggested that the Scottish Episcopal Church was in a special way the heir to this particular Christian tradition, writing in his rather wonderfully entitled 1872 book, *Feamainn Earraghaidheill* (Argyllshire Seaweed): 'This Celtic Christianity we think to be somewhat represented, if not altogether preserved, in our Highland & Island Episcopal Churches. They have something of the primitive nature of the Celtic Churches, and the same absence of identity with Rome.'

Although he had poor health and spent much time in Italy and England, Ewing travelled extensively round his far-flung diocese, which, as it still does, took in the Outer Isles as well as Argyll, and he rallied and strengthened Episcopalians beyond their traditional strongholds in Appin and Ballachulish. Like the MacLeods, he was deeply affected by the agricultural distress among the inhabitants and bemoaned the Clearances, although he saw emigration as the only answer to rural over-population. Based first briefly on Bute and then for three years in Duntroon Castle as a guest of the Malcolms of Poltalloch, he established his episcopal residence from 1852 at Bishopton, Lochgilphead, next to the newly built Christ Church Episcopal Church designed by William Butterfield. A window to the left of the altar in this church depicts him clad in his bishop's robes opposite two striking windows commemorating his wife, Katharine, one showing her as a small girl being held by an angel and the other as a mature lady in a blue dress holding a set of pan pipes. The east window above the altar shows a lone male figure in a boat raising his hands to the sky with a mitre above him. Ewing and his wife are buried in an enclosure in the church grounds with a fine Celtic Cross commemorating this most consciously Celtic of Argyll churchmen.

Perhaps the most atmospheric of Argyll's Episcopal churches is St Columba's, Poltalloch, built during Ewing's Episcopacy between 1852 and 1854 as an estate church for the Malcolm family, who lived in the large house nearby on the ridge above the Kilmartin Valley. It is quintessentially English and the kind of building you would expect to find on a Gloucestershire estate. Lighter and less gloomy than most of Argyll's other Episcopal churches, its Gothic atmosphere is enhanced by the heavily wooded surroundings it now occupies close to the spooky ruins of Poltalloch house. As Frank Walker rightly observes, 'no later Episcopal churches match this cool reserve' although All Saints, Inverary (1885–6), has its own spiritual power.[3] Also worthy of note is the more modest St Bride's Episcopal Church in North Ballachulish, built in 1875, with its windows to Columba, Bridget and Patrick, and touching icon of Bridget with oyster catchers at her feet painted in 1912. Immediately outside its entrance porch a magnificent high-standing Celtic cross commemorates Alexander Chinnery-Haldane, Ewing's successor as Bishop of Argyll and the Isles, who continued his love-affair with all things Celtic and furthered his mission to make Iona a place of living Christianity, notably through the building of Bishop's House in 1893 (page 186).

Argyll's Episcopal Cathedral, St John the Divine in Oban, is rather disappointing. Begun as a parish church in 1863, it was extended and altered in fits and starts over the next hundred years. Still unfinished, it lacks any unifying theme or spiritual heart. Oban's Church of Scotland Parish Church, built on the Corran Esplanade in the 1950s and designed to be a 'stately church in the style of a Cathedral' is not much better. Stark and bland, its strongly Scandinavian feel – the octagon topped tower was based on that of Stockholm Town Hall – seems somehow out of place on the seafront. The Roman Catholic Cathedral just along the Esplanade is in every respect a much more impressive building than the principal Episcopalian and Presbyterian places of worship in this, the largest of Argyll's urban centres.

15

The Cowal Peninsula – George Matheson of Innellan

Among the more intriguing interactions between Argyll's physical and spiritual landscapes is the influence that the Cowal peninsula, and Innellan in particular, exerted on George Matheson, the great Victorian devotional writer and preacher. It is all the more intriguing because Matheson was blind and the landscape had its effect through sound as much as through sights remembered from his boyhood.

Cowal is an area of stark contrasts. Just a few miles from the douce retirement villas and weekend homes for Glasgow businessmen that stretch down its eastern coast are some of Argyll's wildest and most inaccessible places, reached via seemingly never-ending single-track roads, like the one that leads up Loch Striven to Inverchaolain and those penetrating its remote western shores, now marketed to tourists as 'Argyll's Secret Coast'. It is a perfect microcosm of Argyll as a whole, not least in the number of its lochs and the ever-present proximity of the sea. Cowal is a very watery place, with Loch Fyne on one side, Loch Long on the other and Loch Riddon, Loch Striven and Holy Loch between them, giving the land the appearance of a lobster claw or fingers pointing out into the sea. It even has its own mini-Loch Awe in the form of the long inland Loch Eck. Most people come to Cowal by crossing the Firth of Clyde from Gourock to Dunoon. In days gone by many more travelled further into Argyll that way, journeying on by steamer through the Kyles of Bute and round the Cowal peninsula to Loch Fyne. The voyage across the Clyde to Cowal made a deep impression on Alexander Ewing who wrote that with its combination of cloud and sunshine, well-ordered homes and everlasting hills, he felt as though he was 'passing through a parable of life itself'. It led him into a deep meditation 'of the onwards and whither of the human soul and human history'.[1]

George Matheson was similarly affected by the scenery and seascape of Cowal. He was first captivated by it as a boy when he came, like so many others from Glasgow, to spend summer holidays there. At that stage, despite suffering severe inflammation at the back of his eyes, he could see fairly well. Gradually throughout his childhood and teenage years his vision faded until by the age of 18 he was effectively blind. He retained to the end of his life a vivid visual memory from his childhood of the colours and contours of Cowal, and especially of its sea, sunsets, clouds and skies. They became idealised and spiritualised in his mystical theology with the result that, in the words of his friend David Sime, 'at times his talk of the visible universe was like that of a spirit'.[2]

Matheson came to Innellan, then a Chapel of Ease in the Parish of Dunoon, as Church of Scotland minister at the age of 28 in 1868. A year or so after arriving, he suffered a severe crisis of faith. As he put it, 'I found myself an absolute atheist. I believed nothing: neither God nor immortality.'[3] He tendered his resignation to the Presbytery but it was not accepted and he was told that he was a young man and his views would change. Largely through reading German philosophy, he regained his faith in a much more liberal and mystical form, which he described as 'Broad positive'. For the rest of his time in Innellan, despite his blindness, he devoted himself to preaching, visiting and writing poems, devotional meditations and serious works of theology in which he sought to show there was no incompatibility between Christianity and evolution and to champion natural theology. His theology was described by a reviewer as at once 'distinctly and decidedly evangelic' and 'modern, liberal and original'. His reputation as a preacher led people to take their holidays in Innellan just to hear its blind minister. In 1873 it became a parish in its own right and when Matheson left the resort in 1886 to go to a charge in Edinburgh, there was consternation among local hoteliers and boarding house proprietors at the loss of one of the main tourist attractions.

George Matheson spent much time alone in the study of his Manse, which overlooked the Clyde. Sometimes if the light was good he could just catch a shadow of one of the many passing steamers.

More often it was their sounds that caught his imagination. David Sime recalled an evening spent with Matheson in his study when a strong breeze was blowing over the Clyde and an ocean liner was sailing past. Standing by the window, the blind minister commented to his companion:

> That weird music comes up here from the ocean like the far off music of another world, a symphony of great nature. How varied and multiform it is! I often listen to it, when sitting here alone, or perhaps sometimes in the depth of night. It puts one in reverie. And that? Listen! The monotone of that passing steamer, decisive and clear, how finely it blends with Nature's majestic music!
>
> It is the symphony of Nature we are listening to, with the occasional siren-note; but in the most solitary clachan of our mountains and glens, you will sometimes see – I daresay you have already seen it – the sweet light and the unruffled life of heaven itself. Heaven sometimes begins here, and immortality.[4]

That quotation reveals much about the way Matheson used his hearing to stimulate his imagination. It also points to the powerful role played by the imagery of the Cowal seascape in the formation of his own theology and faith. It is expressed in the opening verse of his best-known hymn: 'O love that wilt not let me go, I rest my weary soul in thee; I give thee back the life I owe, that in thine ocean depths its flow may richer, fuller be' with its message that our souls go back into God's great ocean depths. That hymn was written in the study of the Innellan Manse in just three minutes one evening in 1881. In his own words, 'it was the quickest composition I ever achieved. It was wrung out spontaneously from the heart.' Another line in the hymn, 'I trace (or, as Matheson originally wrote, climb) the rainbow through the rain', perhaps draws on his youthful memories of the frequent interplay of rain and light in Cowal. It also reflects a common theme in his theology – that God is to be found as much, if not more, in the shadows and the clouds as in the light.

Matheson returned to the imagery of the sea again and again in his devotional and theological writings. He made much of it in a book published after he had left Innellan entitled *The Lady Ecclesia*, an allegory about the development of the Spirit of Christ in the Church and in the individual. The kingdom which the Lady Ecclesia has inherited from her ancestors, and which forms the background of the allegory, is an island and the book is full of descriptions of the surrounding ocean and its sounds – the sighing of winds, the moaning of waves, the passing to and fro of ships and the infinite distance that lay beyond. The sea epitomised for him the ideas of self-abandonment and sacrifice which were at the heart of his faith. Its capacity to absorb so much, to bring together the millions of drops of rain which collect first in streams and then form rivers that flow down to the ocean, symbolised the all-embracing, encompassing, gathering-in love of God, as expressed in his wonderfully inclusive hymn 'Gather us in, Thou love that fillest all', and in his meditation on the text in 1 Corinthians 15.28 that 'God may be all in all':

> Love is an ocean in which no man loses himself; he regains himself in richer, nobler form. The only ocean in which a man loses himself is self-love; God's love gives him back his life that he may keep it unto life eternal.

The Innellan manse from where Matheson heard the sounds of the sea and in which he wrote many of his great devotional and theological works is one of those that has not been sold off and is still the home of the parish minister, who now has to cover Toward and the High Kirk in Dunoon as well. It stands just behind the church where he preached and which now bears his name. The church was enlarged in 1890, and subsequently enhanced by a massive carved pulpit and the fine Stephen Adam east window of Christ as the Light of the World, both fitting memorials to the blind minister and poet who, seeing nothing of the world as it was but filled with visions of how it might be, interpreted the destiny of creation and the point and purpose of human life with the eyes of imagination and faith.

16

Iona Again and the Campbells Again

In charting Argyll's changing spiritual landscape, we keep coming back to Iona and to the Campbells. It is thanks to successive clan chiefs, and especially to the eighth Duke of Argyll, Mac Cailein Mór from 1847 to 1900, that the island's religious buildings were saved and preserved to become the iconic sacred places that they are today.

When we last visited Columba's isle, in the mid seventeenth century (page 148), the Abbey chancel was being used for Protestant worship. This arrangement did not last beyond 1660 – after which there was no minister on the island until the building of the Parliamentary Church in 1829 – and by the mid eighteenth century the entire Abbey was in ruins. The islanders carried off stones and grave slabs for building purposes and the nunnery was used as a cattle byre. Iona continued to attract visitors, many lured there by the appeal of Columba and his spiritual legacy, but they were often appalled by the condition of the buildings and monuments. Visiting in 1772, the Welsh antiquarian, Thomas Pennant, had to bribe a local man to dig away a pile of cow dung on the floor of the nunnery to reveal Prioress Anna MacLean's grave slab. When James Boswell and Samuel Johnson came a year later, they were disappointed to find that virtually nothing remained of the early tombs in the Reilig Odhráin and that the Abbey floor was covered in mud and rubbish. Most of the marble altar had been chipped away by islanders who believed that a fragment would afford protection against shipwreck, fire and other accidents – an indication that the destruction sometimes attributed to iconoclasm may in fact have had more to do with a lingering post-Reformation superstition in the efficacy of relics and holy objects.

Successive Dukes of Argyll, whose family owned Iona from the 1690s, sought to conserve its religious fabric and heritage. In 1757 the third Duke enclosed the Abbey ruins with a wall in an effort to protect them and instructed his tenants to keep both the Abbey and the nunnery free from weeds and other 'nuisance'. John Walker wrote in 1764 of islanders using the Abbey for worship and there was a report in 1788 of local people dancing in the ruins. In 1797 the fifth Duke reprimanded his tenants for removing stones from the Abbey. Visitors were often the chief culprits in vandalising its contents. In 1819 a party of sailors broke off the hands and crozier from the effigy of Abbot John MacKinnon. A naval officer is said to have defaced his face and later souvenir hunters made off with three of the four lions decorating the base of his monument.

Such vandalism contrasted with the reverential and romantic view of Iona taken by its more cultivated visitors. William Wordsworth was somewhat nonplussed to be greeted on landing by a ragged child trying to sell him pebbles from the beach but penned a sonnet praising the spiritual atmosphere enveloping the island despite its rather desolate and dejected state. In the eyes of many visitors, the ruined aspect of the buildings added to the island's spiritual atmosphere. For Dr Johnson, who memorably remarked on their power to make the piety of those who saw them grow warmer, they were 'ruins of religious magnificence' serving as 'melancholy memorials to a lost age of faith'. An anonymous visitor in 1771 waxed even more lyrically: 'Nature has formed Icolumbkill for contemplation. In this solitary recess, sequestered from the follies and tumults which embroil the great world, the serious soul had leisure to think of heaven. Everything inspired sedate thought.'[1]

Columba's busy monastic hub, from which he regularly had to seek peace by going off to Hinba, had now become a place of calm, quiet retreat. Its appeal was enhanced by its perceived isolation and ruined state, the empty buildings speaking more eloquently of the eternal mysteries than when they had been full of monks and nuns. The Romantic Movement enhanced the appeal of ruins and inspired more and more legends to grow up around Columba and the other saints of Argyll. This process gathered momentum in the latter part of the nineteenth century when antiquarianism, romanticism and Christian ecumenism combined to focus on Iona as the icon of that pure and primitive faith which was increasingly being labelled Celtic Christianity.

This renewed interest in Iona coincided with the period when the island's owner was George Douglas Campbell, eighth Duke of Argyll, who had a deep personal interest in its religious history and spiritual significance. An extraordinary polymath, who served as a Cabinet minister in every Whig and Liberal Government between 1852 and 1881, he was a distinguished amateur philosopher, the-ologian, naturalist and geologist, as well as a talented poet and painter and exemplified the intellectual, liberal, mystical Presbyte-rian faith of the Campbells. Fascinated by Iona from his first visit as a teenager, he wrote a best-selling book in 1870 which covered in detailed and scholarly fashion both Columba's life and times and also the Benedictine monastery, its buildings and monuments. Four years later he initiated a major programme of structural repair work in the Abbey, the nunnery and St Oran's Chapel, all of which were in imminent danger of complete collapse. He personally supervised this rescue operation, which took five years and involved substan-tial rebuilding as well as shoring up crumbling walls and removing several feet of rubble. Most of the carved stones which had been lying on the ground were moved to an upright position and placed against walls to afford them some protection. The Duke had hoped to put them under cover but was told this would be prohibitively expensive.

The idealisation of Columba and of Iona reached its apogee in the final decade of the nineteenth century. It manifested itself in roman-ticised paintings like James McTaggart's 'The Coming of Saint Columba' (page 51) and a host of poems, several of which were written by those who were both geographically and culturally far removed from Argyll. Perhaps the most fervent poetic tributes to the enduring spiritual power of Iona came from the pen of Samuel Stone, Rector of the City of London church of All Hallows' On the Wall, who had fallen under its spell on a holiday visit. His 1897 anthology, *Lays of Iona*, the preface of which noted that 'any real interest in Iona did not generally exist until late in the nineteenth century', included a poem eulogising it as 'A second Bethlehem, second Nazareth' and a lengthy hymn which insisted that 'Iona the recluse, not lordly Rome' should be seen as 'England's nursing mother' and concluded with a ringing peroration worthy of 'Land of Hope and Glory': 'Forward, Iona's child, Church-Mother of the free'.

This intense new interest in and enthusiasm for Iona's spiritual landscape in the 1890s was part of a broader movement of Celtic revival and a more general idealisation of the Highlands and Islands and their inhabitants. The lingering influence of James Macpherson's Ossian, the writings of Ernest Rénan and Matthew Arnold on the particular virtues and sensitivities of the Celtic people, and a growing fascination with Gaelic folklore helped to change the popular perception of the West Highlander from half savage barbarian to mystical, spiritual Gael. Agitation by crofters for basic rights of security of tenure and fair rents during the 1880s won much sympathy for the Highlanders' cause and enhanced their romantic appeal. Iona was taken up as a talisman and model by ecumenically-minded church leaders and theologians who desired to heal the denominational divisions that characterised the Scottish church, not least in its various Presbyterian manifestations. Instrumental in this cause was James Cooper, a Church of Scotland minister and later Professor of Ecclesiastical History at Glasgow University. In an important lecture in 1895 he argued that the revival of Celtic Christianity would lead to 'the healing of the divisions in Scottish Christianity'.

Cooper had some intriguing and rather idiosyncratic suggestions as to how the contemporary church might model itself more closely on its Celtic predecessor. He argued that acting in the spirit of Columba, it should draw more on those of high rank and noble birth and use 'the gifted sons of our nobles and chiefs' to provide both leaders and additional lay helpers to assist parish clergy. He also called for the creation of a network of memorials to Celtic Christianity in the form of replica high crosses which he proposed should be erected in 'the numerous spots which are consecrated by saintly memories' as well as in churchyards and by the wayside. 'There is no fear now of superstition connecting itself with them', he added to allay any Presbyterian anxiety, 'they would simply be silent preachers – reminders to the lonely wayfarer of the Saviour's lonelier conflict on the Tree, of His all-victorious love, and of His call to us to be crucified with Him'.[2] In fact, the practice of erecting replica high-standing crosses in graveyards and as memorials was already popular, having begun in the 1860s with the adoption of the

Celtic cross as an accepted marker for the graves of musicians, poets, artists and others with cultural interests, and continued through the early twentieth century. A striking example is the replica Kildalton Cross erected as a First World War memorial at the junction of the roads to Keills and Kilmory a mile south of Bellanoch in Knapdale.

Cooper's most impassioned plea in his 1895 lecture was for the restoration of the abbey buildings on Iona as a living embodiment of the whole Celtic Christian tradition. He envisaged them becoming a theological college, ecumenical retreat house and school of Celtic art and music. Like others, he felt powerfully the cross-denominational appeal of Columba and the potential that his legacy offered to unite Christians of different hues. In reality, Iona at this time symbolised nothing so much as the divided state of the church. Although the eighth Duke of Argyll allowed visiting clergy from both the Episcopalian and Roman Catholic churches to celebrate services within the walls of the ruined Cathedral, this was strongly opposed by many Presbyterians in the Church of Scotland and Free Church of Scotland who had the only churches on the island. A visiting Catholic priest lamented that 'no altar was there for the eucharistic sacrifice … the poor people from the cradle to the grave were living without graces and dying without the blessing of true religion'.[3] Episcopalians fared little better. The island's Free Church minister had to be forcibly restrained when Bishop Ewing ended an open-air service in the ruins with a Latin prayer. An islander later challenged the bishop to say how his ceremonies differed from those of the papists. Ewing's response, 'If you had attended to my prayers you would have perceived a vast difference' was met with the retort, 'Then why don't you pray in a language we can understand?'[4] When Ewing's successor, Alexander Chinnery-Haldane, sought in 1894 to establish a house on the island to be used as a place of prayer, study, contemplation and daily Eucharistic celebration, the parish minister raised a petition of 114 names against this Episcopalian venture. However, the Duke of Argyll was strongly of the opinion that those visiting Iona should be free to worship in their own way and, persuaded that what Chinnery-Haldane had in mind was a place of prayer rather than of proselytising, he granted permission for the building of what became known as Bishop's House. Situated at the end of the village, overlooking the Sound of Mull, it remains the Episcopal Church's base on the island today, providing comfortable accommodation and a Chapel. A pointed arch niche in the east gable contains the only statue of Columba to be found on the island.

The celebrations on Iona to mark the 1,300th anniversary of Columba's death on 9 June 1897 revealed just how far the major denominations were from finding unity in their common Celtic inheritance. Services in Gaelic and English were conducted by the Church of Scotland in the Cathedral, which had been given a temporary roof, 'in thanksgiving for the introduction of the Gospel into our land'. Chinnery-Haldane led clergy from the Episcopal Church in a separate commemoration on the same day in their new retreat house which was formally handed over into the care of the Society of St John the Evangelist, better known as the Cowley Fathers. Roman Catholics, whose request to come to the island on 9 June was turned down, had to be content with a service six days later when 615 pilgrims arrived by steamer for a Pontifical High Mass in the cathedral ruins. The *Oban Times* commented: 'A chance for the millennium was missed at Iona. Instead of three commemorations of St Columba, why not have had one combined celebration in the ancient fane of Iona?'[5]

Two years after these events, in the very last year of the nineteenth century, the Duke of Argyll relinquished ownership of all the ecclesiastical buildings on Iona and handed them over to a trust linked to the Church of Scotland. It was charged with re-roofing and restoring the Abbey Church so that it could be used for public worship and with preserving and, where appropriate, restoring the other buildings. The trustees were also enjoined to allow all branches of the Christian Church to hold services within the restored Cathedral. This was the basis on which the Abbey was re-roofed and fitted out during the 1900s to make it suitable for worship once again. The restoration work was supervised by three leading architects: John Honeyman, whom the eighth Duke had commissioned as early as 1891 to draw up plans for restoring the chancel, Thomas Ross and Peter MacGregor Chalmers. Sharing a strong sense of history and attachment to the Celtic Church, they collaborated in restoring the Abbey to its medieval glory while fulfilling the Trustees' desire that it should 'keep alive the memory of the brave spirit, the pious labours and the noble sacrifices of St Columba'. Work on the restoration was completed in 1913, creating the worship space which is still used today.

It was significant and appropriate that the man responsible for saving and restoring Iona Abbey as a place of Christian worship should have been a chief of the Campbell clan. The initiative of the eighth Duke could be seen as atoning in some measure for the iconoclasm of his seventeenth-century ancestors. It was not, however, born out of any sense of guilt or embarrassment about the past but rather out of his deep love of Iona and a profound admiration for and identification with Columba. Although not without his romantic side, he was enough of a Campbell to view the early monastic structure of the Columban church with a detached, scholarly eye. He had no sympathy with those who wished to turn it into a denominational football, holding that 'it is vain to look, in the peculiarities of the Scoto-Irish Church for the model either of Primitive practice, or of any modern system. As regards the theology of Columba's time, although it was not what we understand as Roman, neither assuredly was it what we understand as Protestant'.[6]

Like others in his family, the eighth Duke of Argyll was drawn to Columba on the basis of a faith expressed in poetic terms. His son, later the ninth Duke, an accomplished devotional poet, wrote a free translation from Gaelic of a hymn attributed to the Iona saint, which perhaps came close to expressing the faith that they shared:

> That I might for ever bless Him who upholds
> All things that are great, or are small;
> Who all the bright glories of Heaven unfolds
> Whose voice in the sound of the sea doth call,
> Whose are the mountains, and shores, and wolds,
> God, the Creator, Preserver of all![7]

The eighth Duke expressed his own religious beliefs, which were complex and infused by a very strong emphasis on natural theology, in a series of books ranging from *The Unity of Nature* and *Primeval Man* to *The Philosophy of Belief* and *The Unseen Foundations of Society*. As these titles suggest, his approach was both rigorously philosophical and deeply mystical. He shared George Matheson's belief that everything was tied into a grand scheme of things coalescing together on the basis of a fundamental but mysterious law of sacrifice, and anticipated George MacLeod's sense of the spiritual in the physical, writing that 'there is no sharp and absolute line of separation between the sacred and the profane, the natural and the supernatural, the material and the spiritual, the duties of our religions and the duties of our daily life'.[8] Indeed, he came close to the doctrine known as panentheism in his insistence that everything points to God and in some sense partakes of the Godhead. A keen ornithologist, he wrote of the song of the willow wren:

> It hath some mystic power to raise
> Dreams of a world unknown

and noted in a description of Glen Shira just north of Inveraray:

> I hear the sound of torrents, and the air
> Is full of liquid murmur from the hills.[9]

This Wordsworthian sense of the capacity of landscape to evoke deep mystical and spiritual presences was inspired by his passionate attachment to the lochs, mountains and glens of Argyll. In a moving passage describing 'one of the happiest days I had ever spent in my life' he recalled standing on the shore of Loch Ba on Mull awaiting a deer drive when he was twenty and feeling that the mass of Ben More could be compared to the 'everlasting hills' of the Psalms:

> There was present to me that day an internal landscape – not of the present or the past, but of the future – into which I gazed with the joy of great hopes, and aspirations more enchanting even than the beautiful combinations of water and woods and mountains which were beneath me, and around me and above me.[10]

The arrangement that the Duke devised for ensuring Iona Abbey's continued future as a place of living Christian worship reflected his own denominational allegiance. Throughout his life he devoted considerable energy to defending Presbyterianism against its Episcopalian and English detractors. He had no time for the narrow dogmatism that shrieked loudly from the rooftops and believed it had a monopoly of the truth. He had first encountered and reacted against it as a youth – when a puritanical nurse rebuked him for whistling on a Sunday, he replied, 'Why not? The birds whistle on a Sunday' – and was disturbed to encounter it again among some of the more Evangelical ministers and members of the Free Church in the aftermath of the Disruption of 1843. What he believed in was rather 'the still small voice that comes to those who love to catch the lowest whispers of Truth'.[11] For him that gentle, eirenic voice found its clearest expression in the broad, national established Church of Scotland, with its mission to bring the ordinances of religion and consolation of pastoral care to everyone regardless of their beliefs and not just to the elect.

This was why the Trust in which he vested the ownership and management of Iona Abbey (or Cathedral as it was called in the founding deeds), while allowing all Christian denominations to use the building for worship, was itself to be firmly tied to the Established Church of Scotland, whose leading officials were appointed ex-officio members. The Duke rightly predicted that 'my deed will be grief to the Roman Catholics, to the Anglicans, and to the Scottish Anglicans, all pretty nearly equally disliked by me'.[12] Despite the flack that he received from these and other quarters, however, the arrangements that he made, tying the future management and maintenance of the Abbey to the national church, have ensured that it has been a place of broad ecumenical worship, with a public universal outreach rather than a narrow denominational identity. He would surely have approved of the agreement made in 1999 to take the Abbey and its buildings into the care of Historic Scotland, with the ecumenical Iona Community leasing them for worship and residential purposes, and of the decision by the Iona Cathedral Trust in 2010 to widen its ecumenical base, while retaining a strong Church of Scotland connection, and to extend its remit 'to advance the education of the public in relation to the history, culture and heritage of Iona Cathedral and the Island of Iona'. Both these recent developments accord with his vision, realized in 1899, of securing the future of what is undoubtedly the most important site in the spiritual landscape of Argyll, and arguably of Scotland as a whole, as a place of living Christian worship and witness.

A huge marble effigy of the eighth Duke of Argyll and his third wife, Ina, is housed in the railed-off south transept at the central crossing in Iona Abbey. In some ways it seems an incongruous intrusion into

Effigies of the eighth Duke of Argyll and Duchess Ina,
South Transept, Iona Abbey

the medieval building, a classic Victorian funerary monument of the
kind you might expect to find in an English cathedral or rather grand
parish church, redolent of over-blown Victorian piety rather than
austere Columban spirituality. To make matters worse it is made
from marble quarried at Carrara in Tuscany rather than on Iona!
Yet it is a wholly fitting memorial to the man who saved the Abbey.
Duchess Ina, herself a McNeill from Colonsay, wanted her husband
to be buried on Iona but his will specified that he was to be laid to rest
with his ancestors at Kilmun. After his death in Inveraray in 1900,
she removed his heart and preserved it in a pickling jar. It is said to
have been taken to Iona and placed under his effigy in the Abbey
when it was constructed in 1912. An adjoining effigy was placed
over her tomb after her death in 1925. Like her husband, she was
devoted to Argyll and left her mark on its spiritual landscape. It was
at her instigation that the interior of the 'English' side of Inveraray
Church was completely remodelled in 1898 to give it a much more
liturgical atmosphere. The centre of the ceiling was opened to house
an imitation clerestory and side galleries were added, with panels
above decorated with Celtic trumpet patterns in brilliant red, blue
and gold. A huge hexagonal pulpit, modelled on the pulpit in the
Baptistery at Pisa, was made by joiners on the Inveraray estate and

Pulpit, Inveraray Church

an elaborate Communion table on twenty legs was erected in the centre of the sanctuary, which was given a Terrazo floor edged with marble and a high screen with elaborate Gothic tracery and a crested canopy.

The eighth Duke's first wife, Elizabeth, who died suddenly at the age of 34 in 1878, is also commemorated on Iona by a simple Celtic cross erected beside the road to the north of the island a couple of hundred yards or so beyond the Abbey. Their eldest son, John, who married Queen Victoria's daughter, Princess Louise, and spent most of his life as Marquess of Lorne before eventually succeeding his father as the ninth Duke, made his own distinctive contribution to Argyll's spiritual landscape by substantially re-ordering the Mausoleum at Kilmun in 1892. He replaced the slated roof with a cast iron dome with twelve skylights, making the interior surprisingly light and airy and banishing the gloomy and dejected atmosphere that had troubled him when he first visited it. Small vaults were built to contain the coffins of the Dukes of Argyll, each with a marble tablet set in front, with substantial platforms above them providing plenty of room for future burials – although the two most recent Dukes have, in fact, been buried on Inishail (page 242). High on the walls above are fine carvings of the Galley Of Lorne with the inscription on one side 'Their sail is furled, their voyage o'er/Their souls have reached Christ's holy shore' and on the other 'Our race forget not those of yore/God takes the load of life they bore'. Among the objects which were left in the mausoleum after the eighth Duke's burial, and now on display in the excellent museum in Kilmun Church, is a striking sculpture by Princess Louise showing an angel reaching down and holding the outstretched hands of the crucified Christ.

Of the eighth Duke's twelve children with Elizabeth, it was their third daughter, Victoria, who had the most impact on the religious life of Argyll. Born in 1854, she was left a cripple by a severe attack of rheumatism when she was five, necessitating braces being fitted to her legs. Despite her disabilities, which were compounded by a life-threatening lung abscess when she was 14, she spent much time visiting poor families on Iona and often dragged herself to the ruined Abbey, which became her favourite place of retreat and contemplation. A companion recalled: 'We visited the people together, and in the evenings we sat in the ruined cathedral to watch the sunsets.

We used to scramble up on the ledge by the south window and sit there. It was rather difficult for her, but she was not to be daunted. I helped her and there were loose stones below to assist us'. Her biographer, Frances Balfour, waxes lyrical about the central place that the abbey ruins played in Victoria Campbell's faith and in determining the course of her life:

> There she had felt her second consecration. No hands setting her apart had been laid upon her. The wind blowing where it listeth, through the cloistered pillars and arches, had blessed her with the peace which passeth all understanding.
>
> Through the nave, whose floor was the thyme-scented turf, her feet had often led her; till by the window, looking over the translucent seas, she heard the call that bade her pass through many waters to the havens whereunto she was called, and where her work and her people awaited her. [13]

The call that Victoria felt, as she gazed out across the Sound of Mull from her favourite window seat in the ruined abbey one day in 1882, was to devote her life to serving the needs of the inhabitants of Argyll's islands. This she did by spending lengthy periods on Iona, Mull, Colonsay and especially Tiree, setting up sewing and craft classes for women, Sunday schools, Bible-reading groups and soup kitchens. She laboured tirelessly to promote employment and spiritual nourishment among the impoverished crofting communities of the islands she loved and where she often had to be carried round on a sedan chair or even stretcher. A special pew constructed at the back of Inveraray Church so that she could attend services in her wheelchair is still there today, more than a hundred years after she died in 1910, a miniature version of the family pew in the gallery above. She is also commemorated on a plaque added to the base of the Celtic cross in memory of her mother on Iona. Her most poignant memorial, however, is surely to be found in the south choir aisle of Iona Abbey, now set aside as a place for private prayer and meditation, where a small plaque set in the east wall under a window looking out over the Sound of Mull records: 'In this church and by this window Victoria, daughter of George, eighth Duke of Argyll, dedicated her life to the glory of God in the service of the people of these islands'.

17

The Folklore and Celtic Revivals

The Celtic Revival movement which flourished in the late nineteenth and early twentieth centuries had a considerable impact on the spiritual landscape of Argyll that is still being felt today. It left a physical legacy in the church architecture and furnishings of conscious Celticists like Peter MacGregor Chalmers, and in the practice of using replica high-standing crosses as grave markers and war memorials (pages 185–6). Its effect was even greater on the imagined landscape of perceptions and presences. It led to a heightened appreciation of the spiritual nature of Argyll's landscape, as expressed not only in its caves, chapels, stones and crosses but also in its rich folklore and traditions pointing to a strong and continuing attachment to the supernatural, the syncretistic and the mystical.

This new interest in the spiritual dimension of local landscape was considerably stimulated by the rise of antiquarianism and historical scholarship. Argyll featured prominently in pioneering scholarly studies such as William Skene's three-volume *Celtic Scotland* (1876–80) and Joseph Anderson's *Scotland in Early Christian Times* (1881). The appearance of new scholarly texts of the lives of Columba and other saints and of early poems and prayers went hand in hand with serious archaeological surveys of both prehistoric and Christian sites. Important excavations in the Kilmartin Glen were informed by a romantic as well as an academic agenda, with an oak grove being planted around the stone circle at Temple Wood to give it a more Druidic feel. Systematic cataloguing and drawing of early Christian and later medieval carved stones bore fruit in the publication of the first comprehensive study of *The Early Christian Monuments of Scotland* in 1904. Even in this serious work of scholarship the illustrations were presented in such a way as to heighten the mystery and romance of their subjects.

These developments helped to foster a new attitude of respect and concern for the many medieval artefacts which were still under threat from religious prejudice as well as indifference. As late as the early 1800s a zealous Protestant iconoclast journeyed from Jura to Keills and offered the boatman £2 to pull down the free-standing cross which he described as 'a Popish relic'.

Alongside these antiquarian and scholarly endeavours, there was a more spontaneous and personal rediscovery of the spiritual power of Argyll's landscape and a desire to interact with it. A striking example is the painting of Christ's crucifixion done in 1887 in a cave on Davaar Island in Campbeltown Bay by Archibald MacKinnon, a local art teacher. The story goes that he awoke from a dream in which he saw the dying Christ surrounded by the sins of the world and went straight out secretly in a boat to the island to paint the scene. It is not clear how consciously MacKinnon sought to continue the early Christian tradition of decorating and hallowing the walls of remote coastal caves but there is undoubtedly something both primal and medieval about his work. He returned in 1934, the year before he died, to touch up the painting which was covered over in 2006 by a red and black depiction of Che Guevara. It has now been restored and is well worth viewing – though I would not advise venturing out to Davaar Island, as my wife and I did, in a gale force wind, which blew us back against the cliffs. It is important to wait until the tide is fully out, walk across the causeway to the island and then head right and south along the path to the foot of the cliffs overlooking Kildalloig Bay. A lengthy scramble over boulders leads eventually to the cave entrance which is marked by a wooden cross. Once inside the damp and dark cave, it is easy to miss the painting by walking past it. It is half way down on the left hand side next to a smaller painting of an angel with the text underneath: 'I have done all this for thee. What will Thou do for me?'

Undoubtedly the most important influence in the late nineteenth- and early twentieth-century rediscovery and re-imagining of Argyll's spiritual landscape was the booming interest in the region's folklore. The most prolific Scottish folklore collectors in this period were a trio of Campbells who devoted themselves to noting down the traditions, legends and stories of the West Highlands recounted to them by native Gaelic speakers. John Francis Campbell, the old-

Crucifixion painting, Davaar Island

est of the three, known in Gaelic as Iain Og Ile, was was born in Islay in 1821 and died in 1885 in Cannes in the south of France, where he is buried under a replica of the Kildalton Cross. His most important work was *Popular Tales of the West Highlands*, published in four volumes between 1860 and 1862. His pioneering work was continued by Lord Archibald Campbell (1846–1913), second son of the eighth Duke of Argyll and father of the tenth Duke, whose published work included *Records of Argyll: Legends, Traditions and Recollections of Argyllshire Highlanders, collected chiefly from the Gaelic* (1885) and *The Children of the Mist* (1890). Lord Archibald, who also initiated and edited a series entitled *Waifs and Strays of the Celtic Tradition*, was, in turn, assisted greatly by the third of the trio, John Gregorson Campbell (1836–91), who was born in Kingairloch, grew up in Appin and was appointed minister of Tiree and Coll by the eighth Duke of Argyll in 1861. He contributed *The Fians; or stories, poems and traditions of Fionn and His Warrior Band* and *Clan Traditions and Popular Tales of the West Highlands and Islands* to the *Waifs and Strays* series and was the author of two posthumously published books, *Superstitions of the Highlands and Islands of Scotland* (1900), and *Witchcraft and Second Sight in the West Highlands* (1901).

These publications had a huge impact on popular perceptions of Argyll's spiritual landscape. They populated it with fairies, enhancing the romance and reputation of places like Fairies' Hill at Kintraw and the Fairies Wood at Nant near Kilchrenan, and also with glastaigs, kelpies, brownies, hags and other supernatural creatures, many of them of a rather malevolent and frightening disposition. They also revealed the remnants of a strongly syncretistic popular culture in which primal pagan superstitions mingled with Christian beliefs. This was something that had caught the attention of earlier observers. In his first report as Prefect-Apostolic of the Roman Catholic Mission to Scotland in 1660, William Ballentine noted that many of those living in the West Highlands were 'addicted to divination', and much given to foretelling the future, habitually using charms and believing in the existence and power of fairies. After his visit to Iona in 1764, Dr John Walker made a similar observation about the inhabitants: 'They have all of them a remarkable propensity to whatever is marvellous and supernatural. They are famous for the second sight, full of visions seen either by themselves or others; and have many wild and romantick notions concerning religion and invisible things.' The late-nineteenth-century folklorists added an element of wistful nostalgia by suggesting that these supernatural syncretistic beliefs and practices were finally disappearing. Commenting on Bishop Carswell's complaint in 1567 that the people of Argyll were more interested in stories of Fionn MacCumhaill than those of the Bible (page 133), John Gregorson Campbell noted 'the same continued to be the case until very recent times'.[1] Despite being a devout minister of the Kirk, he did not express any unease about these lingering echoes of pre-Christian thought patterns and practices among his parishioners and he never passed judgement on them.

A similarly open and accepting attitude characterized the long line of Argyllshire ministers who collected Gaelic songs, stories and legends. Among the first was John Beaton, minister of Kilninian on Mull, who shared his considerable collection of proverbs, riddles and beliefs concerning death and second sight with the pioneer Welsh folklore collector, Edward Lhuyd, at the end of the seventeenth century. Patrick MacDonald, minister of Kilmore, collected many songs in the late eighteenth century. Significant contributors to the late-nineteenth-century folklore revival included Duncan Campbell, minister of Cumlodden from 1889 to 1901, and James MacDougall, minister of Duror from 1871 to 1906 and author of *Folk tales and fairy lore in Gaelic and English collected from oral tradition* (1910). Pre-eminent among early-twentieth-century folklorists was Kenneth MacLeod, minister of Colonsay and Oronsay from 1917 to 1923 and of Gigha and Cara from 1923 to 1947, who collaborated with Marjorie Kennedy-Fraser in *Songs of the Hebrides* and published two books of West Highland folklore, *The Road to the Isles* (1927) and *The Road to Iona* (1933). He is commemorated in stained-glass windows in Gigha Church and in Iona Abbey where a fine full-length portrait of Columba (page 48) bears the inscription: 'Remember in the Lord the Rev Kenneth MacLeod, DD, Pastor and Bard. So long as the Songs of the Gael are sung, his name will endure, 1873–1955.'

It is significant that ministers were so prominent in the folklore revival. The overall effect of what they and other enthusiasts collected, largely from oral sources, was to reinforce the impression of Argyll as a distinctively, if not uniquely, spiritual region full of mystical experience, supernatural presences and closeness to the next world. Whether this was the result of a conscious agenda on the part of the collectors is a matter keenly disputed by modern scholars, nowhere more so than in the case of by far the most influential figure in this whole movement, Alexander Carmichael (1832–1912), famous for his multi-volume collection of poems, charms, blessings, prayer and incantations translated from Gaelic, *Carmina Gadelica* (Songs of the Gael). Born on Lismore, Carmichael came from a family which had lived on the island for centuries and claimed links to Moluag and direct descent from the fair-haired bishop who had supposedly inspired the building of the Cathedral. He took advantage of his job as an exciseman travelling around the West Highlands and islands checking up on illict whisky distilleries to collect material from crofters, cottars and fisher folk. Although much of his work of noting and collecting, which stretched over more than fifty years, was done beyond Argyll in the Outer Hebrides, he drew on John Gregorson Campbell's research on Tiree and himself gathered material on Mull and on the Argyll mainland.

Carmichael was very clearly part of the Celtic revival movement, influenced by the writings of Rénan and Arnold, having a strong sympathy for the plight of the Highlanders during the Clearances and inclined to idealise and romanticise them. The Gaelic scholar Domhnall Stiùbhart has argued that he approached his work with a conscious agenda, seeking to redeem the Gaels and their traditions from both harsh Highland evangelical Presbyterianism and Lowland prejudice, and to present them as ecumenical, tolerant, and mystical. Stiùbhart sees Carmichael as becoming steadily more interested in the spiritual aspects and character of Gaelic culture and oral tradition. Crucial to this process was a stay that he, his wife and some friends made on Iona in 1878, shortly after the Cathedral and Nunnery had been cleaned up and restored on the orders of the eighth Duke of Argyll. Carmichael was deeply affected by the island's spiritual atmosphere and went on to do considerable research on its place names and on Columba. What had started out for him primarily as archaeological and natural history research turned into a much more spiritually focused project to collect hymns, prayers, charms and blessings. Donald Meek has similarly argued that Carmichael deliberately left out a good deal of dark and disturbing pagan material in favour of hymns and prayers when putting together *Carmina Gadelica* in order to forward his particular agenda, which was to present the Gaels as essentially spiritual beings, ecumenical, tolerant, syncretistic as well as civilised and cultured in character.[2]

In fact, I wonder if Carmichael did distort and shape his material to fit a particular agenda quite as self-consciously and deliberately as these two leading modern Gaelic scholars have suggested. He was very much a child of Argyll, deeply and perhaps even unconsciously imbued with its liberal, eirenic Presbyterianism, its distinctive mix of Catholic and Protestant and pre-Christian and Christian influences, and its strongly mystical bent. He deplored the factious and sectarian nature of some Highland Christianity and in particular the narrow evangelicalism increasingly found within the Free Church in the Western Isles. He noted that the negative confrontational attitude displayed there towards what was perceived to be pagan led local people to clam up in the wake of religious revivals and become frightened to share their traditional charms and incantations. In the very different religious atmosphere of Argyll, by contrast, he found much more openness to and acceptance of primal and pre-Christian traditions. Carmichael's enthusiastic engagement with Argyll's spiritual landscape and legacy, like that of the Church of Scotland ministers who were avid folklore collectors, was certainly as much of a spiritual as a scholarly endeavour, but perhaps it was more intuitive and less self-conscious than has been suggested. He was a pilgrim as much as a researcher, as Kenneth MacLeod observed: 'Year in, year out, for nearly sixty years, Dr. Carmichael was on pilgrimage throughout Gaeldom. To many of us he seemed, both in temperament and in activity, as one of the Iona brethren re-born in the nineteenth century.'[3]

Whether or not a conscious agenda lay behind its compilation, there can be no doubting the huge and lasting impact of *Carmina Gadelica*, the first two volumes of which appeared in 1900. Periodically ransacked for modern paperback anthologies of Celtic prayers and blessings, it has done more than any other work to colour modern perceptions of Celtic Christianity and enhance its popular appeal. Although much of its material derives from the Catholic Outer Isles, there is enough from the predominantly Protestant communities of the Argyll islands and mainland to demonstrate their continuing devotion to Columba and other Celtic saints, Michael and the angels, and their recourse to charms and incantations in the face of the perils and chores of hard and often dangerous lives. A cottar on Mull shared with Carmichael a poem invoking Columba,

Bridget, the Virgin Mary, Peter, Paul, John and Jesus to help in
churning butter. Fishermen on Tiree blessed a cross which they wore
as a charm 'against drowning, against peril, against spells, against
sore wounding, against grisly fright'. A story from Mull told of a
widow with a sick cow who saw Columba rowing home to Iona
with twelve companions – she called on him to come ashore and heal
the cow which he duly did. Also collected on Mull was a charm to
be used in case of chest seizure invoking the power of the sun, moon,
rain, dew, stones, mountains, fenny swamps and great surging seas.

What comes across again and again in the pages of the *Carmina
Gadelica* is an intense sense of the presence and immanence of
the spiritual in the physical and of the sacredness of the land and
the natural world. There are several charms testifying to the healing properties of wild plants like St John's Wort (also known as St
Columba's plant) and bog myrtle. Pearlwort was seen as especially
blessed because it was supposedly the first plant on which Christ
placed his foot when he came to earth, or in other versions when
he rose from the dead. Placed over the door lintel, it kept away evil
spirits. Placed under the right knee of a woman in labour, it had
a soothing effect. Carmichael noted its use as a love philtre, taken
by love-sick maidens as a drink with the juice from its leaves being
pressed into pure water from a sacred well. He specifically remarked
on the use of water from Tobar Bhaodain, St Baodan's Well behind
Ardchattan Priory, for this purpose. An almost pantheistic sense
of God's presence in nature is combined with a primal invocation of
physical elements and appeal to a heroic figure from Argyll's history
– in this case, Somerled – in this waulking song from the Rinns in
Islay:

> O apple tree, may God be with thee,
> May Moon and Sun be with thee,
> May east and west winds be with thee,
> May the great Creator of the elements be with thee,
> May everything that ever existed be with thee,
> May great Somerled and his band be with thee.[4]

Alexander Carmichael died in Edinburgh in 1912. His coffin, draped
with a tartan plaid, was conveyed to Oban by train and thence to

Lismore by the Macbrayne's steamer *Fingal*. He was buried in the island graveyard under a headstone engraved with a Celtic cross with interlacing spirals and the inscription: 'Be my soul in peace with thee, Brightness of the mountains. Valiant Michael, meet thou my soul'. In his obituary, Kenneth MacLeod captured what was perhaps the central element in Carmichael's spiritual character and what made him so clearly an Argyll man:

> He spoke of our cult, of our ways, of our beliefs; he seldom spoke of our 'superstitions' – never, indeed, in his later days. What our race thought as to the relations of man to man, and of man to the world and to the other-worlds, was all sacred in his eyes: the broken cry of the pagan as well as the stately Praise of Iona, the unconscious worship of God through His sun and through His moon, as well as the conscious worship of God through Him who was born of the Virgin Mary. St. Columba, in our great days, grafted the vine on to the oak, — who are we, then, and what are we, that we should be wiser than our best?[5]

If Carmichael and other folklorists were inclined to romanticise and over-spiritualise both the inhabitants and landscape of the West Highlands, they appear paragons of sober restraint in comparison with some of the artists and writers more closely associated with the Celtic Revival whose evocation of a misty spirit land focused particularly on Iona. Among the subjects chosen by John Duncan, the leading artist of the Celtic Renaissance, were Columba on the Hill of the Angels (1904), St Bride being transported by angels from Iona to Bethlehem to become Christ's foster-mother (1913), and Columba bidding farewell to the white milk horse on Iona (1925). William Sharp, the leading Scottish literary figure in the so-called Celtic Twilight movement, who often wrote under the pseudonym Fiona Macleod, invested Argyll as a whole and Iona in particular with a dreamy supernatural aura. His important 1896 collection *Lyra Celtica* brought together many evocative verses about Argyll, including a Loch Fyne boat song, a poem about the Cailleach of Bein-y-Vreich, 'the witch of the Cruachan Ben', and Norman MacLeod's 'Farewell to Fiunary', which invokes Fingal's castle and Ossian's song and was written by the future Caraid nan Gaidheal when he left his father's Manse to begin his studies at Glasgow University. Sharp's extensive writings about Iona in the 1900s were hugely influential in creating the image that has remained to this day of an island of dreams and visions with only the thinnest of boundaries between this world and the next.

Sharp, who penned the poem that begins 'Deep peace of the running wave to you' and is often mistakenly taken to be an ancient Gaelic blessing, was fascinated by pagan–Christian synthesis. His *Spiritual Tales* (1903) included three stories set on Iona with the theme of the closeness of the natural and spiritual worlds. The first began with a long conversation on the shore between Columba and a Druid called Ardan about the ancient and the new wisdom. Afterwards, Ardan chanted a rune to the monks, telling them to listen to the Birds of Sorrow. Early the following morning a robin in Columba's cell sang a lament for Christ and called on the saint to summon all the birds on the island together and bless them. This he did and a great peace descended. The second story told of Columba blessing flies and fishes. The third described his visions of a Druid, a seal man and a moon child bound together in a 'deep peace'. An extended meditation on Iona, published in 1910, focused not on the physical landscape of beaches, rocks and fields, nor even the familiar spiritual landscape of sacred memories and presences, but rather on 'Iona the metropolis of dreams. None can understand it who does not see through its pagan light, its Christian light, its singular blending of paganism and romance and spiritual beauty.' Among the many dreams that Sharp shared, in what became a kind of reverie, was that Christ would come again upon Iona, possibly in the form of a woman. He then turned his attention to Columba: 'I doubt if any other than a Gael can understand him aright. More than any Celt of whom history tells, he is the epitome of the Celt.' What particularly appealed to Sharp about the saint was his visionary and prophetic power: 'He was the first of our race of whom is recorded the systematic use of the strange gift of spiritual foresight, "second-sight".' He also applauded Columba's closeness to the Druids, writing approvingly of the 'half-Pagan, half-Christian basis upon which the Columban Church of Iona stood'. It was, however, to the image of Iona as 'an Isle of Dreams' that he kept returning: 'Here for century after century, the Gael has lived, suffered, joyed, dreamed his impossible, beautiful dream.'[6]

Sharp's work is suffused by a sense of melancholy and by both the image and the reality of death – that theme which pervades so much of the spiritual landscape of Argyll. He and his fellow enthusiasts for the Celtic Twilight movement have been accused of indulging in a kind of cultural necrophilia and preferring the objects of their admiration to be dead or dying. There is a constant sense of longing in his writings for a time that has long gone, and of lament for 'a doomed and passing race'. A poem in *Lyra Celtica*, entitled 'The Sorrow of Delight', echoes George Matheson in its statement that, 'Joy that is clothed in shadow is the joy that is not dead'. Sharp makes much of the 'tragic gloom' which colours both ancient and contemporary Scoto-Celtic poetry and notes that 'the Spirit of the Gaelic earth does not make for mirth .... A strange melancholy characterises the genius of the Celtic race.' He ends his book on Iona with intimations of death but also of resurrection:

The Celt has at last reached his horizon. There is no shore beyond. He knows it. This has been the burden of his song since Malvina led the blind Oisìn to his grave by the sea. 'Even the Children of Light must go down into the darkness.' But this apparition of a passing race is no more than the fulfilment of a glorious resurrection. The Celt falls, but his spirit rises in the heart and the brain of the Anglo-Celtic peoples, with whom are the destinies of generations to come.[7]

William Sharp died in 1905 at the age of 50 in Sicily. His grave within Castello di Maniace is marked by a replica Iona cross.

18

Inveraray Bell Tower and Two Other Memorials to the First World War

Among Argyll's more bizarre tourist attractions is the bell tower at All Saints Church, Inveraray. Incongruously Episcopalian in the way that it dominates the skyline of this most Presbyterian town, it was built by Niall, the tenth Duke of Argyll, as a memorial to Campbells killed in the First World War.

Duke Niall was steeped in the legends and folklore of Argyll and unusually open to supernatural experience. He claimed to see the Galley of Lorne, crewed by the spirits of his ancestors, passing above Loch Fyne on its aerial journey to the original Campbell heartland of Loch Awe. On summer evenings he would often go down to the River Aray and blow a horn to summon 'the wee people'. He firmly believed in fairies, believing them to be 'the spirits of a race of men who ages ago lived in earth mounds, which are what they frequent' and describing them as 'little green things which peer at you from behind trees, as squirrels do, and disappear into the earth'.[1]

Unusually for a Campbell, he was a strong Episcopalian, worshipping from 1914 to 1949 in All Saints, which had been built in 1886 for Amelia, the second wife of the eighth Duke of Argyll. As well as the bells, he gave the church a reproduction of a painting of the face of Christ by Gabriel Max based on the supposed imprint on Veronica's handkerchief. It has a curious haunting quality with the eyes sometimes seeming open and sometimes closed. The bells were cast in Loughborough in 1921. The lorry bringing them to Inveraray stalled twice on the Rest and be Thankful and the bells had to be unloaded and left on the roadside provoking amazement among passers by and local shepherds. They were initially hung in a small Bell House at the east end of the church. The 128-foot tower was not completed until 1931. The Duke himself assisted in its construction by transporting stones in a wheelbarrow and carrying them up the steps of the tower.

Each of the bells has an individual dedication – one to Mary and the others to the Celtic saints Moluag, Columba, Mund, Brendan, Maelrubha, Blaan, Brigid, Molaise and Murdouch (about whom I can find out nothing). Campanologists come from near and far to ring them. The tower, which is open to the public throughout the summer, is well worth visiting – although too rapid an ascent or descent of the 176 steps in the narrow circular staircase can induce giddiness. A display in the ground-floor chamber records the Duke's musings on this very personal project, which has added another land-mark to Argyll's spiritual landscape about which he felt so deeply:

> These walls thus built will for ages remind the passing traveller of those hid battlements of Eternity, from which, as a poet says, ever and anon a trumpet sounds, and rifting clouds unveil the watching Holy Ones – the cohorts of the Blest – the Celtic Saints and those of all climes and tongues – who, having passed through that change called Death by the World of Mortality, now man the bulwarks and bastions of the City Celestial in the Kingdom of Tír na nÓg, which is the Land of the Ever Young.

The death of Duke Niall in Inveraray in 1949 was accompanied by many strange happenings. A large number of birds invaded the castle, music was heard in various parts of the house, said by those who heard it to come from 'The Little Harper', and mysterious lights appeared reflected in the waters of Loch Fyne. A dark and indistinct figure was seen peering through the glass door in the entrance porch to the castle but when it was opened there was no one there. It was said to be Columba come to take the Duke home. The last Duke of Argyll to be buried at Kilmun, he is described on a memorial plaque in All Saints Church, Inveraray as 'To the faith ever faithful, to his country and clan most loyal, a firm friend rich in knowledge of antiquity and history, steeped in the lore of the land where he lived and fittingly commemorated by the peal of bells which he caused

The Argyll Mausoleum, Kilmun Church. Duke Niall was the last Campbell chief to be buried here.

to be set up in this place to sound the praises of God over loch and glen'.

Two other memorials designed to commemorate the First World War deserve mention, although one was never built and the other is now in a somewhat derelict state. James Salmon, a Glasgow architect, drew up designs for a large memorial on the esplanade in Campbeltown made up of a circle of stones reminiscent of the henge monuments found in the Kilmartin Valley, with a huge Galley of Lorne resting on a triumphal arch in the centre. Salmon intended its construction to be a communal effort, noting on his drawing of what he called the 'Celtic Circle' that every man in Campbeltown should bring at least one stone for the dyke and every woman a basketful of earth for the mound. He also suggested that the larger stones could be brought by soldiers representing various regiments. His ambitious plans were rejected in favour of a more restrained but still impressive tall, chunky obelisk with a rugged stone cross in its arched recess, designed by A.N. Paterson.

Perhaps the most unusual war memorial in Argyll is the Tree Cathedral planted in 1921 by Alexander Mackay, the then owner of Glencruitten Estate on the eastern outskirts of Oban just beyond the golf course. Set in the middle of thick woodland and modelled on St Andrews Cathedral, it is laid out on an east–west axis complete with cloisters and chapter house. Double hedges form the outside walls, the pillars are represented by narrow yew trees, the altar cross and choir stalls are fashioned out of clipped golden yew and a Japanese maple forms the great East Window. Mixed heathers were planted in the nave and transepts to give the effect of a mosaic floor although these have now been replaced by grass. The Cathedral is consecrated ground and members of the Mackay family are buried there.

The Tree Cathedral is prominently featured in *Morvern Callar*, a novel written in 1996 by Alan Warner, who was born and grew up near Oban. He relocates it to the Pass of Brander on the north bank of Loch Awe near the Cruachan power station and describes it being used for weddings and baptisms in the summer. The Tree Church, as it is called in the book, is a recurrent symbol of hope and redemption in an otherwise very bleak story. On the final page, Morvern Callar, a supermarket checkout operator whose boyfriend has committed suicide, staggers through the snow to pray there. Here is an interesting modern engagement with, and re-appropriation of, Argyll's spiritual landscape in what is overall a very secular and nihilistic novel. A public right of way runs through the Glencruitten woods and there are currently plans to improve access and restore the Cathedral of Trees as a living sacred space open to the local community and to pilgrims and visitors.

19

Two Twentieth-century Monuments to Columba

Columba's continuing presence has always been keenly sensed in Argyll. In recent times it has seldom been felt more intensely than in the early 1930s when it helped to inspire two projects that have had a major impact on both the spiritual and physical landscape of the region: the building of the Roman Catholic Cathedral in Oban and the restoration of the buildings around Iona Abbey. Both were long-term projects – work on the Cathedral began in 1932 and was not complete until 1959, while restoration of the Abbey buildings started in 1935 and was finished in 1965.

Little has been said in this book about the Roman Catholic presence in Argyll in the three centuries following the Reformation. As is made clear in John Watts' excellent recent study, *A Record of Generous People*, it was very small, as it still is (page 6), and for much of the time largely hidden and underground. A survey at the end of the seventeenth century showed that only Col and Tiree had a significant Catholic population. There are occasional reminders in the landscape of the period of harsh penal laws, like the stone with a hollow in it at the foot of Dun Mhuirich beside the road between Tayvallich and Keills. Known as 'the priest's stone', it is said to have been used for baptisms by itinerant priests. The Catholic population was boosted by immigration in the later nineteenth century: Irish immigrants brought over to work in the quarry at Bonawe funded the building of the Catholic church in Taynuilt. The restoration of the Scottish dioceses in 1878 finally enabled the Roman Catholic church to establish a full and public presence. Largely on the basis of its transport links to the Catholic strongholds of Barra, Eriskay, South Uist, Moidart and Arisaig, Oban was chosen as the seat for the bishopric of Argyll and the Isles, which had just 16 priests, half of whom were too aged or infirm to carry out duties. Initially a holiday house on the Esplanade, used as a summer retreat by Jesuit priests, served as the episcopal base and place of worship, but in 1886 a corrugated iron building known as the 'Tin Cathedral' was erected with the financial support of the third Marquess of Bute, who insisted that it provide daily sung Mass and set up a choir school next door. By 1932 enough money had been raised to start building a proper cathedral around the iron one which was no longer water-tight. Construction work had to be halted several times because of financial problems but the cathedral was worth waiting for. It is one of the most imposing and dignified church buildings in Argyll.

The architect for St Columba's Cathedral, Oban, was Giles Gilbert Scott, best known for the Anglican Cathedral in Liverpool, Battersea Power Station and for designing Britain's traditional red telephone boxes. The first Cathedral anywhere in the world to be built entirely of granite, its restrained Gothic exterior provides a prominent land-mark on the seafront for those entering Oban harbour by ferry. Inside, the impression is of lofty simplicity and austerity. Of all the Roman Catholic places of worship that I know, it is the most Presbyterian – even a Covenanter would feel at home in it. There are no stained-glass windows and the only statues are positioned discretely at the very back of the nave. Appropriately given its dedi-cation, Columba is depicted at various points – twice on the reredos as well as in the dramatic painting by Nathaniel Westlake hanging over the entrance door, which shows him calmly standing in a boat as he is banished down Loch Ness by pagan druids. Woven into the main altar cloth in Gaelic is the verse from Psalm 34 that Adomnán described Columba copying just before his death: 'Those who seek the Lord shall not lack for anything'.

Columba's stock was particularly high in the 1930s. A biography by Lucy Menzies, published in 1920, inspired a rash of hagio-graphical studies and the lingering impact of William Sharp's work was still being felt as Iona came to be seen as an ever more sacred and holy place. Anna Buchan, writing under her nom de plume O. Douglas in 1933, had the heroine of a novel describe Columba's island as 'a fairyland, a place to be left to dream, where nothing could be too wonderful to happen'.[1] In fact, the island was about to

Painting of Columba being sent down Loch Ness, St Columba's Cathedral, Oban

be transformed through the vision and energy of George MacLeod, who almost single-handedly set in train the project which brought it back to being the base for a Christian community as influential as Columba's original monastery.

MacLeod was a scion of the great Morvern dynasty of ministers. His grandfather was Norman Macleod of the Barony, his great-grandfather 'Caraid nan Gaidheal' of Campbeltown and his great-great grandfather the first MacLeod minister of Morvern. Although he did not himself grow up in Argyll, he was deeply conscious of this ancestry and it informed his theological outlook, which combined evangelical simplicity, muscular Christianity and mysticism. Ron Ferguson rightly starts his fine biography of MacLeod in Fiunary and it was to the manse there, given to him by the Church of Scotland when it was no longer needed for the Morvern parish minister, that he often returned in his old age.

MacLeod, who holidayed on Iona for a month every year, became increasingly convinced through the early 1930s that a project focused on rebuilding the living quarters of the Benedictine Abbey could foster the community spirit which he felt was desperately needed as a counter to the prevailing individualism of the age. In 1935 he put a paper to the Iona Cathedral Trustees proposing that skilled craftsmen and Divinity students who were candidates for the ministry should collaborate on restoring the buildings with a view to making them a Church of Scotland seminary which would incul-cate in all ministers the values of brotherhood and communal life. His hope was that candidates for the Church of Scotland ministry would spend six months of each of their three years of training on Iona. The Trustees agreed to his proposal and in the summer of 1938 MacLeod took out his first party of students and craftsmen, several of them unemployed shipyard workers from his parish in Govan, Glasgow. These summer work camps went on until 1965, by which time the cloisters, refectory, chapter house and dormitories had all been rebuilt.

George MacLeod exemplified an approach that I have suggested has been very prominent in the religious history of Argyll in which the past spiritual landscape is appropriated, romanticised and adapted for a new use. He had a passionate commitment to Columba and what his monastic community stood for. Ringing in his ears was the prophecy supposedly uttered by the saint shortly before his death:

Iona of my heart, Iona of my love,
Instead of monks' voices there shall be lowing of cattle:
But ere the world comes to an end
Iona shall be as it was.

MacLeod was a shameless romantic and had no qualms about inventing stories about Columba or using other people's phrases without attribution as though they were his own, as he famously did with the English mystic Evelyn Underhill's observation that Iona was 'a very thin place'. He was also a deeply faithful and prayerful man, whose beautifully crafted prayers, juxtaposing references to stones and angels, express the theme of finding the spiritual in the material that we have already encountered in the devotional writings of George Matheson and the eighth Duke of Argyll.[2]

Despite his energy and charisma, George MacLeod did not get quite what he wanted on Iona. When the Abbey buildings were finally finished and ready for occupation in 1965, the Iona Com-munity, which he had set up in 1939 to foster brotherhood among his all-male team of ministers and manual workers, voted against his seminary plan and chose rather to make the Abbey a place for retreats, conferences and training. This is essentially what it has remained ever since. Although the Community, which now numbers around 270 members and over 1800 associate members of both sexes and many different denominations, has its headquarters in Glasgow, Iona remains its spiritual home. Hundreds of guests come every year to stay for a week in the Abbey or in the MacLeod Centre, built on the hill above it in 1988, to focus on issues of justice and peace. Thousands more visitors to the islands attend services in the Abbey led by a resident group of staff and volunteers.

Iona Abbey remains a living Christian hub focused on building community, engaged spirituality and creative worship. Visitors sometimes express surprise and disappointment that there are no cowled monks walking quietly around the cloisters. Instead the buildings are filled by boisterous young volunteers from all over the world who come to work as cooks, cleaners, sacristans and maintenance workers to support the ministry of hospitality. Guests staying at the Abbey and the MacLeod Centre share the common life by helping in washing up, cutting vegetables and cleaning the toilets. Accommodation is basic, although not as basic as at the Community's third island centre, Camas Tuath, an old fishing hut on the Ross of Mull, which is used for youth groups. Morning and evening worship in the Abbey Church flows naturally into and from the life and work of the day. The atmosphere of evangelical simplicity, practical muscular Christianity and devotion tinged with open-minded mysticism is one that Macleod's Morvern forbears, and indeed Columba himself, would recognise and approve.

20

An Episcopalian Traveller and a Free Church Pilgrim

A spate of romantic travel writing about Argyll in the early twentieth century presented it as a Celtic dreamland, full of archaeological and historical interest as well as misty spirituality. Two writers were particularly prolific and influential: Mary Donaldson, who was born in Croydon in 1876 and moved to Ardnamurchan in 1927, and Thomas Ratcliffe Barnett, who was born in Renfrewshire in 1868 and served as a United Free Church minister in Edinburgh.

M.E.M Donaldson, as she always styled herself, made long expeditions on foot through the Western Highlands in the 1920s, wearing distinctive clothes made to her own specifications to ease mobility over rough and rocky terrain whilst remaining resistant to the weather and the midges, and pulling behind her 'Green Maria', a leather-covered wheeled wooden box containing photographic equipment and her 'night and toilet requirements.' Her very popular *Wanderings in the Western Highlands and Islands* (1923) and *Further Wanderings, Mainly in Argyll* (1926) recounted, as expressed in the subtitle of the latter volume, 'history, traditions, ecclesiology, archaeology, romance, present conditions, crofters' life, wild life, humour, literature, Folklore &c'. They are still well worth reading for their detailed historical, topographical and antiquarian information. She also wrote more romantic volumes, such as *The Isles of Flame, a Romance of the Inner Hebrides in the Days of Columba* (1913).

Although brought up in a strictly Presbyterian household, Mary Donaldson forsook the faith of her childhood and became an enthusiastic Episcopalian. Although not a fan of the clan Campbell, she conceded that 'all the Campbells I have met have invariably been delightful enough to be MacDonalds. I like to think they were descendants of the three Campbells who fought for the Prince at Culloden'.[1] She was very critical of Presbyterianism's hold over Argyll, and especially its influence on architecture, complaining that Lochgilphead, Inveraray, Port Ellen, Tobermory and other towns

> have been erected on strict Calvinistic principles to enter a pro-test, as permanent as may be, against the natural beauty of the situation. This is accomplished by building the most grimly and gauntly ugly structures to devastate, as much as man possibly can, the God-given scenery. The angels must weep as they look down on these evidences of man's perversity which so nearly succeeds in destroying every vestige of the loveliness so lavishly bestowed by the Creator's hand.[2]

T. Ratcliffe Barnett first took to walking through the West High-lands to provide therapeutic release from the harrowing experience of ministering to wounded and shell-shocked soldiers during the First World War. He made much of nature's redemptive, curative powers and was influential in developing the idea of the spirituality of landscape understood in terms of both natural and human features which he felt could not be separated. His 1933 book, *The Land of Lorne*, which like many of his published works went into numerous editions, presented Argyll as first and foremost a spiritual landscape 'full of places of pilgrimage'. Alongside detailed descriptions of its saints, crosses and stones, he also explored its supernatural and otherworldly presences.

Barnett identified and emphasised many of the features in Argyll's spiritual landscape that have already been noted in this book. He made much of the theme of death, writing that 'from end to end the whole of Argyll is strewn with castles of the dead', while acknow-ledging that there were certain special places where he felt a sense of the presence of the dead particularly acutely:

> I never loiter in Appin but I keep looking over my shoulder. For there is still an aura of ghosts about its glens and hills and a feeling along its shores that the dead are watching to see if the living are ever going to redd up some old scores that have never been settled.[3]

He devoted a whole chapter of his book to ghosts and another chapter to auras, freits and second sight. Like Duke Niall of Argyll, he was very open to encounters with fairies, as in this description of his experience while standing on top of the chambered cairn of Achnacree near Benderloch:

> It was a stifling afternoon in August. It seemed to me that in the silence the music of the Wee Folk, whether they were fairies or tiny Picts, came floating up out of the darkness. It was a plaintive sort of music, with a dropping cadence, and a tragic sharpening of the note. Those who were fairy-glamoured in the old, old days were often lured down into these earthen dwellings and were seen no more. Being no longer fairy-glamoured, I crept away on tiptoe through the trees, and over the moss for home.[4]

It is striking that Barnett, the Free Church minister, was much more open than Donaldson, the Episcopalian, to supernatural presences and experiences. While she could see only Calvinist ugliness in Inveraray, he found a very different quality in the Campbells' planned town:

> Inveraray is still half Fairy Burgh and half Real Town, with the bird-haunted woods thrown round her, and the waves of Loch Fyne lappering about her doorsteps. In the evening the woods are full of twilight wonders, and when the full moon rides high above Duniquoich the glades of Glen Shire are peopled with spirits of wandering men who have come back to visit the shielings and fight their battles over again.[5]

These may seem strange words to come from the pen of a Free Church minister in the 1930s, but the fact was that this evangelical Presbyterian could identify totally with Argyll's mystical spirituality. In many ways Barnett was a very prescient and forward-looking commentator. He called for the preservation of the stones at places like Keills, 'for winds and weeds and weather are playing havoc with these relics of the past which can never be replaced'. He envisaged his travels through Argyll as a pilgrimage and spiritual journey rather than just the wanderings of a tourist or antiquarian. His last and most poignant book, entitled *Scottish Pilgrimage in the Land of Lost Content* and published in 1942, four years before his death, has several chapters on Argyll. As will be discussed in Chapter 22, preservation and pilgrimage are two of the most important current themes and concerns in terms of the management and promotion of Argyll's spiritual landscape. For that, Ratcliffe Barnett must take some of the credit, as he must too for that sense of wistfulness, suggested in the title of his valedictory volume, which so often colours how that landscape is perceived.

The Keills Cross, which Barnett called for to be better preserved. It now stands in the shelter of the re-roofed Keills Chapel.

21

Craig Lodge and Other New Religious Communities

In the constant process of reconfiguring Argyll's spiritual landscape new religious communities spring up, consciously relating to past traditions and existing features of the landscape. Some have already been mentioned, like the Living Stones Christian Centre in Kilmartin (page 38). Inevitably, Iona remains a favourite place for setting up new religious communities. In 1997 a Catholic House of Prayer was opened in a prominent position just off the track that leads up the hill from the village. Known as Cnoc a'Chalmain, or the Hill of the Dove, it comprises residential accommodation and an oratory where Mass can be celebrated and where the Blessed Sacrament is reserved, providing a permanent Roman Catholic base on the island alongside the Episcopalian Bishop's House, the Church of Scotland Parish Church and the ecumenical Iona Community centres in the Abbey and the MacLeod centre. The Findhorn Foundation has a retreat house called Traigh Bhan on the north of the island.

The largest and most flourishing of the recently established religious communities in Argyll is Craig Lodge Family House of Prayer, based close to Dalmally, that ancient place of desert retreat, and just over two miles from St Conan's Kirk. Occupying an old hunting lodge on the north side of the River Orchy once owned by the Breadalbane Campbells, it annually welcomes over 2,000 guests, some of whom come for guided retreats and others simply to take a break in the peaceful surroundings.

The House of Prayer is the result of the vision of Calum MacFarlane-Barrow, whose father was an Episcopal priest in Argyll for nineteen years before converting to Roman Catholicism in 1928, and his wife Mary-Anne. He bought the Lodge in 1977 to run as a guest house, but a series of visits through the 1980s by members of the family to Medjugorje, the village in Bosnia-Herzegovina where six young people experienced apparitions of the Virgin Mary, resolved him to turn it into a house of prayer and retreat, which he did in 1988. The ethos of Craig Lodge is very much based on that of Medjugorje. Calum Macfarlane Barrow describes its particular mission and charism as being 'to share the messages delivered by Our Lady and put them into everyday life by encouraging one another to grow in holiness'. The text of the latest monthly message, which still comes from the Virgin to one of the original visionaries, Marija Pavlovic, is posted on the dining room wall. There are numerous statues of Mary in the house and grounds and the style of worship in the Chapel is intense and charismatic, with much emphasis on the gifts of the Holy Spirit.

The Craig Lodge community is made up of fourteen members drawn from five families who live and work locally and ten young volunteers who contract to come for a year, living a simple monastic-style life that involves a mixture of prayer, Scriptural study and manual work, giving up alcohol, smoking and exclusive relationships, and having limited access to television and the internet in order to open themselves more to God and to others. The sprawling lodge, which can accommodate around forty overnight guests, hosts regular guided weekend retreats and also welcomes those who come predominantly from Glasgow and the Central Belt to enjoy the scenery and peaceful atmosphere. Guests are free to join in the twice-daily worship as much or as little as they wish. The Community is increasingly involved in educational work throughout Argyll and the Isles, and organises annual youth and adult pilgrimages to Iona.

Craig Lodge is very much in the van of contemporary movements across the church variously known as fresh expressions, modern monasticism and lay-led renewal. In many ways it provides a modern version of the monastic ideal, which both Columba and Conan implanted on Loch Awe in the seventh century. Ruth Black, who runs the retreat house, believes that it very much follows in that tradition and that its location is far from being coincidental. It is used as a testing ground for potential vocations by several religious orders. During one of my own stays there while researching this book, I met a young man from Finland who was working as a volunteer, having been sent by the Franciscan Friars of Renewal to help discern whether he should join them.

In the true tradition of Celtic monasticism, it is far from being a remote rural retreat unconnected with the world and isolated from its problems. A simple shed behind the main lodge buildings serves as the base for Mary's Meals, the charity set up by Magnus Macfarlane-Barrow in 2002, which provides a daily meal for over 750,000 children in the developing world, so enabling them to attend school when they would otherwise have to work. A pattern of engagement in and retreat from the world is one of the ways in which Craig Lodge continues to espouse the distinctive practices of Irish monasticism as pioneered by Columba and his followers across Argyll. Others include the deep undergirding of regular prayer, the emphasis on evangelical witness and the prevailing atmosphere of structured, ordered and disciplined living.

Calum Macfarlane-Barrow, himself a Campbell of Kilmory on his mother's side and deeply imbued with Argyll's spiritual history and heritage, likes to think that the Columban monastery of Cella Diuni was in fact located just a few miles north east of his own new community in the foothills of Beinn Eunaich which, according to some authorities, takes its name from Adomnán. He is also deeply conscious of Craig Lodge's proximity to one of the main pilgrim routes to Iona and is very keen that it should have an important role as a hostel and retreat for those walking or cycling the projected Iona – St Andrews pilgrim way, which he would ideally like to see routed over the hills around the north of Ben Cruachan to avoid the narrow and busy Pass of Brander before plunging down into Taynuilt and then going on to Oban via Glen Lonan, another ancient pilgrim trail.

Craig Lodge sits very naturally in Argyll's spiritual landscape, not just in geographical terms but also because of its evangelical simplicity and its hardy muscular Christianity. Although it is very Catholic and very charismatic, there is an openness, a gentleness and an emphasis on healing, which accords with the region's liberal mystical traditions. Calum Macfarlane-Barrow has, indeed, made a significant new addition to Argyll's spiritual landscape by establishing a Way of the Cross up the steep hillside behind the former hunting lodge. Its fourteen stations lead up to a large white-painted wooden ringed Celtic cross. Planning regulations only permit the cross to be erected for 28 days every year and for the rest of the time it lies on the grass. When the cross is hauled to its upright position it can be seen for miles around, including by the those making their way along the busy A85 tourist route to Oban.

A few hundred yards behind the cross, standing over 1,000 feet high but sheltered from the full blast of the wind in a dip of the ground, a beehive cell has been constructed out of rocks gathered from the surrounding hills, and covered with grass. Several of the Macfarlane Barrow family and other members of the community have spent a night there on their own sleeping on its bare wooden bench. This cell, modelled on those found on Eileach an Naoimh in the Garvellachs, links directly back to the Irish-inspired monasticism of 1,200 years ago. Indeed, it summons up even more ancient associations, commanding a superb view over Loch Awe with its fairy and Fingalian sites as well as its early Christian monasteries, graveyards and chapels and of Ben Cruachan with its primal power as the dwelling place of the Cailleachan. Here is a new living link to Argyll's deep and many layered spiritual legacy and history.

Beehive cell in the hills above Craig Lodge

Other recently established communities are on a much smaller scale. In a remote part of Morvern, towards the end of a narrow road from Acharacle that runs alongside the River Shiel, an old boat house has been converted into a small Orthodox chapel, filled with icons of Finnan, Moluag and Columba. It is the base of the Community of St Finnan and St Nicholas, established in the mid 1990s by Father Christopher Wallace under the Ecumenical Patriarch in the Russian Orthodox tradition. Combining his priestly duties with his work researching parasitology on fish farms, Father Christopher celebrates the Liturgy in English there at least once a month to a small congregation. He sees Finnan, who is said to have lived for some time as a hermit on the Green Isle in nearby Loch Shiel, as a direct inspiration. There is also a project to establish an Orthodox monastery in the grounds of Kilnian Parish Church at Torloisk on Mull, which was built in 1755 and abandoned for worship in the mid 1980s. Father Seraphim Aldea, a Romanian monk who studied in England, hopes to build a nunnery there dedicated to the Celtic Saints, but there has been some local opposition to his plans.

Although it is perhaps not quite a new religious community, it is worth mentioning the creation by the Church of Scotland of a new Presbytery of Argyll in 2004. Formed by uniting the Presbyteries of South Argyll, Lorn & Mull and Dunoon, its bounds are similar to those of the old Synod of Argyll and more or less coincide with the former County of Argyll, although excluding the parishes of Morvern and Ardnamurchan, which remain in Lochaber Presbytery, and including the island of Bute plus a small area of Perthshire and Stirlingshire around Crianlarich. It embraces over one hundred parishes, the great majority of which are now conjoined in linkages and a total of 155 ecclesiastical buildings (including manses). The parishes of Barra and South Uist have recently joined the Presbytery and Luss is keen to come in.

It is good that Argyll is now one unit as far as the Church of Scotland is concerned. This has encouraged a deeper consciousness of its particular religious heritage, as reflected in this statement written by David Kellas, minister of Kilfinan and first Moderator of the new Presbytery, and read out at its first meeting held in Inveraray Church on 2 March 2004:

We take into our care the islands of the West: Iona, where Columba first planted the tree of life; Lismore where Moluag laboured whose staff still recalls us to the Way, the Truth and the Life; the great isles of Mull, Islay, Jura, Bute and all the little islands. We take in blessing the noble lands of Dalriada, first Kingdom of the Scots, of Lorn, of Kintyre, of Cowal. We embrace parishes rich in the history of the mighty men of old, rich in the tradition of men and women of faith down the ages. All around us the ancient stones look down, a remembrance that the search began many thousands of years ago. We offer to the men and women of Argyll Jesus Christ, the Word of God, the end of our search and the start of a wonderful journey.[1]

The ancient stones look down
Above: Ruins of St Fillans
Chapel, Green Isle
Below: Early Christian carved
stone on Inishail

22

Preservation, Pilgrimage and Painting

What is happening to Argyll's spiritual landscape today? As always, it is being refashioned and reimagined, especially, perhaps, through preservation and conservation projects, pilgrimage initiatives and the creative activities of artists.

The material heritage of Argyll has never been better cared for. Conservation projects are preserving important objects and sites and providing better access and interpretation, allowing more people to enjoy and gain an appreciation of them than ever before. Carved stones and crosses have been brought in out of the wind and rain and put under shelter. New museums and interpretation centres have sprung up across the region. The Kilmartin House Museum, established in 1994 in the old manse, where my mother recalled going for her church membership classes, provides a superb insight into the religious, cultural and political atmosphere of the surrounding valley of ghosts. The legacy of Columba and his successors on Iona can now be much better understood thanks to Historic Scotland's installation of new interpretation panels around the Abbey and refurbishment of the museum in the old infirmary in 2013. The latest addition to Argyll's museums is the imaginatively conceived display on the Campbells in the entrance area of Kilmun Church, and the adjacent Argyll Mausoleum opened to the public for the first time in 2015. The next, as and when funding allows, may well be the Lamont Burial Asle adjoining Kilfinan Church, which is due to be refurbished and reopened to house and display the important collection of stones there. Alongside these conservation projects, ruined and abandoned churches have been rebuilt, a good example being St Columba's Roman Catholic Chapel at Drimnin at the end of the Morvern peninsula, built in 1837, abandoned in the 1930s and restored between 2008 and 2012 as a venue for worship, music and art.

It is all very different from the pilfering and casual re-appropriation that so often characterised the approach of past generations to sacred buildings. There is a new attitude of reverence towards historic remains. Indeed heritage has almost become the new religion. There is also what amounts to a huge new academic industry involved in recording, classifying and interpreting what remains of the past. Not everyone is happy with these developments. Some feel that something has been lost with this new focus and that by subjecting ancient stones to sophisticated X-ray analysis and displaying them in beautifully lit glass cases, we are robbing them of their raw spiritual power and reducing them to being, in the words of one of George MacLeod's prayers, merely 'fit subjects for an analyst's table'. Frank Walker complains that the re-roofing and restoration of Keills Chapel has turned a place of worship into a storage shed.[1]

The re-roofed Keills Chapel and replica high-standing Cross

I can understand these concerns but I believe they are misplaced. The chapels at Keills and Kilmory had long ceased to be places of worship before they were roofed over to house and protect the stones which lay around them. It may be that those chapels which are still in a ruined and roofless state speak more romantically and eloquently of a long-gone age of faith, but the stones that are now so well preserved and interpreted retain their spiritual power and message. Some of the structures built to house them are undoubtedly less aesthetically pleasing than others – the bus shelter-like edifice at Kilberry and the hut at Saddell spring to mind – but if they were not protected, the ancient stones of Argyll would simply deteriorate and not speak to us at all. It is true that their witness is perhaps most effective and eloquent when they are sited in places still being used for worship, as with the crosses at the back of Kilmartin Parish Church and the ancient fonts in Achahoish and Lochgoilhead churches. But it is surely much better to re-use church buildings no longer required for worship to display and explain the surrounding spiritual landscape rather than let them rot away or turn them into domestic dwellings.

There is, in fact, much to be said for those churches which are still used for worship doing more to make themselves places which explore and interpret the spiritual heritage of their area. This is already being done imaginatively in some of Argyll's more remote churches. The back wall of Kilchattan Church on Luing is covered with information panels on Celtic saints and nearby holy places such as the Garvellachs. The nearby Kilbandon Church on Seil has an excellent video presentation that visitors can activate to gain a sense of the religious history of the island as well as of the church's present mission. There is scope for other churches to adopt similar creative strategies to enhance their evangelistic outreach by linking it to the legacy of the past. The Gaelic half of Inveraray Parish Church, for example, could become a museum of Argyll's Christian history. Kilmun Church has shown how part of a church building can be taken over and used as a museum without in any way detracting from its sanctity or suitability for worship.

Argyll is full of parish churches still functioning as places of worship, even if only on the basis of occasional Sundays and with congregations barely into double figures. They are for the most part, thank God, open all the time. Some are making a real attempt to attract visitors by providing a ministry of hospitality, like St Conan's Kirk which opened a tea room in its gatehouse in 2014. Nearly all these churches attract more tourists through the week than worshippers on Sunday mornings. There is a huge opportunity to turn these tourists into pilgrims, giving them a spiritual experience that will deepen or challenge their faith. It is beautifully expressed in a notice on the door of Christ Church Episcopal Church in Lochgilphead: 'May all who come to this place as Visitors find here the presence and love of God and leave here as Pilgrims'.

There is an extremely thin dividing line between tourism and pilgrimage, as has been recognised by the travel industry, which has recently identified what it calls 'faith tourism' as one of its fastest-growing sectors. Several places in Argyll have long been expert in bridging this gap, perhaps nowhere more so than Iona. Research that I have undertaken there suggests that most of those who come for a week at the Abbey, the MacLeod centre, Bishop's House or the Catholic House of Prayer see themselves very clearly as pilgrims with a committed religious motivation. Others visiting the island for a few days and staying in hotels or bed and breakfast places prefer the terms spiritual seekers, adventurers or wanderers. Those who come to Iona just for a day-trip mostly describe themselves as tourists. They can become pilgrims, by sharing in the Abbey's daily prayers for peace and justice at noon, finding themselves moved by the imagery of a window or one of the high-standing crosses, or challenged by one of the banners or displays reflecting a current campaign of the Iona Community.

Pilgrims gathering at the foot of St Martin's Cross, Iona

There are other, more overt pilgrim experiences to be had on Iona. Several groups regularly make pilgrimages there. Among the hardiest and most adventurous are those who take part in Scottish Cross, an annual walk to the island during Holy Week. In the Roman Catholic tradition, but open to all, it began in 1997 and has grown steadily since. Pilgrims stay in village halls and youth hostels along the way, carrying a cross and arriving on Iona on Easter Sunday. Since 2011 the preferred route has been to start at Corran on Loch Linhe and walk via Glenfinnan and Acharacle to Kilchoan, crossing by ferry to Tobermory and then on across Mull via Salen, Pennyghael and Bunessan to Fionphort. The Orthodox Friends of Iona have made several pilgrimages and there is an annual Catholic youth pilgrimage from Craig Lodge, which in 2014 involved twenty-six children and ten helpers. Every Tuesday in summer there is a six-mile pilgrimage around the island itself, led by Iona Community staff and volunteers and open to all. It departs from St Martin's Cross at 10am and takes in many of the key features of Iona's spiritual landscape, including the nunnery, Martyrs' Bay, the Hill of the Angels and the Bay of the Coracle, where participants are invited to pick up two pebbles from the shore, one to cast into the sea as a token of a burden of which they want to rid themselves, and the other to take home as a symbol of a new resolve or intention. The pilgrimage later goes on to a supposed hermit's cell made up of a circle of stones in the lee of the hill known as Dun-I. In fact it is a relatively modern sheep fold. Today, as in the past, Argyll's spiritual landscape is not without its imaginary additions.

Several new initiatives are arising in response to the growing interest in faith tourism and pilgrimage, and a realisation that Argyll has so much to offer in these areas. A recent example is the Cowal 'Cradle of Christianity' Pilgrimage Trail, which is being developed by the rural parish churches of the Cowal peninsula as one of a number of projects to engage creatively with local communities. Under the title 'Faith Tourism, Heritage and Pilgrimage' it aims to create a pilgrimage route for walkers, cyclists, motorists, coach parties and sailors linking the historic sites of Kilmun, Kilfinan, Kilmodan, Colintraive and Inverchaolain. Another recent initiative is the 'St Columba Pilgrim Journey' promoted as one of six Scottish pilgrim journeys in 2012 by Scotland's Churches Trust to encourage people to visit historic churches. This web-based resource provides maps and information for those going by car or bicycle. The St Columba Journey goes from Campbeltown to Lochgilphead via Tarbert and then divides with one route going up Loch Fyne to Inveraray and the other up the west coast to Oban with detours to Crinan, Seil and Luing. There is an Islay and Jura loop and the main route goes on across Mull to Iona and then returns via Mull to cross into Ardnamurchan and on to Mallaig and up the Great Glen. Those undertaking this pilgrimage are invited to carry a passport which can be stamped at certain designated destination hubs. In Argyll these include the Lorne & Lowland and the Highland parish churches in Campbeltown, the parish churches at Tarbert, Inveraray, Kilmelford and Bowmore, Iona Abbey and the Scottish Episcopal and Roman Catholic cathedrals in Oban.[2]

A longer pilgrimage in the footsteps of Columba can be made by following a trail devised by the Colmcille partnership, which aims at fostering links between Ireland and Scotland based on their shared Gaelic heritage. It starts at Glen Colmcille in Donegal and takes in Columba's birthplace on Lough Gartan and other sites associated with him in Northern Ireland before crossing from Antrim to Kintyre and continuing from Southend to Dunadd and then on to Iona.[3] New long-distance walking trails, like the 57-mile long Cowal Way opened in 2003 and the 87-mile Kintyre Way opened in 2007, are making these and other pilgrim ways more feasible and appealing.

Argyll will have a significant role in the proposed long-distance pilgrim way across Scotland from Iona to St Andrews, which is being championed by politicians, led by Roseanna Cunningham MSP, and church leaders. Around a third of its 185-mile route would pass through Argyll, including thirty-five miles across Mull. Considerable work has already been undertaken on mapping the best route, which as far as possible will use existing forestry tracks and core footpaths. Perhaps the biggest challenge is how to avoid the busy A85 through the Pass of Brander. Possibilities include routing the pilgrim way north along the bank of Loch Etive and then through Glen Noe, or skirting the lower slopes of Ben Cruachan before dropping down into Glen Orchy. There will be considerable opportunities for churches along the way to offer hospitality and worship to pilgrims and it is possible that there will be spurs off the main route, for example along the old pilgrim path through Glen Lonan, which would offer an alternative way between Oban and Taynuilt.

A significant recent initiative to promote pilgrimage has been centred on the parish of Luss, which was only transferred from West Dumbartonshire to Argyll in 1996 and now stands at the gateway to the county as it is approached on the main road from Glasgow and the South. In pre-Christian times it was known as Clachan Dhu, or the Dark Hamlet, possibly because of rituals which took place there or because the sun took a long time to rise over the high hills above this side of Loch Lomond. The name Luss, thought to be derived from the Latin *lux* for light, possibly dates from Kessog's conversion of the area from paganism to Christianity in the early sixth century. His death at the hands of pagans, supposedly around 520, made him an early Christian martyr and inspired a cult which led to Luss becoming a major place of pilgrimage in the Middle Ages. Although the present parish church, a fine example of Victorian Gothic, dates only from 1875, it houses several important ancient artefacts, including a very early font, possibly over 1,000 years old, and a head which may date from the sixth century and could represent Kessog. Both these objects, together with an early medieval effigy, were taken from the old medieval parish church at the time of the Reformation by parishioners anxious about iconoclasm, and hidden near the cairn marking the supposed site of Kessog's death. They were discovered again in the mid eighteenth century when General Wade's military road was being built up the side of Loch Lomond.

In the summer of 1998, Dane Sherrard, then minister of Bishopbriggs, was making a day trip to Inveraray. He stopped en route at the semi-ruined church of Arrochar at the head of Loch Long, and felt called to restore it to use. He applied for the vacant linked charge of Arrochar and Luss and became minister later that year. As well as restoring Arrochar Church, he also transformed Luss Church during his fifteen years in the parish. To pay for the restoration and on-going maintenance costs, he capitalised on its potential for weddings on the romantic shores of Loch Lomond, installing fixed closed-circuit cameras so that services could be beamed live on the internet anywhere round the world. A seven-minute sound and light presentation was also installed, allowing the church's many visitors to gain an insight into the history of the parish.

Dane Sherrard was especially keen to make Luss once again a place of pilgrimage. He created a series of pilgrim pathways on the glebe, a 23-acre field on the banks of Loch Lomond. Radiating out from a central wooden cross are paths themed around the stories of Saints Francis, Columba and Kessog. Access to the glebe, which is surrounded by water on all sides, was provided via a bridge built in 2006 by a squad from the Royal Engineers Regiment to replace one that had been washed away in 1993. Similar projects involving the military could well help to build the infrastructure for other new pilgrim ways in Argyll. With the Army's relocation from Germany to Britain, there is a desire to work on projects which will connect with local communities. I received an enthusiastic response when I suggested to a conference of army chaplains that a valuable practical expression of such engagement might be the construction by soldiers of bridges and paths for new pilgrim trails.

A residential hostel for pilgrims, made up of redundant porta-cabins from the nearby nuclear submarine base at Faslane, was built

Statue of Kessog on the pilgrim trail in the glebe at Luss

in the grounds of Luss Manse in 2006. Opened by Prince Charles and christened the Pilgrims' Palace, it can accommodate thirty-six people in comfortable bunk beds. During Dane Sherrard's ministry, groups of young people from around the world stayed there while working on the pilgrim pathways through the glebe land, as did Prince's Trust teams working on local environmental projects. The Manse garden also houses a Pilgrim Centre and Heritage Room. In 2011 Luss became Scotland's first Green Pilgrimage city, taking its place alongside the Golden Temple at Armritsar, Jerusalem, Trondheim, Canterbury Cathedral and other pilgrim sites linked in a global network committed to sustainable, eco-friendly pilgrimage. Dane Sherrard hoped to provide electric-powered cars so that overseas visitors could make carbon-neutral pilgrimages around Argyll. Although he retired from Luss in 2013 with some of his dreams still unfulfilled, his vision has not died. Several primary schools in Argyll and Bute are continuing to engage in pilgrim activities which he initiated. Promotion of pilgrimage and faith tourism is a major aim of both the Presbytery of Argyll and the tourism department of Argyll and Bute Council.

Pilgrims' Palace, Luss

Encouraging people to journey through Argyll as pilgrims has enormous potential to stimulate the region's rural economy through more occupancy of guest houses and bed and breakfast establishments and better patronage of local shops and suppliers. This is what has happened in Galicia, another region of Europe which has a Christian symbol as its corporate logo (in its case a communion chalice) as a result of active promotion of the Camino to Santiago di Compostella. Developing pilgrimage also enables every church, however small, to tell its story and have a new outreach in terms of welcoming strangers.

For those unable, for whatever reason, to make a physical journey, there are other ways to gain something of the experience of pilgrimage. Virtual pilgrimages to and round Iona and other sites can be accessed on the internet, and photographs and paintings provide icon-like images of the landscape for spiritual contemplation and meditation. Argyll's spiritual landscape has long appealed to painters, as we have already noted in respect of William McTaggart and John Duncan (pages 51 and 203). Iona, of course, has been a particular magnet, drawing the Scottish colourists, notably Francis Cadell and Simon Peploe, and many other artists. Setting off from Oban a few years ago with a group of pilgrims, I talked to a trio of female artists en route for a week painting and drawing on Iona who saw themselves also as pilgrims.

Argyll is probably the most painted part of Scotland and must surely have the densest concentration of resident artists. Several have been drawn there by the spiritual qualities of its landscape and none more so than John Lowrie Morrison, indisputably Argyll's best-known and most popular artist. Born in Glasgow in 1948, he moved to Argyll in 1973 to teach art at Lochgilphead High School and turned to full time painting in 1998. From his studio in Tayvallich he produces nearly 1,000 paintings a year, the great majority landscapes of Argyll and its islands. A devout Christian, he is a Reader in the Presbytery of Argyll and former Session Clerk for the linked parishes of Tayvallich, Bellanoch and Inverlussa. He says that he was initially drawn to Argyll because of its landscape and especially the light which he sees as divinely inspired:

> The light is my reference to God. God's light permeates our minds, our souls, our very being. In Argyll the light works in a very special way – it passes over – there is a special relationship between light and dark. I see it as an allegory of the human soul which I express through the technique of chiaroscuro. This is usually seen in terms of dark and light or black and white. For me it is contrasting dark and colour.[4]

Morrison, or Jolomo as he signs himself in his paintings, prays before every new painting, 'handing it over to God' and often again during the painting process. Steeped in the geology, history and folklore of Argyll, he occasionally paints churches – Kilninian at Torloisk on Mull and Kilfinan are his favourites – sometimes at a crazy angle 'because I want to portray them full of people singing' and with gravestones standing in front 'to show the dead as well as the living'. Most of his paintings are landscapes and seascapes, suffused with the blue and purple that he regards as the distinctive colours of Argyll. His favourite season is autumn and his favourite time to paint is in the gloaming as the sun goes down and the landscape is turned purple, which he sees as a deeply sacramental colour enhancing the spiritual feel of Argyll.

Jolomo is not the first person to identify blue and purple as Argyll's primary colours. Writing in 1933, Thomas Ratcliffe Barnett summed up what he saw as its distinctive landscape: 'in the lurk of the craggy hollows blue and purple shadows play hide-and-seek when the rays of the setting sun sklent across the land'. Barnett, too, felt that 'the greatest glory of a highland day in the west comes when the sun goes down' and gave a particularly vivid description of looking out from Kilmory Knap to 'the plum-coloured islands' and 'the rim of purple mountains seen against the glow of sunset … The whole sky was shaded upwards in delicate washes to a zenith of velvet blue, a dusky tent of God lit with a crescent moon and a single star.'[5]

In recent years John Lowrie Morrison has become increasingly drawn to painting beaches with footsteps going down to the sea between tufts of long grass. This image has recurred in paintings set on Iona, Oronsay, Colonsay, Gigha, Mull, Jura and along the west coast of Kintyre and Knapdale, with Carsaig Bay an especially favourite location, as reflected in the painting on the front cover of this book, which is entitled 'An evening gloaming, Carsaig Bay, Knapdale'. He sees the footsteps in the sand as icons and metaphors for life and death: 'the path down to the beach draws you down to the sea and draws you back to God'. There are echoes here of George Matheson's image in 'O love that wilt not let me go' of giving one's life back to God 'that in thine ocean's depth its flow may richer, fuller be'. Like Matheson, Jolomo is drawn to darkness, shadows and gloaming as much as to the light and the bright primary colours that fill his paintings with hope. In that respect, he reflects and represents an abiding feature in Argyll's spiritual tradition and landscape.

Conclusion
Death and the Landscape Beyond

A recurrent theme of this book has been the way that death stalks the landscape of Argyll. Kilmartin Valley seems to have been designed and laid out as a ritual landscape of the dead. The early Christian and later medieval carved stones were first and foremost grave markers, and the high-standing crosses may well have been erected as waypoints on processional pilgrim routes to shrines and tombs. Coffin roads criss-cross the region, putting death into place names like Carraig nam Marbh, the Rock of the Dead, on the south side of Loch Feochan near Kilninver, which is said to be where the bodies of nobles, after being carried overland, many on a route which went through Glen Orchy to Loch Awe and then via the Streing of Lorne, were embarked on galleys to be sent to Iona where they would be carried along the Street of the Dead before burial. A well-established coffin road across Mull starts at the similarly named Port nam Marbh on the north side of the entrance to Loch Spelvie.[1] It is still possible in several places around Argyll to see the cairns made up of piles of small stones that were erected where coffins were rested on their long journeys to burial grounds. The best examples that I know are beside Clach na Criche (The Boundary Stone), the outcrop of volcanic magna on the road near Fiunary in Morvern, which marks the boundary between the parishes of Killintaig and Kilcolmkiel.

The most inescapable reminders of the omni-present reality of death are the numerous graveyards and cemeteries scattered around Argyll. They are often sited in seemingly very remote regions, high up on the slopes of hills or shrouded by trees, and always surrounded by stone walls. Some, like Cladh a' Bhile, are very ancient, many are overgrown, often with a crumbling chapel in their midst, while

others are still very much in use and well-tended. Almost as ubiquitous are the grander monuments, mausoleums and burial aisles and
enclosures erected to house the bodies of the rich and well-to-do,
most of them Campbells.

These graveyards have become important places of pilgrimage. People come from all over the world to visit them in order to
trace their ancestors, thanks partly to the growing fascination with
family trees and genealogy. Indeed, they have become among the
most visited parts of Argyll's spiritual landscape. Many people
enjoy walking round them simply because of their atmosphere and
the interesting artwork and inscriptions on the gravestones. We feel
a sense of timeless peace and tranquillity as we walk among the
ancient lichen-covered tombs, which have taken on the character
of works of art or historical monuments. Those who erected and
engraved them saw them in a very different light. Often marking
tragically early, diseased and violent deaths, their prime purpose was
to remind those still alive of the frailty of our human clay and the
reality of mortality.

Symbols of mortality on a tombstone in Keil Churchyard,
Lochaline

An unusually high proportion of Argyll's gravestones are engraved
with the chilling words 'Memento Mori' (Remember Death) and symbols of death such as the skull and crossbones, hourglass, trumpet

(to sound the last trump) and scythe of the Grim Reaper. Travellers to the region have long commented on this feature of its landscape. After visiting Glenorchy Church in 1819, the poet Robert Southey observed that 'it seems the custom to engrave skulls, and other such hideous emblems of mortality upon tombstones'. On her tramps through Argyll more than a hundred years later, Mary Donaldson was similarly struck by the popularity of the skull and crossbones device on gravestones, suggesting slightly cheekily that it was 'more suitable, surely, for marking the graves of pirates or pagans than of professing Christians!'[2]

These stark images are sometimes accompanied by verses reminding those who stop to read them of their own mortality. An early eighteenth-century table tomb in Kilmun Churchyard has a Gaelic verse which, when translated, reads: 'As long as you are alive, before your body becomes cold, frequently remember death'. Inscribed on the gravestone in Kilmartin Churchyard of Elizabeth McFarlane, who died in 1809, are the words:

> It is God that lifts our comforts high
> Or sinks them in the grave
> He gives and then he takes away
> He takes but what he gave

Perhaps most pointed of all is the verse under a carving of an hourglass on the back of the gravestone in Kilfilan churchyard of Duncan Thomson, who died at the age of 52 in 1814:

> My glass is run
> And yours is running
> Be wise in time
> Your day is coming

No other part of the British Isles has such a concentration of these macabre symbols and verses. Why is this? In her book on Kilberry Church, Marion Campbell suggested that it is because these were the only symbols allowed on gravestones after the Reformation. But that would surely apply to the rest of the country and does not explain the exceptional emphasis on death in Argyll's graveyards. Is it, I wonder, just one aspect of a broader theme in the imagined spiritual landscape of Tír na nÓg, the land of the west and the setting sun? It is surely striking that some of the most beautiful evocations of the Argyll landscape, from Adomnán's musings about Iona in the late seventh century to Norman MacLeod's depiction of Morvern in the mid nineteenth century, have been made in the context of how wonderful it would be to die or be buried there (pages 87 and 173).

Argyll remains a place where people come to die, or at least to live out their latter days. It is a favourite destination for the retired and has the highest proportion of inhabitants aged over 65 of any Scottish local government region (22 per cent as against a national average of 17 per cent). This proportion is set to rise steeply in the context of increasing outward migration of the young and those of working age. The overall population of the county is projected to decline by 13.5 per cent by 2037. Depopulation is, of course, nothing new in Argyll. Many of the graveyards that now seem so remote were once close to thriving clachans and settlements that long ago disappeared, mostly in the late eighteenth and nineteenth centuries when changes in farming forced so many people to emigrate. For a long time Argyll was over-populated, its meagre and unproductive land unable to sustain the number of inhabitants, many of whom were eking out a bare existence. Now the situation is very different and the sense that the region is emptying and dying is exacerbated by the fact that outside the urban centres many houses are second or holiday homes, only occupied for a small part of the year.

Argyll's churches too seem to be dying. Several have been sold and are now used for other purposes – a former parish church in Oban houses the town's tourist centre, while one in Campbletown is a heritage centre. Some smaller village churches have been converted into dwellings and others have undergone rather more dramatic transformation, like the former Kilcalmonell Free Church at Clachan in Kintyre which, for a time, was used for growing cannabis. Although many rural parish churches remain open, their congregations tend to be small with Sunday worship being held only once or twice a month. Appropriately perhaps, they are often most alive and at their fullest for funerals.

It is on the islands, where depopulation is often greatest, that death haunts the landscape most obviously and evocatively. There is, of course, a long association between the ideas of dying and cross-ing over water. It is there in Greek mythology where the souls of the newly dead are rowed across the Styx by the ferryman, Charon, and in many primal religions where the dead are believed to cross rivers or seas to enter the next world. Within Christianity, this connection is powerfully represented in the image of crossing the Jordan River and in the baptismal ritual of drowning in water in order to be born to eternal life. Perhaps because of their particular association in Celtic folklore with Tír na nÓg, Argyll's Atlantic islands have long been particularly sought after as places to be buried. Iona, of course, is pre-eminent in this regard with its Street of the Dead and early graveyard in Reilig Odhráin, to which the bodies of nobles and also kings, if not quite as many of the latter as the guidebooks suggest, were brought across the sea.

Prominent figures still come to Iona to be buried. The most recent was John Smith, the Labour Party leader who died in 1994. He was himself a son of Argyll, born in Dalmally, raised in Ardris-haig, where his father was head teacher of the primary school, and educated at Dunoon Grammar School. The family's roots lay in Allt Beithe, a small settlement in the hills above Tarbert, which was decimated by a cholera plague in 1845. The only inhabitant to escape death was a two-year-old boy who went on to become Smith's great-grandfather.

Argyll's islands are particularly well endowed with graveyards. Here more than anywhere the dead outnumber the living and dominate the landscape. In part this is because of severe rural depop-ulation. Jura is a case in point, with three extensive graveyards on an island which now has fewer than 200 inhabitants but once had over 1,000. Each was also the site of a chapel: Kilchianiag near the sea by Inverlussa towards the north end; Cill Chaluim Chille in a field at Tarbert half way up the island; and Cill Earnadail at Keills, on a hillside above the main modern settlement at Craighouse. It was in this last burial ground, situated, like so many in the West Highlands, beside a fast-flowing stream to carry the spirits of the dead down to the sea, that I had the deeply moving experience a few years ago of participating in a traditional island funeral where, after lowering the coffin into the earth, we shared a dram of Jura malt whisky and an oatcake around the graveside.

Alexander Ewing was particularly taken by Eilean Munde in Loch Leven just north of Ballachulish, where the earliest burials were of those converted to Christianity by St Munn and who wished to lie near his cell. He was amazed to discover, on a visit in 1872, that it was still much sought after as a final resting place, not least by people from as far afield as the United States who sometimes came over while they were still alive to 'await their end near the venerable churchyard'. He met one elderly American who had arrived in Ballachulish close to death but subsequently recovered his health and was uncertain what to do next.[3]

Grave of the twelfth Duke of Argyll, Inishail

I find two of the island graveyards on Argyll's inland lochs especially atmospheric. Inishail, also known as the Island of Rest or the Green Isle, lies in the northern part of Loch Awe. Its graveyard is reached by taking a boat round to a little beach on the west side of the thickly wooded island and clambering up through dank vegetation to the yew trees, which spread their dark pall over the inevitable ruined chapel that stands on what may be the site of the nunnery founded by Findoca. The burial plot contains several effigies of armoured figures in characteristically muscular Christian poses and an intriguing altar frontal. It has been suggested that early Campbell chiefs were buried there before the building of the collegiate church at Kilmun, but there is no evidence for this and it seems more likely that they were laid to rest at the other Kilmun close to Davalich and overlooking the old Campbell stronghold of Innis Chonnell further down Loch Awe. However, the remains of the two most recently deceased

Dukes of Argyll do rest on Inishail. It is said that the eleventh Duke, who died in 1973, did not want to lie with his forebears in the Argyll Mausoleum at Kilmun because of its proximity to the Polaris nuclear submarine base then located in the Holy Loch. So his ashes were interred on Inishail where his father, Walter Campbell, a grandson of the eighth Duke, was already buried. He is commemorated by a high-standing Celtic cross. The twelfth Duke, who died in 2001, is buried in a railed enclosure in long grass beyond the graveyard. His massive tombstone, with his name Ian engraved in large letters below a boar's head, is already overgrown and looks somewhat forlorn, a reminder that even the mighty MacCailean Mór is mortal.

Green Isle

The other island graveyard that I find particularly haunting is situated at the northern extremity of the old county of Argyll on the Green Isle, or St Finnan's Isle in Loch Shiel. The county boundary for long ran down the middle of the island, which is now wholly in Inverness. Protestants from Argyll were buried on its southern slopes and Catholics from Inverness on the northern side. It is said to be the oldest burial place still in use today anywhere in Western Europe and is reputedly the site of Finan's hermitage. Burials are thought to have begun there in the sixth century and it is sometimes claimed, rather fancifully, that since then there have been around 60,000 interments.

Father William Fraser, for many years the local Catholic parish priest, told me that it was very difficult when digging a new grave to find a piece of ground that was not already full of bones. I went out there one beautiful summer morning in a boat from Acharacle. The island is covered with crosses, some very ancient and now at crazy angles, which point towards the sky. It has recently been cleared of scrub and undergrowth and is easy to walk over. At the top is the small ruined chapel of St Finnan with its ancient bell kept in a recess behind

Early carved Christian stone on Green Isle

the altar. Although there are plenty of the characteristically graphic symbols of mortality found across Argyll, including a particularly gruesome skeleton-decorated tombstone, the Green Isle is not in any way gloomy or spooky.

The nearby parish church at Acharacle offers on its welcome table a leaflet about bereavement and the practical things that need to be done when someone has died. In a lifetime of visiting churches across the British Isles, I have never come across anything similar. Maybe the spiritual landscape of Argyll does not just inspire thoughts of death and dying but also offers some pointers for coming to terms with it. The coffin roads with their cairns and the traditional customs associated with West Highland funerals underline the importance of ritual and process in mourning, and its communal dimension. The numerous gravestones and mausoleums serve as reminders of the benefits of naming and acknowledging the reality of death. Another remote Argyll church, Inverchaolain on Loch Striven, reached by a long single-track road from Toward Point, although now only used for two services a year, is kept open and seems to have found a new role as a place where people who have been bereaved go for consolation and reflection. The porch has become a shrine where cards, photographs and prayers are pinned up in memory of loved ones who have died. When I visited it one autumn afternoon two groups of families, who had clearly come from a considerable distance away, were scattering ashes in the graveyard. This is an interesting and creative use for a redundant church, which seems to have been developed spontaneously, and perhaps highlights another way in which Argyll's landscape of death may serve an important pastoral purpose.

Graves on Green Isle

Death looms large in several books set in and about Argyll. Neal Ascherson's *Stone Voices: The Search for Scotland* begins with a vivid description of driving across mid-Argyll to visit his dying mother in Lorn and the Islands Hospital in Oban. Alan Warner's *Morvern Callar* is a bleak reflection on the emptiness in the aftermath of sudden death set around Oban and on the north side of Loch Awe. Another bleak novel, J. MacDougall Hay's *Gillespie*, set in Tarbert, Loch Fyne, where the author grew up as the son of a steamship agent, is also full of death. All three books share a sense of the landscape of Argyll outliving death. In Ascherson's case, it is the solid eternity of the stones that will outlast everything. In *Morvern Callar* it is the calming influences of the Cathedral of Trees and Loch Awe which somehow keep Morvern going after her boyfriend's suicide. In *Gillespie* it is the eternal aspect of the land as the source of inspiration and life, and the conviction that it is beautiful and 'full of God'. In reality, as well as in fiction, Argyll's landscape out-lives death. The gravestones have become part of that landscape and survive long after the names which they commemorate have been eroded and forgotten. The lochs, rivers and seas continue to flow. The rain still falls. We are back to the enduring power of stone and water.

Most religions teach that there is something beyond death. For Christians it is a new heaven and a new earth and the sure and certain hope of resurrection from the dead. It so happens that Acharacle Church, so close to the graveyard on the Green Isle, presents a parable of resurrection as well as offering practical help to those facing bereavement. The church was saved from structural collapse by being completely rebuilt between 2006 and 2014 at a cost of over £200,000, much of it raised by the local community. Other churches across Argyll are engaged in similar projects to bring new life and hope in the midst of what could seem like a relentless tide of death and decline. Resurrection is, indeed, one of the key themes in the story of Argyll's spiritual landscape with its constant reinvention, adaptation and re-imagining. Old stones have been re-used again and again to create new buildings.

There is another motif that has long characterized the imagined and imaginal spiritual landscape of Argyll. It gives us glimpses and intimations of another world. For Celtic dreamers it is the world of eternal youth, of Tír na nÓg, fairies, second sight and supernatural presences. For Christians it is glimpses of Heaven. George Matheson experienced such intimations as he listened from his Innellan Manse to the 'Symphony of Nature' on the Clyde and reflected, 'Heaven somehow begins here, and immortality'. For T. Ratcliffe Barnett they came as he stood on a summer's day at Crinan harbour looking out to the islands in the open sea and to the great flats of Mòine Mhór 'steeped in the shimmering light of the west':

You may think you have come to a cul-de-sac of the world. But, before long, you will be quite sure that where the world ends heaven only begins … When the sun goes down in all its glory, the outgait to the west from Loch Crinan is like the forecourt of heaven.[4]

Skeleton tombstone, Green Isle

Notes

Please see Bibliography and Further Reading (p. 252) for full details of publications listed in Notes.

Introduction

1 Omand, *The Argyll Book*, pp. 241, 242.
2 MacLeod, *Morvern*, pp. 16, 200.
3 Walker, *Buildings of Scotland: Argyll and Bute*, pp. 264–5.
4 O'Donoghue, *The Angels Keep Their Ancient Places*, p. 35.
5 Boswell, *Journal*, 21 October 1773. Johnson made the remark while staying at Lochbuie on Mull.
6 Barnett, *The Land of Lorne*, p. 144.

2 Kilmartin Valley

1 Ritchie, *Archaeology of Argyll*, p. 67.
2 Lines, *Sacred Stones*, p. 131.

3 Dunadd and Dál Riata

1 Butter, *Kilmartin*, p. 80.
2 Campbell, *Witchcraft & Second Sight*, p. 223.
3 Lane & Campbell, *Dunadd*, p. 259.
4 Campbell, *Saints and Sea-kings*, pp. 18–19.
5 Campbell, 'Were the Scots Irish?', p. 291. See also Lane & Campbell, *Dunadd*, pp. 32–36.

4 Columba's Footprints

1 Smyth, *Warlords and Holy Men*, p. 100.
2 Clarkson, *Columba*, p. 56.
3 Donaldson, *Further Wanderings*, p. 7.

4 See Clancy, 'Annat in Scotland', p. 112; Campbell, *Argyll*, p. 150; Pallister, *Argyll Curiosities*, p. 4.

5 The Saints of Argyll

1 Butter, *Cill-names and Saints in Argyll*.
2 Adomnán, *Life of Columba*, p. 126.
3 Ritchie, *Archaeology of Argyll*, p. 182.
4 Marsden, *Sea Roads of the Saints*, p. 75–6.
5 Marsden, *Sea Roads of the Saints*, p. 68.
6 Macquarrie, *Legends of the Scottish Saints*, p. 346.
7 Butter, 'St Munnu in Ireland and Scotland', pp. 36, 38.
8 Sprott Towill, *Saints of Scotland*, p. 182.

6 Early Christian Carved Stones and Crosses

1 Royal Commission on the Ancient and Historical Monuments of Scotland, *Argyll*, VII, p. 57.
2 See Montgomery, *The God-Kings of Europe*.
3 Ritchie, *Archaeology*, p. 200.
4 Ross, *Memoir of Ewing*, p. 429.

7 Cells, Chapels and Caves

1 Ross, *Memoir of Ewing*, p. 429.
2 Ritchie, *Archaeology*, pp. 189–191.
3 Ritchie, *Archaeology*, p. 182; Clancy, 'Annat in Scotland'.
4 Meredith-Lobay, *Contextual Landscape Study* pp. 21 & 86.
5 MacDonald, *Clerics and Clansmen*, p. 263.
6 Markus, *Power and Protection*.
7 Ritchie & Harman, *Exploring Scotland's Heritage*, p. 103.

8 Monastic Foundations – The MacDonalds' Contribution

1 On Somerled's contribution, see Angus MacMillan, 'The Emergence of Early Governance in Argyll' in McClure, *A Land That Lies Westward*.

10 Bishops and Books – Lismore and Carnasserie Castle

1 MacDonald, *Clerics and Clansmen*, pp. 19–60.
2 MacDonald, *Clerics and Clansmen*, p. 77.
3 MacDonald, *Clerics and Clansmen*, p. 61.
4 MacGregor, 'Creation and Compilation'.
5 Carmichael, *Lismore*, p. 116.

6 Meek, 'The Reformation and Gaelic Culture' in Kirk (ed.), *The Church in the Highlands*, p. 41. See also Omand, *The Argyll Book*, p. 235; MacGregor, 'Church and Culture' in Kirk, *op.cit.*, pp. 1–35.

7 Meek, 'The Gaelic Bible' in Wright (ed.), *The Bible in Scottish Life and Literature*, pp. 9–23.

8 Dawson, 'The Protestant Earl & Godly Gael' in Wood, *Life and Thought in the Northern Church*, pp. 337–363.

11 The Campbells are Coming – Kilmun, Campbeltown and Inveraray

1 Walker, *Argyll and the Islands*, p. 6.

2 McKechnie, *The Lamont Clan*, p. 1.

3 Macdonnell, *Clan Donald*.

4 Boardman, *The Campbells*; Dawson, 'Clan, kin and Kirk' in Amos et al., *The Education of a Christian Society*; MacGregor, 'The Campbells'.

5 Campbell, *Scotland As It Was and As It Is*, p. 34.

6 Sellar, 'The Earliest Campbells'; see also Campbell, *History of Clan Campbell*, I, pp. 3–16, and Boardman, *The Campbells*, pp. 10–11.

7 See Easson, 'The Collegiate Churches of Scotland'; Boardman, 'Pillars of the Community' in Oram, *Lordship and Architecture*, pp. 123–159; Boardman, *The Campbells*, pp. 142–159; Campbell, *History of Clan Campbell*, p. 124.

8 Dawson, 'The Protestant Earl' in Wood, *Life and Thought*, pp. 348–9.

9 Macdonnell, *Clan Donald*, p. 90.

10 Royal Commission on the Ancient and Historical Monuments of Scotland, *Argyll*, IV, p. 150.

11 Dawson, 'The Protestant Earl' in Wood, *Life and Thought*, p. 349; Pallister, *Villages of Southern Argyll*, pp. 44–5.

12 Buchan, *Highland and Lowland*, p. 7.

13 *Glenorchy Parish Church*, p. 18.

12 Parish Churches

1 MacDonald, *Clerics and Clansmen*, p. 264.

2 Gillies, *The Viking Isle*, p. 72.

13 Morvern Manse – The MacLeod Dynasty

1 MacLeod, *Morvern*, p. xx.

2 MacLeod, *Morvern*, p. 6.

3 MacLeod, *Morvern*, p. 13.

4 MacLeod, *Morvern*, p. 15.

5 MacLeod, *Morvern*, p. 19.

6 MacLeod, *Morvern*, p. 104.

14 Episcopal Argyll – Alexander Ewing

1 Marion Lochhead, *Episcopal Scotland in the Nineteenth Century*, pp. 165, 168, 173.
2 Ross, *Memoir of Ewing*, pp. 137–8.
3 Walker, *Buildings of Scotland*, p. 38.

15 George Matheson of Innellan

1 Ross, *Memoir of Ewing*, p. 124.
2 Macmillan, *Life of Matheson*, p. 69.
3 Macmillan, *Life of Matheson*, p. 121.
4 Macmillan, *Life of Matheson*, pp. 284–5.

16 Iona again and the Campbells again

1 Sharpe, 'Iona in 1771', p. 197.
2 *The Divine Life of the Church*, II, p. 15.
3 Bradley, *Celtic Christianity*, p. 147.
4 Bradley, *Celtic Christianity*, p. 148.
5 Bradley, *Celtic Christianity*, p. 149.
6 Campbell, *Iona*, p. 41.
7 Campbell, *Passages From the Past*, II, p. 540.
8 Campbell, *Autobiography*, II, p. 451.
9 Campbell, *Autobiography*, II, p. 560.
10 Campbell, *Autobiography*, I, p. 233.
11 Douglas, *Autobiography*, II, p. 577.
12 Balfour, *Lady Victoria Campbell*, p. 284.
13 Balfour, *Lady Victoria Campbell*, p. 279.

17 The Folklore and Celtic Revivals

1 Campbell, *The Fions*, p. xi.
2 Stiùbhart , *Life & Legacy of Carmichael*, pp. 4, 21, 82.
3 *Celtic Review*, October 1912, p. 122.
4 Carmichael, *Carmina Gadelica* , p. 445.
5 *Celtic Review*, October 1912, pp. 118–9.
6 MacLeod, 'The Three Marvels of Iona' in *Spiritual Tales*, Vol. 1, pp. 55–84; 'Iona' in *Works*, Vol. IV, pp. 95, 130, 134, 241, 244–5.
7 MacLeod, *Works*, Vol. IV, p. 246.

18 Inveraray Bell Tower and Two Other Memorials to the First World War

1 Lees-Milne, *Ancestral Voices*, p. 246.
2 Warner, *Morvern Callar*, p. 36.

19 Two Twentieth-century Monuments to Columba

1 Douglas, *The Day of Small Things*, p. 202.
2 See, for example, his prayer 'Man is made to rise' in *The Whole Earth Shall Cry Glory*, pp. 24–25.

20 An Episcopalian Traveller and a Free Church Pilgrim

1 Donaldson, *Wanderings*, p. 10.
2 Donaldson, *Further Wanderings*, p. 38.
3 Barnett, *The Land of Lorne*, p. 64.
4 Barnett, *The Land of Lorne*, p. 58.
5 Barnett, *Scottish Pilgrimage*, p. 56.

21 Craig Lodge and Other New Religious Communities

1 Reproduced by permission of David Kellas. Other quoted passages in this chapter are taken from interviews at Craig Lodge in May 2014.

22 Preservation, Pilgrimage and Painting

1 Walker, *Argyll and the Islands*, p. 62.
2 http://www.scotlandspilgrimjourneys.com/pilgrim-journeys/5/st-columba-journey
3 http://www.colmcille.org/slicholmcille
4 Interview with author, 11 September 2014.
5 Barnett, *Land of Lorne*, pp. 12, 44.

Conclusion – Death and the Landscape Beyond

1 The coffin route across Mull is described in detail in McGrigor, *Paths of the Pilgrims*, pp. 24–5.
2 Donaldson, *Further Wanderings*, p. 304.
3 Ross, *Memoir of Ewing*, p. 592.
4 Barnett, *Land of Lorne*, pp. 11, 27

Bibliography and Further Reading

Adomnán of Iona, *Life of St Columba*, ed. & trans. R. Sharpe (Harmondsworth: Penguin, 1995).

Ascherson, Neal, *Stone Voices: The Search for Scotland* (London: Grant Books, 2002).

Balfour, Frances, *Lady Victoria Campbell* (London: Hodder & Stoughton, 1911).

Barnett, Thomas Ratcliffe, *The Land of Lorne* (Edinburgh: Chambers, 1933).

Barnett, Thomas Ratcliffe, *Scottish Pilgrimage* (Edinburgh: John Grant, 1942).

Boardman, Stephen, 'Pillars of the Community: Campbell Lordship and Architectural Patronage in the Fifteenth Century' in Oram and Stell, *Lordship and Architecture* (2005), pp. 123–59.

Boardman, Stephen, *The Campbells 1250–1513* (Edinburgh: John Donald, 2006).

Boardman, Stephen and Williamson, Eila (eds), *The Cult of the Saints and the Virgin Mary in Medieval Scotland* (Woodbridge: Boydell Press, 2010).

Boswell, James, *Journal of A Tour to the Hebrides with Samuel Johnson LL.D.* (London: Charles Dilly, 1785).

Bourke, Cormac (ed.), *Studies in the Cult of Saint Columba* (Dublin: Four Courts Press, 1997).

Bradley, Ian, *Celtic Christianity: Making Myths and Dreaming Dreams* (Edinburgh: Edinburgh University Press, 1999).

Brown, Ian (ed.), *Edinburgh History of Scottish Literature*, 3 vols (Edinburgh: Edinburgh University Press, 2006).

Buchan, John, *Highland and Lowland* (author's private collection: unpublished typescript of talk given in 1927).

Butter, Rachel, *Kilmartin: Scotland's Richest Prehistoric Landscape* (Kilmartin: Kilmartin House Trust, 1999).

Butter, Rachel, *Cill-names and Saints in Argyll: a way towards understanding the early church in Dál Riata?* (PhD thesis: Department of Celtic, University of Glasgow, 2007).

Butter, Rachel, 'St Munnu in Ireland and Scotland: An Exploration of His Cult' in Boardman & Williamson (eds), *Cult of Saints* (2010), pp. 21–42.

Campbell, Ewan, *Saints and Sea-kings. The First Kingdom of the Scots* (Edinburgh: Canongate Books, 1999).

Campbell, Ewan, 'Were the Scots Irish?' *Antiquity*, Vol. 75 (2001), 285–92.

Campbell, George, 8th Duke of Argyll, *Iona* (London: Strahan, 1870).

Campbell, George, 8th Duke of Argyll, *Scotland As It Was and As It Is*, 2 vols (Edinburgh: David Douglas, 1887).

Campbell, George 8th Duke of Argyll, *Autobiography*, 2 vols (London: John Murray, 1906).

Campbell, John Douglas Sutherland, 9th Duke of Argyll, *Passages From the Past*, 2 vols (London: Hutchinson & Co., 1907).

Campbell, John Gregorson, *The Fions: or, Stories, poems, & traditions of Fionn and his warrior band* (London: David Nutt, 1891).

Campbell, John Gregorson, *Witchcraft & Second Sight in the Highlands & Islands of Scotland: Tales and Traditions* (Glasgow: James MacLehose, 1902).

Campbell, Marion, *Argyll – The Enduring Heartland* (Kilmartin: Kilmartin House Trust, 2001).

Campbell of Airds, Alastair, *A History of Clan Campbell*, 3 vols (Edinburgh: Polygon, 2000–2004).

Carmichael, Alexander, *Carmina Gadelica: hymns and incantations,* (Edinburgh: Floris Books, 1992).

Carmichael, Ian, *Lismore in Alba* (Perth: D. Leslie, n.d.).

Clancy, Thomas, 'Annat in Scotland and the Origins of the Parish', *Inness Review* Vol. 46, No. 2, Autumn 1995, pp. 91–115.

Clancy, Thomas and Pittock, Murray (eds), *The Edinburgh History of Scottish Literature*, 3 vols (Edinburgh: Edinburgh University Press, 2006).

Clarkson, Tim, *Columba* (Edinburgh: John Donald, 2012).

Dawson, Jane, 'The Protestant Earl & Godly Gael: The Fifth Earl of Argyll and the Scottish Reformation' in Wood, *Life and Thought in the Northern Church* (1999), pp. 337–63.

Dawson, Jane, 'Clan, kin and Kirk: the Campbells and the Scottish Reformation' in N.S. Amos, A. Pettegree & H.V. Nierop, *The Education of a Christian Society* (Farnham: Ashgate, 1999), pp. 211–42.

Donaldson, Mary, *Wanderings in the Western Highlands and Islands* (Paisley: Alexander Gardner, 1920).

Donaldson, Mary, *Further Wanderings – Mainly in Argyll* (Paisley: Alexander Gardner, 1926).

Douglas, O., *The Day of Small Things* (Thomas Nelson, 1933).

Driscoll, Stephen, *Alba: The Gaelic Kingdom of Scotland AD 800 – 1124* (Edinburgh: Birlinn, 2002).

Duncan, A.A.M., *The Edinburgh History of Scotland. Volume 1, Scotland: The Making of the Kingdom* (Edinburgh: Oliver & Boyd,1975).

Easson, D.E., 'The Collegiate Churches of Scotland', *Records of the Scottish Church History Society*, Vol VI, No. 3 (1938), 193–215.

Ferguson, Ron, *George MacLeod* (London: Harper Collins, 1990).

Foster, Sally, *Picts, Gaels and Scots* (London: Batsford, 1996).

Gaskell, Philip, *Morvern Transformed* (Cambridge: Cambridge University Press, 1968).

Gillies, Freddy, *The Viking Isle* (Gigha: Ardminish Press, 2002).

Glenorchy Parish Church (Lochawe: Glenstrae Press, 2012).

Kirk, James (ed.) *The Church in the Highlands* (Edinburgh: Scottish Church History Society, 1998).

Lane, Alan and Campbell, Ewan, *Dunadd: An Early Dalriadic Capital* (Oxford: Oxbow Books, 2000).

Lees-Milne, James, *Ancestral Voices* (London: Chatto & Windus, 1975).

Lines, Marianna, *Sacred Stones, Sacred Places* (Edinburgh: Saint Andrew Press, 1992).

Lochhead, Marion, *Episcopal Scotland in the Nineteenth Century* (London: John Murray, 1966).

MacArthur, Mairi, *Iona* (Grantown-on-Spey: Colin Baxter, 1997).

McClure, J. Derrick, Kirk, John M. and Storrie, Margaret (eds), *A Land that Lies Westward: Language and Culture in Islay and Argyll* (Edinburgh: John Donald, 2009).

MacDonald, Iain, *Clerics and Clansmen: The Diocese of Argyll between the Twelfth and Sixteenth Centuries* (Leiden: Brill, 2013).

Macdonnell, Ian, *Clan Donald & Iona Abbey* (Melbourne: privately published, 2012).

MacGregor, Martin, 'Creation and Compilation: The Book of the Dean of Lismore and Literary Culture in Late Medieval Gaelic Scotland' in Brown et al. (ed.), *Edinburgh History of Scottish Literature* (Edinburgh: Edinburgh University Press, 2006), I, pp. 209–18.

MacGregor, Martin, 'Church and Culture in the late Medieval Highlands' in Kirk (ed.), *The Church in the Highlands*, pp. 1–35.

MacGregor, Martin, 'The Campbells: Lordship, Literature and Liminality', *Textual Cultures*, Vol. 7, No. 1 (Spring 2012), 121–57.

McGrigor, Mary, *Paths of the Pilgrims* (Dalkeith: Scottish Cultural Press, 2006).

McKechnie, Hector, *The Lamont Clan* (Edinburgh: Clan Lamont Society, 1938).

MacLeod, Fiona, *Spiritual Tales* (London: David Nutt, 1903).

MacLeod, Fiona, *The Works of Fiona MacLeod* (London: Heinemann, 1910).

MacLeod, George, *The Whole Earth Shall Cry Glory* (Glasgow: Wild Goose Publications, 2007).

MacLeod, Norman, *Morvern: A Highland Parish*, ed. Iain Thornber (Edinburgh: Birlinn, 2002).

MacMillan, Angus, 'The Emergence of Early Governance in Argyll', in McClure, *A Land That Lies Westward* (2009), pp. 103–22.

Macmillan, Donald, *The Life of George Matheson* (London: Hodder and Stoughton, 1907).

Macquarrie, Alan (ed.), *Legends of Scottish Saints: Readings, hymns and prayers for the commemorations of Scottish saints in the Aberdeen Breviary* (Dublin: Four Courts Press, 2012).

Macquarrie, Alan, *The Saints of Scotland* (Edinburgh: John Donald, 1997).

Markus, Gilbert, *Power and Protection: The Torbhlaren Bell, its Shrine and the Relic Tradition* (Kilmartin: Kilmartin House Museum, 2009).

Marsden, John, *Sea Roads of the Saints* (Edinburgh: Floris Books, 1995).

Meek, Donald, 'The Reformation and Gaelic Culture' in Kirk (ed.), *The Church in the Highlands* (1998), pp. 37–62.

Meek, Donald, 'The Gaelic Bible' in Wright (ed.), *The Bible in Scottish Life and Literature* (1988), pp. 9–23.

Meredith-Lobay, Megan, *Contextual Landscape Study of the Early Christian Churches of Argyll: The persistence of memory* (Oxford: Archaeopress, BAR, 2009).

Montgomery, Hugh, *The God-Kings of Europe: The Descendants of Jesus Traced though the Odonic and Davidic Dynasties* (San Diego, CA: Book Tree, 2006).

Muldoon, James (ed.), *Varieties of Religious Conversion in the Middle Ages* (Gainseville, FL: University of Florida Press, 1997).

O'Donoghue, Noel, *The Angels Keep Their Ancient Places* (Edinburgh: T & T Clark, 2001).

Ó hÓgáin, Dáithí, *The Sacred Isle: Belief and Religion in Pre-Christian Ireland* (Woodbridge: Boydell Press, 1999).

Omand, Donald (ed.), *The Argyll Book* (Edinburgh: Birlinn, 2006).

Oram, Richard and Stell, Geoffrey (eds), *Lordship and Architecture in Medieval and Renaissance Scotland* (Edinburgh: Royal Commission on the Ancient and Historical Monuments of Scotland, 2005).

Pallister, Marian, *Villages of Southern Argyll* (Edinburgh: John Donald, 2004).

Pallister, Marian, *Argyll Curiosities* (Edinburgh: Birlinn, 2007).

Pallister, Marian, *Lost Argyll* (Edinburgh: Birlinn, 2003).

Paterson, Raymond Campbell, *No Tragic Story. The Fall of the House of Campbell* (Edinburgh: John Donald, 2001).

Raine, Kathleen, *Collected Poems* (Ipswich: Golgonooza Press, 2000).

Ritchie, Graham (ed.), *The Archaeology of Argyll* (Edinburgh: Edinburgh University Press, 1997).

Ritchie, Graham and Harman, Mary, *Exploring Scotland's Heritage: Argyll and the Western Isles* (Edinburgh: Royal Commission on the Ancient and Historical Monuments of Scotland, 1985).

Ross Alexander, *Memoir of Alexander Ewing* (London: Daldy, Isbister & Co., 1877).

Royal Commission on the Ancient and Historical Monuments of Scotland, *Argyll: An Inventory of the Monuments*, 7 vols (Glasgow: HMSO, 1975–92).

Sellar, W.D.H., 'The Earliest Campbells – Norman, Briton or Gael', *Scottish Studies*, Vol. xvii (1973), 109–25.

Sharpe, R., 'Iona in 1771', *Innes Review*, Vol. 63, No. 2, (Autumn 2012), 161–259.

Smyth, A.P., *Warlords and Holy Men, Scotland AD 80–1000* (London: Edward Arnold, 1984).

Sprott Towill, Edwin, *The Saints of Scotland* (Edinburgh: Saint Andrew Press, 1982).

Stiùbhart, Domhall, *The Life and Legacy of Alexander Carmichael* (Port of Ness: The Islands Book Trust, 2008).

The Divine Life of the Church (Scottish Church Society Conference 2nd Series), Vol. II (Edinburgh: J Gardner Hitt, 1895).

Tolan-Smith, Christopher, *The Caves of Mid Argyll* (Edinburgh: Society of Antiquaries of Scotland, 2001).

Walker, Frank Arnell, *Argyll and the Islands: An Illustrated Architectural Guide* (Edinburgh: Rutland Press, 2003).

Walker, Frank Arnell, *The Buildings of Scotland: Argyll and Bute* (New Haven & London: Yale University Press, 2005).

Warner, Alan, *Morvern Callar* (London: Vintage, 1996).

Watts, John, *A Record of Generous People: A History of the Catholic Church in Argyll & The Isles* (Glasgow: Ovada Books, 2013).

Webb, Sharon: *In the Footsteps of Kings: A New Guide to Walks In and Around Kilmartin Glen* (Kilmartin: Kilmartin House Trust, 2013).

Westwood, Jennifer and Kingshill, Sophia, *The Lore of Scotland* (London: Random House, 2009).

Williams, Ronald, *The Heather and The Gale: Clan Donald and Clan Campbell during the Wars of up Montrose* (Colonsay: House of Lochar, 1997).

Wood, Donald (ed.), *Life and Thought in the Northern Church c.1100–c.1700* (Woodbridge: Boydell Press, 1999).

Wright, David (ed.), *The Bible in Scottish Life and Literature* (Edinburgh: Saint Andrew Press, 1988).

Index